PRAISE FOR
PROFIT WITH PRESENCE

"This book is one of the few books you'll ever read that has the potential to profoundly and positively impact every aspect of your life. Life changing! I plan to gift it to everyone I care about."

—STEVE WILEY, author, speaker, and founder, The Lincoln Leadership Institute at Gettysburg

"How do you make a difference, make a profit, and live a life of purpose? Dr. Eric Holsapple shows you the way in *Profit with Presence*. It's a must-read guide for any leader."

—LARRY KENDALL, author of *Ninja Selling*

"A powerful and practical personal road map for those of us who are inspired to use business and business education for a better world."

—DR. BETH A. WALKER, dean, College of Business, Colorado State University

"This book is long overdue. In a world where businesses are increasingly called to pursue profits with purpose, *Profit with Presence* sheds light on the hidden value of practicing mindfulness as the key to achieving this goal. Through a series of personal experiences and evidence-based inquiry, Eric Holsapple shows how the practice of mindfulness can improve our daily lives and result in large-scale changes at the organizational and system level. Be present is the answer!"

—**SANJAY RAMCHANDER,** dean, McCoy College
of Business, Texas State University

"To reap the rewards in the business of life, you must be present to win. *Profit with Presence* builds a gentle but sturdy bridge between two dimensions of modern life that can appear seemingly at odds: mindfulness and money. Dr. Holsapple skillfully shows us how to open commerce between our inner self and the outer world, creating a wealth mentality that profits anyone willing to do the inner work. Make no mistake about it: Holsapple means business! Take up this book, and you will be richer for it."

—**ANDREW HOLECEK,** spiritual
teacher, author of *Dream Yoga*

"Eric is a gifted leader and teacher. I have learned countless lessons from him, which have helped me realize incredible joy and fulfillment in my life and business. This book will help anyone who wants to make a valuable contribution in their life!"

—**ERIC THOMPSON,** president, Colorado
Professionals, Windermere Real Estate Services

"Dr. Eric Holsapple offers deep insights from his many years of truth-seeking and personal development. His book is a must-read if you are looking for a unique perspective and practical pathway to greater peace and prosperity."

—**DR. JOE PARENT**, best-selling author of *Zen Golf, A Walk in the Wood: Meditations on Mindfulness with a Bear Named Pooh*; and many other works

"The growth Eric has achieved both mentally and physically and written down so clearly throughout this entire book has made those close to him grow beside him. We all will forever be grateful."

—**DON MAROSTICA**, former Loveland City Council Member, former Colorado State Representative, former Director Colorado Office of Economic Development and International Trade

"*Profit with Presence* exceeded my expectations! This book has provided a framework, with detailed examples, that will have a lifelong impact on anyone who reads it. One of the quotes—'Transformation means the only thing that's permanent is your state of mind, until you say otherwise'— is one of many impactful lessons learned here. I would recommend this to everyone on my leadership team."

—**CHAD MCWHINNEY**, cofounder and executive chairman, McWhinney Real Estate Services

"Eric Holsapple has created a bridge between spirituality and materialism that has never been thought or dreamt of. This is an oasis of an open heart for those who have spent their time only calculating numbers and money and an amazing gift of practicality and opportunity to create money for those who have only lived philosophically."

—**RAY CRIST**, founder, The Jaguar Path,
School of Yoga and Shamanism

"In *Profit with Presence*, Eric weaves together his vast leadership experience, extensive business knowledge, and years of dedicated mindfulness practice—providing readers with the motivating tools, clear vision, and strategic-planning tools necessary to thrive as a mindful leader. Read this book to begin enhancing your affluence, influence, and inner peace."

—**LARISSA HALL CARLSON, M.A.** Mindfulness Studies,
Ayurvedic yoga specialist, Ayurvedic practitioner

"I love Dr. Holsapple's practical and useful techniques for mindfulness in leadership. He describes a path for practical mindfulness to reduce stress, reduce overthinking, improving decision-making, and increasing creativity while also improving profit and increasing employee well-being."

—**TINA KUHN**, author of *The Manager's Communication Toolkit* and *The E Suite: Empathetic Leadership for the Next Generation of Executives*

"I've been blessed to know Eric for over thirty-five years, and *Profit with Presence* perfectly captures his journey and provides inspiration for the rest of us to improve our lives through the Twelve Pillars of Mindful Leadership. In a world fraught with senseless violence and conflict, the Pillars demonstrate that success in business and life can rise above the chaos we all encounter. The world needs mindful leadership now more than ever, and I know that *Profit with Presence* will positively impact the leaders of today and more importantly, the future."

—**BRUCE JAMES**, shareholder, former CEO, and managing partner, Brownstein Hyatt Farber Schreck, LLP

"In *Profit with Presence*, Dr. Eric Holsapple shows us that commercial and material success need not be at odds with living a mindful, intensely present life. Presence can create abundance in all facets of our lives and in all types of organizations. Truly a must-read."

—**DEVIN FERREY**, partner, FR Corp

"A book I wish I had an opportunity to read forty years ago when I was launching my own quest for success and achievement as a leader in the military and later in business! Dr. Eric Holsapple convincingly argues that one need not face a choice between Presence and Mindfulness and the tenets of success. It's never too late to get started, and this book delivers the framework to do so!"

—**BRIGADIER GENERAL ROB CARMICHAEL**, USA, retired, chief strategy officer, Maine Savings FCU

"Mindfulness does not only live in yoga studios or in solitude. Holsapple demonstrates that it is crucial for a healthy workplace and intentional leader."

—**FAISAL HOQUE**, *Wall Street Journal* and *USA Today* best-selling author of *Lift* and *Everything Connects*

"The bibliography, in and of itself, is a gold mine for all those who aspire to lead with presence. But this book is not just a wealth of information, it is based on wisdom from years of application. Everything offered has been processed and applied directly to Eric's life and leadership experience as a CEO. If it's in this book, it's been tested and verified. This new paradigm for leadership and business is exactly what is needed most in the world now. Eric's method will save you decades of time and place you right on the cutting edge."

—**MICHAEL JOSPÉ**, founder and president, Earth-Based Institute

"Offers a plethora of high-focus processes to achieve knowing oneself, creating a purpose, and manifesting one's calling. Dr. Holsapple creates a business-profit application with an active structure of principles and activities to manifest and fulfill: 'To thine own self be true.'"

—**ROGER STRACHAN**, PhD, founder, Center of Creative Choice and Wilderness Encounters

"Much has been written on leadership and on the power of presence, but little has been written on the power of blending them. In this stunning book, Dr. Eric Holsapple shares his experiential journey of combining the two. In practical ways, Eric lays out that our work, our life, and our spiritual practice can be an integrated cohesive whole, instead of seemingly disconnected fragments. This book is not theoretical; it's a street-tested spiritual work path."

—**FRED SHOEMAKER**, author of
Extraordinary Golf: The Art of the Possible

"As someone who has been in leadership almost my entire career, Eric has challenged me to think outside the box I've been living in. WOW! What a thought-provoking, powerful ride through areas many have not explored or don't know how to. Thank you for this must-read, *Profit with Presence*."

—**JOHN REED**, CEO, Maine Savings
Federal Credit Union

"Dr Holsapple's approach to mindfulness in business, *Profit with Presence*, is a practical guide that challenges and empowers us readers to make the differences we know the world needs. The optimism embedded in his methods provides an inspirational boost to manifest positive and lasting change in ourselves and the world around us, both in our professional and personal lives."

—**JOSH BEARD**, partner and
manager, liquor store services

"*Profit with Presence* is precisely what the world needs now. As our political, social, and economic systems tell us we are more divided than ever, *Profit with Presence* tells us otherwise. And more importantly, it gives practical tools to tap into that interconnectedness, to overcome the constraints of daily life to live more intentionally, more mindfully, and all-around better lives. As business leaders, elected officials, and other community leaders, Eric's book is a lens through which, individually, we can get there; then collectively work to make the world more united."

—**LEAH JOHNSON**, former elected
official, author of *Finding Fantastic Joy*

"*Profit with Presence* opened my eyes to the benefit of living life with purpose without feeling bad about economic and material successes. After reading and reflecting on Dr. Holsapple's Twelve Pillars of Mindful Leadership, I have a clear understanding, and peace, about accepting others' perspectives, and the grace to work with them. A must-read for CEOs and a great mind asset for any stage of their career."

—**CHRISTOPHER R. KING**, president
and CEO, DPC Companies

"Dr. Holsapple has created a pathway for those of us in business who are looking for something beyond profit—not to ignore or forget profit, but to go beyond being driven solely by profit. Going beyond the way we normally operate, which is to bring Presence and our full Selves to our work. Very grateful for this work being brought more and more into the mainstream. It is a conversation that is needed and this book is a powerful piece of that."

—**AARON HENDON**, managing broker, eXp Realty

PRAISE FOR
LIVING IN THE GAP
MINDFUL LEADERSHIP PROGRAM

"The program changed my life in a way I never thought possible and didn't even think I needed. I have built lifelong connections and friendships from this program. The program has given me the tools to live a better life."

—**NATE MELCHOIR,** principal, Dunton Commercial

"Living in the Gap gives you the tools, and relationships and awareness, to live a soul-directed life that allows you to live on purpose in joy and gratitude."

—**AMANDA POMBAR,** Nature-Connected guide

"This program held my feet to the fire to truly be the man I want to be. I now feel confident that I can not only achieve whatever I put my mind to, but that I have the tools to be fully aligned every day."

—**DAVID RAFFELOCK,** founder, Profound Purpose

"Beyond expectation. The length and journey of the program makes it unique and special. Transformational change takes time and effort. It must be repeated and reinforced."

—MATTHEW HENRICHS, CBRE

"Going through this nine-month, intensive program has been the single greatest, most impactful thing I've ever done for myself. I've always had the ideas, or the 'wish I could,' for leading the kind of life I want, but never really had the tools, intention, routines, or roadmap to really create that vision. Now I do. It's up to me."

—JOHN COVERT, Zonda Home

"I trusted the process and let the work do itself. At one moment it all clicks and comes together and it really launches your purpose in life! Just have to take action!"

—MARK GOMES, branch manager, Key Bank

"This is the cutting edge of personal development; you owe it to yourself and the people around you to be successful in all things."

—SAM WHITE, Capital Fund

"Living in the Gap has provided the tools to facilitate a breakthrough and lasting change in my healthy lifestyle and productivity."

—ROSS CARPENTER, Newmark Merrill

"Living in the Gap is a simple, yet incredibly effective system for anyone that is looking for a deeper meaning in life."

—LANCE EBERHARD, Colliers International

"This program has opened my eyes and heart to what I want, how I can get there, and the support and habits I need to do it."

—BAILEY CHARLES, LC Home

PROFIT

WITH

PRESENCE

PROFIT

— WITH —

PRESENCE

THE 12 PILLARS OF
MINDFUL LEADERSHIP

DR. ERIC J. HOLSAPPLE,
CEO LC REAL ESTATE GROUP

GREENLEAF
BOOK GROUP PRESS

Published by Greenleaf Book Group Press
Austin, Texas
www.gbgpress.com

Distributed by Greenleaf Book Group

For ordering information or special discounts for bulk purchases, please contact Greenleaf Book Group at PO Box 91869, Austin, TX 78709, 512.891.6100.

Design and composition by Greenleaf Book Group
Cover design by Greenleaf Book Group
Illustrations by Erica Ellis of Ellis Designs, LLC

Excerpts from BHAGAVAD GITA: A NEW TRANSLATION by Stephen Mitchell. Copyright © 2000 by Stephen Mitchell. Used by permission of Harmony Books, an imprint of Random House, a division of Penguin Random House LLC. All rights reserved.

Publisher's Cataloging-in-Publication data is available.

Print ISBN: 979-8-88645-010-1

eBook ISBN: 979-8-88645-011-8

To offset the number of trees consumed in the printing of our books, Greenleaf donates a portion of the proceeds from each printing to the Arbor Day Foundation. Greenleaf Book Group has replaced over 50,000 trees since 2007.

Printed in the United States of America on acid-free paper

23 24 25 26 27 28   10 9 8 7 6 5 4 3 2 1

First Edition

I dedicate this book to my partners and the employees at
LC Real Estate Group and our nonprofit, Living in the Gap,
who were the inspiration for Living in the Gap Workshops and
this book. I love and appreciate you and the difference you
are making in yourselves, your families, and your communities.

They are Mindfully Creating Community in Loveland, Colorado.

This book's purpose is to share the opportunity for
mindful business with the world, and to support the
Mindful Leadership Program at our nonprofit, Living in the Gap.
Thank you.

CONTENTS

FOREWORD . . . . *xxi*

PREFACE . . . . *xxv*

INTRODUCTION *1*

PART 1—CONCEPTUAL FRAMEWORK

CHAPTER 1 Presence 11

CHAPTER 2 Transformation 29

CHAPTER 3 The Precession Effect 39

CHAPTER 4 Spiritual Cross-Training 45

PART 2—THE TWELVE PILLARS OF MINDFUL LEADERSHIP

PILLAR 1 Be Present and Practice Mindfulness 55

PILLAR 2 Identify Your Purpose in Life 85

PILLAR 3 Create Clarity, Vision, Intention, Commitment, and Habits . . 115

PILLAR 4 Success Is a Mindset of Be-Do-Have 141

PILLAR 5 Show Up, Take Action, and Detach from Results 150

PILLAR 6 Be Responsible, Practice Nonjudgment and
Compassion 160

PILLAR 7 Foster Relationships with Your Word and Listening 167

PILLAR 8 Be in Flow, Create Affluence and Influence 191

PILLAR 9 Be Grateful, Give Generously, and Serve 199

PILLAR 10 Acceptance Means to Stop Resisting and Complaining 209

PILLAR 11 Take Everything Impersonally and Let Life
Flow through You 220

PILLAR 12 Beginner's Mind Means to Know Nothing Absolutely
and Be Curious 226

PART 3—PRACTICING MINFULNESS IN YOUR BUSINESS AND CONCLUSIONS

CHAPTER 5 The Mindful CEO 243

CHAPTER 6 The Mindful Corporation 250

CHAPTER 7 Conclusion: Toward a New Cultural Worldview 273

AFTERWORD 293

ACKNOWLEDGMENTS 295

LIVING IN THE GAP Additional Resources 301

APPENDIX 1 Summary of Chapters and Pillars, Exercises, and
Mindfulness Practices 303

APPENDIX 2 Yoga Is the Science of Consciousness 341

APPENDIX 3 Mindfulness Research 356

NOTES 361

BIBLIOGRAPHY 377

ABOUT THE AUTHOR 387

FOREWORD

As Peter Drucker famously said, "The best way to predict the future is to create it." Eric Holsapple has figured out a strategy to do just that for himself, family, friends, college students, work associates, partners, and business friends. Now, even those business professionals around the world in need of a new paradigm can learn to create their futures.

Eric didn't have a book to follow. He has done it on his own by trial and error. This required drive, intensity, hard work, ingenuity, integrity, enthusiasm, and empathy. The wonderful thing about Eric is that he is sharing his approach with the rest of us, so that anyone can also live the life they've imagined.

I met my cousin Eric many years ago at our long-standing family reunions at the farm in Worthington, Massachusetts. He seemed much younger than me at the time, and he always chauffeured my Aunt Betty Jane to the event. He later came into my business life at a time when I was at my lowest. Eric showed me a path back and stood by me until I had come back. He is a natural entrepreneur from the tip of his toes to the top of his head. I have watched his business success climb to unimagined heights and circle the globe. He's participated in my leadership experiences in Gettysburg on numerous occasions. I have spoken for him while he ran the Colorado State University Everitt Real Estate Center and have participated in his Living in the Gap workshops.

I have watched him grow not only his impressive home building and real estate holdings but also his relationship with his family, friends, and partners. Most impressively, Eric has grown into a man who is making a tremendous difference in the world of business. By spreading mindfulness, not for money, but through his nonprofit enterprise, Living in the Gap, Eric has helped to profoundly change many lives.

Eric also comes highly recommended by his close friend Larry Kendall. The two of them taught together for ten years at Colorado State. Larry is the founder of the Group Real Estate Firm and wrote the best-selling book *Ninja Selling*, named after his popular workshops. Larry has been personally and professionally impressed by Eric, who shares a philosophy of changing lives through business, which makes a lot of sense. He is so impressed with Eric that he introduced him to Greenleaf Publishing. This introduction allowed Eric to get his story out to the business world as quickly and professionally as possible.

The message of this book is very important. I have always been fascinated by the stories of very successful people. What motivates them? What did it take to get there? What could I learn from them to apply in my own life? *Profit with Presence* is a wonderful story about an amazing person who has created an extraordinary family, life, company, and local and university communities. He has influenced all these communities in positive ways and now has decided to share his methods with the world of business.

This is a page-turner that I didn't want to put down. It's also structured to be as gradual, or as deep, as you want to go with individual choices. There are no "shoulds" or "have-tos" involved. The astute reader will not only learn what Presence can bring in the way of peace and joy to their life but also get a glimpse of eternity and the opportunity to enhance their Soul—all this while making a profit and a unique difference in ways that are important to them.

I hope that people who read this book will come away with that message. I know I will enthusiastically recommend it to all of our clients. Eric Holsapple has made a huge impact in many lives. *Profit with Presence* can help you do the same to run the business—and also live the life—of your dreams.

—**STEVE WILEY,** founder and president of the Lincoln Leadership Institute at Gettysburg, Gettysburg, Pennsylvania, 2023

"Steve Wiley is the best speaker you've never heard of!"

—ABC NEWS

"The most powerful performance training available."

—USA TODAY

PREFACE

In 2018, I was in San Francisco with several of my partners of LC Real Estate Group. We were attending a transformational workshop called Atlas Project and had been asked to come up with our vision for the world. This was a daunting task, and I had a hard time sleeping that night as I pondered my vision. I viewed the world as being a complete mess, with division, violence, and frankly, so much mindless behavior.

I got up early, even though we had gone to bed late, did my usual morning routine, and went out for a run along the waterfront. I turned a corner and almost stepped on a homeless person. Homeless people were everywhere, and this was before the coronavirus pandemic that devastated the city and the world. As I stepped over the person, my little inner voice said, *Why doesn't someone do something about this?* And more shocking was the immediate response from the same voice, *Why don't you do something?*

I went back to my room and wrote a poem about it and read it in front of the seminar group later that same day. This was not typical for me. I had begun writing poetry only a few weeks earlier at the age of sixty. Something was shifting in my inner landscape. That day, I came up with my vision of the world—"World transformation starts with me"—which became the impetus for the Living in the Gap workshops, where we train businesspeople in mindfulness, and later the writing of this book, *Profit with Presence*.

Businesspeople need an entry to mindfulness that is practical and useful. The tools in this book provide that on-ramp while also pointing to ways to take mindfulness as far as a person wants to go. My hope is that this book is an answer to what some purists classify as a McMindfulness approach, meaning one that lacks depth and waters down the amazing tools of mindfulness just to make money.

Business has added to many issues, including the ills of social media and the Industrial Revolution, that have contributed to divisiveness, climate degradation, and a lack of Presence more generally. We don't talk to each other anymore, and we need to restart genuine communication. The divisiveness, violence, and mindlessness in the world and issues such as climate change are not only troubling to citizens but also bad for business. Mindful action by business leaders can help this situation greatly. This book asks the business community to step up to the plate, and it gives them tools to do so.

I believe business is the key because business leaders are in a position to make a difference. Business matters, and business has influence on communities through its innovation and production and has influence on politics through its affluence and visibility. Any CEO who promotes social change in lieu of profit, as opposed to *Profit with Presence*, will not be CEO for long. In contrast, this book documents that mindfulness has increased company productivity, reduced health-care costs, and gives businesses a competitive edge, and this is my experience with our company as well.

The world can be an unsettling place, especially recently, with division guiding politics, education, race, climate, the economy, and virtually everything. The coronavirus, in addition to illness and death, became socially divisive and made connection and corporate culture a challenge because companies must now navigate the Great Resignation, remote work, pressures of inflation, and more.

If we can provide a path for business to promote social change with growth and profit potential, then CEOs and their stakeholders will listen. Following the Twelve Pillars of Mindful Leadership provides an approach in which mindfulness can increase the bottom line while reducing stress, diminishing divisiveness, and improving relationships. By fostering better relationships and practicing nonjudgment and compassion, we can begin to truly see and hear other people and reduce discord. We will still disagree, but everything does not have to be an argument.

By improving relationships with fellow employees, we can maintain connection. And by giving employees these tools, they can improve their families' homelife, churches, communities, and schools. Through mindfulness, we can not only maintain but also improve corporate culture. It will take more effort and intention in a world of remote work, but it can be done. It has to be done.

Businesses employ people on both sides of the political divide and of all genders and races, and it controls their livelihoods, so it has a unique ability to bring people together for a common cause to do good in the world as well as create profits. Besides, businesspeople generate the majority of the wealth in the world, and wealthy businesses and people who obtained their wealth through business, either directly or indirectly, fund politics and other causes that matter in our society.

The simple truth is that political divisiveness is bad for business. Political ideologies have no place in business in most instances. South

Africa was at the precipice of civil war at the end of apartheid, not much different from what the United States is facing now, other than it was worse, and it was the business community that came together and forced the politicians to mend fences, as told by Barbara Walter in her book *How Civil Wars Start*.[1]

It does not appear that the politicians in the United States and elsewhere are going to become less divisive on their own any time soon. The business community has the means to get politicians' attention through its affluence and make the left and right work together. I believe this is a huge opportunity for mindful leadership, and it was a large motivation for me to write this book.

Affluence increases influence, and in my experience making money can be a key factor in making significant differences in the lives of your family, employees, customers, and communities and in the world. Making money to make a difference in the quality of lives, including your own, is mindfulness. Everyone matters, and if you are a business professional, you are a difference maker. What difference do you choose to make?

There are lots of reasons to practice and promote mindfulness, and the reasons I have discovered and put to use over the last thirty years are outlined in this book and its Twelve Pillars of Mindful Leadership. There is no time to lose, and the best time to start is *now*.

Why does it matter?

Because you matter.

I hope you enjoy reading *Profit with Presence* and practicing its tenets. I wrote it for you.

INTRODUCTION

Money, profit, and even business more generally often appear to be dirty words to some in the mindfulness community and its culture. My aim is to help you take a different approach and join others in promoting mindfulness and offering a path in which business is invited into the mindfulness conversation, not only as a welcomed participant but also as a catalyst for change. Business is a powerful force for change. In 1942, Joseph Schumpeter defined the essential force of capitalism as "creative destruction" and having the ability to constantly evolve as it chases profit.[1]

Capitalism has the ability to revolutionize the economy from within, destroying the old one and creating a new one, seemingly almost instantaneously. For instance, business transformed the world through expanding the internet, which only became widely available in the mid-1990s, leading to the Dot Com boom in the late 1990s, and the social media boom of the last decade. Much good has come from these business revolutions, but it also came at a cost: separation, divisiveness, internet security issues, and seemingly, promotion of mindless behavior around the globe.

But what if business found that mindfulness could also be a positive influence on long-term profits and survival in a world of divisive politics, the Great Resignation, and the spawning of remote work? As you will read, Aetna documents over $2,000 per employee in health-care savings and $3,000 per employee increase in productivity due to mindfulness practices they implemented.[2] SAP documented a 200 percent return on investment on their mindfulness training, and said they believed mindfulness gave them a competitive edge. We have experienced higher productivity, less absenteeism, and higher bottom line results across the board for our company.

And what if the entire mindfulness community welcomed business to the conversation and helped businesses find ways to train their people to be more mindful while being productive participants in the creation of profits?

The mindful business revolution has already started, and many companies—from Aetna and Google to my company, LC Real Estate Group—are encouraging employees to practice mindfulness. *Profit with Presence* aims to aid the conversation and accelerate the next phase of creative destruction, in which business promotes mindfulness within, transforms the world, and is a leader in solutions to the problems facing the world today.

Our attention spans are at an all-time low when we need to focus. A confluence of factors is driving a higher level of risk, stress, and divisiveness. While the internet offers accessibility to the world, it's part of the mindlessness problem because it steals our attention and can promote division between people and nations through the amazingly effective tools of social media.

We are a society simultaneously on information overload and at an analytic low point. We simply cannot process the abundant amount of information coming at us from all directions, so we analyze virtually none of it. At a time when the need to focus is paramount, we often find we lack the ability to do so.

We have trained ourselves to scroll, to click the Like button, to be drawn to divisiveness, and to avoid empathy. We judge and stereotype, rather than listen and analyze, because it's quicker. We let others analyze, give us our opinions, and call it news. Different opinions are healthy; different facts are ludicrous.

Everything is faster, except our ability to process the changes. We have adapted to this fast-paced world by not focusing specifically on things, because humans are not capable of focusing on multiple stimuli at the same time. Multitasking causes our minds to skip from one thing to another, never fully integrating any of the information. We have sacrificed depth to take in the breadth of what is coming at us.

Each of us needs to take back our focus. We need to start noticing when we are not present. We need to start listening to each other and stop judging everyone with scant evidence. The tools outlined in this book will show you how. The immense problems we are facing are solvable. Just look at how far we have come in the last 100 years. We simply need to grow our consciousness and reside in Presence while taking mindful actions. Even the social problems are solvable. The only question is whether we are willing to give up our arguments and grievances for real empathy, progress, and Presence.

This book is about how you can take back your focus and make a real difference for yourself, your family, your business, your community, and the world. I know you can because I have, and I have seen many others do the same. Not perfectly, but just by noticeably improving Presence. My business career started when I worked at our family campground in Maine. I worked at the local mill during high school, then at K-mart and an auto dealership, where I was promoted to service manager during college. After I earned my MBA, I went into real estate. Within a few years, I became the North American president for an Australian group and started my own company shortly afterward. So I know about self-generated business success.

But I was not satisfied or fulfilled with business success. I decided to return to college to get my PhD in economics at Colorado State University so I could teach. While at CSU, I started Yoga, and a few years later, my oldest brother, Bruce, a poet, introduced me to meditation. Through Yoga, meditation, and mindfulness, I found my Soul and my purpose: Presence and to share Presence with the business community.

I know business has a critical role in the world; it is far from being irrelevant or counterproductive. It can be the linchpin that promotes mindfulness, reduces divisiveness, and provides the solutions to the myriad problems facing us today.

I'm going to share what I have learned about how to be happy, successful, and present now, today, rather than having to wait until you have accomplished your goals. In my experience, this mindset I describe does not lead us to abandon our goals. It instead improves our ability to take the actions required to accomplish our goals.

This book is for CEOs, leaders, and professionals who want to be more mindful and make positive changes for themselves, their families, their businesses, their communities, and the world. I lay out a methodology, the Twelve Pillars of Mindful Leadership, that will allow you to accumulate more wealth while being present, thus making a positive difference along the way. Learning from the example of my journey and others', you will find strategies to help you be a mindful professional.

This is a book of my personal experiences, learning these principles myself, sharing with my company, and launching the Living in the Gap Mindful Leadership nonprofit. The primary flavor of the book is experiential, but my experiences are backed up with research. During my research, I was flattered to see how my experiences matched what I found there.

I invite you to join the mindful business movement and become part of the solution. Find peace, happiness, meaning, and fulfillment while staying productive and making a difference. *Profit with Presence.*

Mindfulness

Mindfulness is the state of being aware of what you're sensing and feeling in the moment, without interpretation or judgment. Practicing mindfulness can help you achieve your dreams by looking inside yourself to change the outside world. Google's mindfulness program is called Search Inside Yourself.

Extensive research and studies over the past fifty years have provided us with solid, measurable evidence on the benefits of mindfulness. Some of the research is discussed in the chapters, where appropriate, and more is summarized in Appendix 3. Here is a quick summary of the benefits of mindfulness:

- Reduces overthinking

- Reduces stress in the workplace

- Boosts creativity and innovation

- Improves focus

- Improves memory

- Lowers emotional reactivity

- Improves relationships and communication skills

- Helps achieve better health

For all these reasons and more, bringing mindfulness to the workplace is an investment that pays out real dividends. We need to infuse more mindfulness into our culture.

Culture

Culture is a funny thing, except it's not that funny.

We have been told by our parents, and also teachers, coaches, bosses, politicians, and the media, that if we do all the right things, we will be successful, secure, happy, and content. Things like getting a good education, getting a good job and working hard, getting married, raising a family, having the ideal suburban home—and maybe a second home in the mountains or on the coast—and taking dream vacations are symbols of a secure, prosperous, and happy life.

Society has programmed us to believe that achieving these things is success and will make us happy, and we have chosen to believe it. The truth is, success begets success; in other words, success is a mindset, not a destination. Culture has promoted a do-have-be life: we *do* the right things to *have* nice things and, someday, get to *be* happy. The problem is that it is a lie. I call it a cultural lie.

The social order teaches us to live for the future at the expense of the now. Production and consumption are presented as the be-all and end-all. Someday, when you are successful, you will magically be present to enjoy your success. It sounds clichéd, but tomorrow never comes.

Being present is a practice. If we practice our whole lives not being present, so that we can *do* all the things culture has laid out for us to be successful, we form the habit of not being present to what is in front of us. The longer we practice not being present, the harder the habit is to break. In the West, we have conditioned ourselves so that, despite having all our physical needs satisfied, we think only more will satisfy us—the third house, luxury hobby car, private plane, or even traveling to space. Even billionaires seem to only want more. What I see in the press certainly confirms that many have that life view. When I look at the current billionaire space race, I wonder if this isn't what is really going on.

The median worldwide income is less than $2,000 per year according to the Global Rich List. That means half the households in America makes more than thirty times the median worldwide income.[3] Mental health professionals agree happiness is a multifaceted experience that's achieved through mindset, not money.[4] So despite having enough physical resources to be happy, secure, and content compared with the rest of the world, many Americans still feel discontent with their situations.

How is this possible?

The truth is, you cannot become successful; you can only be successful in the moment. You cannot become present; you can be present only in the moment. You cannot become happy; you can be happy only in the moment. Being present takes practice, and we need practice to offset the training we have had in not being present. If you have sacrificed Presence for future success, happiness, and fulfillment, you have bought into the cultural lie, as I did for a long time. Without this realization, after reaching the level of material success you set out to achieve, your conditioning may simply lead you to desire more.

Of course, there are instances of billionaires practicing mindfulness and giving back. For instance, Bill Gates, who with his former wife Melinda has donated over $50 billion to world humanitarian needs through their foundation, meditates regularly.[5] And there are many more examples. My financial contributions to the Colorado State University Real Estate program and other worthy causes, exceeding $1 million, tie directly to my mindfulness practice. My practice makes me more compassionate and generous.

There is certainly nothing wrong with wanting to be a billionaire, but what's your *why*? What's the purpose for the wealth? Wealth, or profit for that matter, is not a valid purpose in itself.

The good news is, you do not need to sacrifice the accumulation of material wealth to practice being present or to find your true purpose. The Twelve Pillars of Mindful Leadership system will allow you to accumulate more wealth and be present while making a bigger, more positive impact on the world.

Affluence

When I first started studying mindful concepts, I thought I had to give up all material possessions to achieve some enlightened state. I have since learned that it's not so for everyone. I wasn't willing to give up my material possessions, although I continuously work on not being attached to material possessions. Fortunately, I learned that affluence increases influence and that wealth meant I could make a bigger difference.

There are renunciates who give up everything and even beg for food as part of their practice. In contrast, I am a householder, which means I have numerous responsibilities, including my home, business, and family. My spiritual journey doesn't include renouncing material goods or my way of life. Having to choose between business and spirituality is a false choice. You can have it all—nice things, dramatic experiences, great relationships, Presence, spirituality—while making a positive impact on the world.

Remember the mindfulness benefits. They can help you achieve all this, if you become aware of the cultural lie and choose a different path. Robert Frost said it well: "Two roads diverged in a wood, and I— / I took the one less traveled by / And that has made all the difference."[6]

PART 1

CONCEPTUAL FRAMEWORK

When the world view catches up with the facts, the old paradigm will be replaced with a new biocentric model, in which life is not a product of the universe, but the other way around. [1]

—Robert Lanza

This section of the book explores the concepts of Presence, transformation, the precession effect, and spiritual cross-training that are critical to grasping the material presented in the Twelve Pillars of Mindful Leadership.

I was never a good student of science. Math came easy, but science was a four-letter word to me. I slouched out of challenging science classes in high school and in college and opted for funny book physics versus the real deal. I say that to let you know that I will not lose you by going deep into quantum physics. I will instead reveal another way to come at science: spirituality or Presence. I will hopefully also address the topic sufficiently so that those more scientifically minded will be positively impacted by what follows. The topics of science and spirituality are converging in the research world today, and it's quite exciting.

To me, despite the magnificent achievements of science, which have dramatically impacted, if not improved, the lives of people across the entire planet, most astounding are the questions science has yet to answer definitively: Why are we here? What is the nature of reality? What is consciousness? Why do we love? Where do we go when we die?

There are some key concepts to understanding Presence and much of the literature in the area of science, spirituality, or consciousness. One of the bridges between science and spirituality or consciousness is the distinction of duality and nonduality, which we explore in the next section.

Chapter 1

PRESENCE

We've come to believe that the core capacity needed to access the field of the future is presence.[1]

—SENGE, SCHARMER, JAWORSKI, FLOWERS

P resence is typically defined as the state of existing, or being, and being present in the moment.* Presence has many layers, like an onion, and encompasses states of consciousness, awareness, and spirit. Consciousness is defined as the state of being awake and aware of one's surroundings. Awareness is defined as the knowledge or perception of a situation or fact. Spirit is defined as the nonphysical part of a person that is the seat of emotions and character, the Soul.

---

*   This and all definitions in this chapter not cited come from the *Oxford English Dictionary*, Oxford University Press, 2022, https://www.oed.com/.

Reading the literature, it seems differentiating the terms "consciousness," "awareness," and "spirit" can be tricky. Carl Jung used spirit as analogous to consciousness, and consciousness and awareness are also often used interchangeably.[†] The main distinction adopted here is they all possess the power of recollection and self-reflection, and their opposites do not. This implies that we are possibly always conscious, just not always able to immediately recall or reflect on the experience. This distinction will be expounded upon throughout this chapter and the balance of the book.

When I use the word *Presence* with a capital *P*, it represents being in the moment, or the now, being conscious, and being fully aware of our internal state and external surroundings, being with spirit, being meta-conscious, and specifically includes being aware that you are aware. Other words or concepts often used interchangeably with Presence are being in the zone, being in flow, and being in the gap.[‡] Presence is being used to represent this entire category of experience in which we can recall or reflect on our experiences.[§]

I don't find it critical to this work to understand the subtle differences between consciousness, awareness, and Spirit in most instances. Sometimes certain terms within the category of Presence, especially consciousness, reveal different meanings individually or are specially cited in research, and will be used that way when appropriate.

Let's start the discussion of Presence by exploring the differences between the world of "nonduality" where Presence resides, and the world of "duality" in which science, material success, and profit reside.

[†]   Thus, spirituality necessarily entails the exploration of consciousness and Presence.

[‡]   Living in the Gap is the name of a nonprofit I formed to promote Presence in the business community. It means to live in Presence.

[§]   My apologies if this simplification for clarity of message is troubling or offensive to any readers. I do not deny there are instances where one term or another is more appropriate and will endeavor to use the term directly and correctly in those instances.

Duality and nonduality

Science is the world of duality. You can study it, dissect it, observe it, and understand it. If it can't be measured, then it doesn't exist.

Presence and Spirituality are in the world of nonduality—consciousness, awareness, love, compassion, trust, and belief. If you believe it, then it's true.

Nonduality is an experience and state of being or oneness. Nondual experiences are explained through language, a tool of duality with subjects and objects. We must use language, or "duality," to explain nonduality to others, which is very limiting. We experience Presence, love, compassion, trust, or belief, but not everything can be explained satisfactorily through language. Completing the exercises provided will give you access to experience Presence directly and personally. For this inquiry into Presence, it's your experience that matters most, and I will do my best to describe in words what is possible to experience through Presence.

On the other hand, language is often necessary for communication between humans. For example, there is the famous saying, "The finger pointing at the moon is not the moon."[2] Using the analogy of the finger being language, describing something with words will always be lacking compared with direct experience of the same thing for yourself. I was staring into a full moon the other night and wondered if any written script could approach the beauty of experiencing the dramatic, radiant moon. I don't think so, do you? Poetry perhaps comes the closest to providing adequate linguistic descriptions of experience, and my brother Bruce wrote a poem about the moon that is appropriate to share:

> & the moon said
> are you looking for a symbol?
> I am a symbol—
> of all that is
> marvelous[3]

The point is to realize we are attempting to describe reality with our language, and that it's not a perfect or seamless translation of the actual experience. Bruce points us back to our own experience of the moon, which is impactful, but what about explaining experiences that we haven't had, or realized we had, ourselves? That is much more difficult and limiting.

Sometimes we hear people say, "I am not even here," or "I don't even exist," or "I am one with everything."

But what do they mean?

First, it is essential to note whether they are talking in relative terms—that is, in relation to something else—or in absolute terms, independent and free from any restriction, limitation, or exception.

Certainly, I exist, but am I independent? I can survive a few days without water, a couple of weeks without food, or several minutes without air, so I am not independent, because I need these things and more to live.

Similarly, describing or analyzing something in relative terms, such as "I see a tree," like you're two independent things, is the world of duality. But this is not the whole story, because according to some ancient Eastern philosophy, and some new Western scientific research we introduce later in this chapter, the tree may not even exist without you the observer. The answer to the age-old question, "If a tree falls in the woods, and there is no one around to hear it, does it make a noise?" is a resounding no according to these theories. The nondual world is absolute and is the world of oneness. There is only seeing, hearing, tasting, touching, or smelling, inclusively. Thus, duality is a relative concept, and nonduality is a concept describing absolute experiences.

In *The Case Against Reality*, Donald Hoffman talks about what we see versus what's really there.[4] Reality is defined as the world, or the state of things as they actually exist, as opposed to our idea of them. For instance, Hoffman describes the body or a face as an icon, or a dashboard for what's really there—a bundle of vibrating energy. So, in absolute terms, I don't exist at all as an independent self. I am a bundle of vibrating energy within an intricate web underlying all existence.

Or as Lynne McTaggart says in her classic book, *The Field*:

> At our most elemental, we are not a chemical reaction, but an energetic charge. Human beings and all living things are a coalescence of energy in a field of energy connected to every other thing in the world. This pulsating energy field is the central engine of our being and our consciousness, the alpha and omega of our existence.[5]

So, in absolute terms, I may correctly assert that "I don't exist" as an independent entity. But in relative terms, that's absurd. I exist in relation to you. Similarly, the concepts of space and time are real and essential in the relative world, and don't even exist absolutely.

Climate change impacts us all and is an example of absolute interdependencies. We may be exposed to the dramatic weather patterns, burning, and flooding around the globe regardless of how responsible we act independently, as they may be caused by the activities of other humans sharing the planet. Our actions or experiences are rarely truly independent, and almost always interdependent.

People's independence is a myth, yet independence is real and valuable. How is this possible?

Because I can be independent relative to others, but in absolute terms, we are all one and dependent on each other; and dependent upon air, water, food, and other basic necessities, even the climate. Both can be true in different contextual frameworks.

Breaking the myth of independence and accepting the reality of interdependence may be a key benefit of mindfulness, and it can help us see the value of contributing to others and our communities and set us on a path of making a difference in the world. This points us to the possibility of accepting the marvels of Presence itself as the most important aspect of life. It's residing in Presence that allows one to experience the interdependence of all things and experience the essential oneness of life in absolute terms.

It turns out that the concepts of duality and nonduality are both necessary to live a meaningful life in which you accomplish things in the material world and make a profit.

The meaning of life

Bernardo Kastrup, following Carl Jung, says the meaning of human life resides in our ability to self-reflect, be "meta-conscious," or reside in Presence, and our ability to know that we are experiencing life. And that we are (intentionally) separating ourselves as "subjects" who are "aware we are aware," and this distinguishes human life from other forms of life.[6] I love this blending of duality (subject–object), with nonduality (oneness), as it points to the essentialness of both concepts. This is the necessary yin and yang of our meaningful human existence with Presence.

While Presence may be primary and essential for meaning and sustainable success and happiness, it's duality, subject and object, that makes life actionable. This makes both concepts relevant for a happy and meaningful life in which you achieve things personally or for your family, and for successful and meaningful business operations that also make a profit. If business exists to support life, the purpose of business must be consistent with the purpose of life. Thus, I believe we were given a body to enable intentional actions with Presence, and we are in business to make *Profit with Presence*.

When someone says, "The meaning of life is to be happy," it's the same as saying the meaning of life is Presence. Happiness happens in the gaps of thought yielded by Presence.

If Presence is the meaning of life, how do you become Present?

It requires you to practice mindfulness, in whatever form works best for you. You will find a variety of suggested mindfulness practices in the remainder of this book and some very simple ways to get started.

Now, let's look at how Presence impacts our lives in the material or physical world, and in the world of business.

The movie of life and business

Rupert Spira uses the analogy that we are the movie screen of Presence, and the life of experience is being played out as a movie on the screen.[7] Like a movie screen that is not impacted by the contents of the movie, our Presence does not change regardless of the contents of our experience in the material world. The movie plays out as our experience of the material world, but the screen of Presence is not impacted once we establish Presence as our primary state.

For instance, take the movie based on Charles Dickens's book *A Christmas Carol*, featuring Ebenezer Scrooge.[8] Scrooge starts off idealizing the material world and profit, and is a miserable human being, albeit rich. But Scrooge has an epiphany, finds Presence, and changes his fundamental nature to be caring and giving to Tiny Tim and others. Far from this being a failure, it changes Scrooge's life to one of meaning and purpose, both personally and in business.

In one movie version of the book, actor Jim Carrey plays Scrooge. And as Carrey once said in real life, "I wish everyone could experience being rich and famous, so they would see it wasn't the answer to anything."[9]

The basic choice being presented in this book is to accept Presence as something of primary importance and the true source of success and happiness, rather than a counterforce of material success and profit; alternatively, you can continue living a false life chasing profits to make you successful and happy.

The movie screen of Presence is there for both possibilities; however, only those who acknowledge Presence as something of primary importance have a happy ending in the movie of life. Without Presence, you may have material wealth beyond imagination, but success and happiness will necessarily remain elusive. That was my life for many years.

Success and happiness are states of being that reside in Presence, and are only sustainable to those who also reside in Presence. Presence inherently means to be successful and happy regardless of the outcome of experience, which takes trust. Presence also supports us to take intentional actions in the face of adversity to provide sustainable success and profit in the material world.

To be clear, I am saying you can have it all if you get your priorities straight. I am *not* proposing that we abandon capitalism, only that we accept Presence as primary and materialism and profit as secondary. This is how capitalism can work for everybody, while we support capitalism as the best method of achieving sustainable success and happiness, or *Profit with Presence*. You simply need to de-Scrooge yourself by residing in Presence, and this book will show you how.

This is my experience and belief, and I will spend the rest of this chapter further explaining and offering published books and research supporting my experience and belief; the rest of the book will show you how to reside in Presence en route to material success and profit, not in lieu of material success and profit.

So, let's look into recent Western research to see what additional support we can find for Presence as the primary purpose in life.

Research

Albert Einstein said that "pure logical thinking cannot yield us any knowledge of the empirical world; all knowledge of reality starts from experience and ends with it."[10] I believe Einstein was possibly the most spiritual scientist in history, but after his passing, Western science seemingly avoided topics such as consciousness, which were left as a mystery for many years. Western science is now fully engaged in the conversation and research of consciousness; however, the Eastern thinkers whom I have studied have been engaged in this conversation and research for thousands of years.

The reason for introducing this relevant research is twofold: One is to stimulate your curiosity and motivate you to explore for yourself the possibilities embedded in the rich world of Presence where the richest research may be your own mindfulness exploration.

Second is to make these theories actionable in your personal and professional life, and in the world of business. To make these theories actionable requires enough conceptual knowledge to create at least the possibility for you that the world works this way, along with enough simplification to allow you to take action. Requiring simplification is fortunate, as there are many authors more qualified than I to delve into the intellectual disparities between the various theories. My expertise is how to apply these concepts to personal and professional life and to the world of business, which is the primary focus of this book.¶

With those caveats, let's explore recent relevant Western scientific research.

Most representative of the surge of recent research may be the books on biocentrism co-authored by Robert Lanza, one of *Time Magazine's*

¶ I admittedly do not give equal treatment to the theories of materialism or physicality, as they have been explored exhaustively and dismissed as unviable by the authors cited in this section.

Top 100 Most Influential People, and *Consciousness Unbound*, a collection of academic articles on consciousness written by the leading scholars in the field and edited by Edward Kelly and Paul Marshall.

Beyond Biocentrism maintains that life is not a byproduct of the universe, but its very source.[11] Dr. Lanza takes the common assumption that the universe led to the creation of life and argues that it's the other way around. This empowering model states consciousness is what gives rise to our sense of there being a universe when the world we experience around us is, in fact, created in our consciousness. *Beyond Biocentrism* proposes there aren't two worlds, the real one and the one in your head, but there is only the one. Where the visual image is perceived is where it is located. This theory maintains "there is nothing outside of perception, how could there be?"[12]

In *Consciousness Unbound* and other personal publications, philosopher Bernardo Kastrup describes analytic idealism. Kastrup is leading the calvary of academics who are finally fully embracing the study of consciousness. He proposes the physical world is merely an image in the individual mind of the observer; each one of us perceives our own physical world as defined by the context of our own observations. He believes there is only one universal consciousness, and that mind and consciousness are synonymous. According to this theory, consciousness is bound, or circumscribed into human form, and can become unbound, thus explaining phenomena such as telepathy and clairvoyance.[13]

Consciousness as a secondary phenomenon is the theory of materialism or physicality, and these theories are adamantly refuted by Lanza, Kastrup, and others espousing biocentrism, analytic idealism, and other theories that entail consciousness as a primary phenomenon.

Let's contemplate the depth and breadth of what is being proposed and then expand the exploration of analytic idealism.

Lanza, Kastrup, et al. propose that consciousness gives rise to our sense of a universe when the world we experience is created in our consciousness, and thus there is nothing outside of perception. Biocentrism and analytic idealism assert that consciousness is a primary basis of the universe. We are possibly consciousness itself; thus, we are also possibly the basis of the universe.

A person's mind is typically described as the element of a person that enables them to be aware of the world and their experiences, to think and to feel, that enable the faculties of consciousness and thought. For our purposes and following Kastrup, it's appropriate to consider the mind as synonymous with consciousness and Presence. According to analytic idealism, the whole universe is the mind, but not just your individual mind; the mind is proposed to extend far beyond individual boundaries, and while your mind is limited by human form, it is part of one large universal mind (Mind).

This is how idealism rationalizes the mind, creating our individual universe, while simultaneously sharing the world and experiences with others, who also share one Mind. "We seem to inhabit the same shared world because we are all immersed in, and surrounded by, the ideas of mind-at-large."[14]

Analytic idealism proposes that consciousness, which is analogous to mind, is circumscribed in all physical beings, and all have potential, albeit limited, to access the Mind. The basic facts of reality according to analytic idealism are:

1. There is a definitive correlation between a person's private experience and their brain activity.

2. We all appear to exist in the same universe.

3. There are laws of nature, independent of individual volition.

4. Physical entities are composed of microscopic segments and subatomic particles.

5. There exists in each person "that which is experience" (TWE).

6. There exist private experiences.

7. Brain activity of a person is experienced in the form of perceptions.

8. There is a definitive correlation between 1) above: private experience and 7) above: a person's brain activity and perceptions.

9. The brain has the same essential nature and is made of the same substance as the rest of the universe (i.e., they are in the same ontological class).[15]

Kastrup has dedicated his life to the study of consciousness and has performed more research published in a vast array of academic journals than I can fathom, or frankly completely understand, despite having read six of his books and numerous articles. So, I don't expect to "convince" you of anything, except that Kastrup is a credible source well regarded in academia who points to what's possible:

> "... the entire physical universe may be akin to a 'nervous system' in the specific sense that all its activity may be accompanied by experience. ... a study has shown unexplained structural similarities—not necessarily functional ones mind you—between the universe at its largest scales and biological brains."[16]

The inference drawn is "that which is experience" (TWE) for individuals is associated with the entire universe. To reconcile this inference with the fact that we have individual experiences, and we are not consciously aware of what is going on in the entire universe, Kastrup draws on the concept of "disassociation" from psychiatry: "Similarly, dissociation allows us to explain the existence of separate, private conscious inner lives, whilst preserving the notion that TWE is, and always remains, fundamentally unitary."[17]

Western culture has historically broadly accepted the assumption that reality consists of mind and matter, and that matter is typically considered primary and to exist independently, and that mind, being synonymous with consciousness, is derived from matter. This research reveals or asserts that mind, or consciousness, and Presence actually are the sources of matter. How consciousness has been proposed to be derived from matter is known as the "hard problem of consciousness,"[18] meaning it has been unsolvable. The assertion, if true, means that mind, or consciousness or Presence, is primary, and the hard problem of consciousness has been unsolvable because theories of materialism or physicality, that propose to source consciousness, are not true in reality.

Holy crap! If you are left scratching your head, don't worry—so was I. I first learned of this concept through ancient Eastern philosophies of Buddhism and Hinduism, and am gratified to see Western science now tackling the scientific proof of these important revelations. If you are like me, initially discovering these ideas and viewing consciousness as a primary phenomenon and the source of the cosmos, versus being secondary or a result of the material world or physical body, is quite a shock. After all, that means the entire basis of our lives up till that discovery was misguided, just like those who believed that the world is flat, or the Sun revolved around the Earth; or more directly, our view of the world and reality may have been upside-down.

Having tried these theories on for a while, I can tell you that they ring true to my life and business experiences. I am not saying that I have mastered these concepts, but I believe in them and work at living them every day. I like the analogy between consciousness or Presence in human beings and water to a fish; both are supremely entwined in the other's existence, neither aware of the other's primary importance. Even more important than understanding or agreeing with words on a page, I suggest you experiment with these concepts as you establish or deepen your own mindfulness practice, because being true in your own experience is what really matters.

There is more to unpack in the research of consciousness than I can hope to do justice to in this short section.** The main intent of this research section has been to establish the importance of consciousness, the mind, and other nondual concepts we collectively define as Presence; to share "what's possible"; and to point to where the science of consciousness may be headed: discovering the universe that lives in each of us, rather than each of us living and discovering the universe "out there."

Moving forward, I am going to focus on what is true from my personal experience that is valuable to share, and what is actionable in our personal, professional, and business lives.

Important assertions and implications

Let's summarize the primary assertions and their implications thus far.

Experiencing Presence is the fundamental purpose of human life and business, yielding sustainable success and happiness.

All other perceptions are experienced through Presence. Thus, Presence is primary and all else is secondary, and possibly just a story created by the mind.

Perceptions are made from images, like the dashboard that represents instruments in a car but is not the reality itself.

** For further study, I again point those interested (or simply skeptical) to the bibliography.

We each create our own universe, and together we create the universe (and universal Mind).

The implications of these assertions are extraordinary and enormous.

First, they reason that Presence is reality, and our perception of what we are in the presence of is typically not reality but a representation of reality.

Second, these statements mean that the direction of your life and the possibilities within life are largely within your perception, and much of it inherently within your control. The things not in our control are left for us to accept as "what is," or reality itself.

Third, they imply that the key to life and business is recognizing Presence as the fundamental purpose of life and business. Business is established to support life, and it's untenable that the purpose of business might diverge substantially from the purpose of life. It's also important to point out that this does not imply that matter, or profit, is not real or important in a relative sense, only that Presence is of primary importance in an absolute sense. Presence is what makes the physical world and profit possible and sustainable in the long run.

Fourth, these assertions suggest that matter- or physical-first models and the profit-first model in business have possibly outlived their usefulness. The materialist paradigm is no longer believable and has left the planet in dire straits. The world is full of division and degradation with no physical solution in sight. The materialist or physicalist view, while effective in the short run, has proven not to be sustainable in the long term, in my opinion. The researchers referred to in this chapter have rejected the materialist and physicalist theories of consciousness out of hand.

The four listed assertions and their personal and professional implications are key to having a sustainable, happy, and successful personal life and business career. How we know matter is through experience, and experience lives in the mind, thus this is as far as one really needs to go to know it's the mind that is driving the bus of matter.

If you want to be steady, dependable, reliable, successful, and happy, it's mind and Presence that can provide these as steady states. Relying on life's experiences will result in your experience of life also being a roller coaster of the same highs and lows life's experiences necessarily yield. Do you know anyone who hasn't had many bad experiences in life—or even *mostly* bad experiences? It's rare. Or anyone who has not died at the end of this miracle called life? Looking to life's experiences for success or happiness is a recipe for disappointment. Not relying on life's physical experiences is how Stephen Hawking lived a successful, happy, and meaningful life despite having amyotrophic lateral sclerosis (ALS).

Residing in Presence will lead you to a sustainably happy and successful life and business career.

Presence further clarified

I want to further clarify the term Presence. I have touched on the similarities of consciousness, awareness, and spirit, and have used the term Presence to represent all three. There is also the term meta-conscious, which implies we are always conscious, however not always able to self-reflect or recall what we have experienced. Following Kastrup's definition of mind, recalling our mind's contents also falls within Presence. Presence shall represent the things we are meta-conscious of experiencing, meaning with recollection or self-reflection. We also explored how the meaning of human life is to discover Presence, which implies being meta-conscious and aware that we are aware.

To demonstrate, close your eyes and focus on listening to your own breathing for the next minute. This is perhaps the simplest and most accessible demonstration of Presence. But take the activity of digestion: As much as I might focus on it, unless something is not digesting well in my system, I am not consciously aware of digestion. It's quite fortunate that so many of our bodily and other activities operate autonomously.

Other more optional functions, like walking or driving a car, also operate without our distinct focus on them once we have trained ourselves to do them repeatedly. That allows us to choose activities we wish to focus our Presence upon, like being with our family or a customer, without these other functions going off-line, and keeping ourselves operating effectively. Can you imagine if everything was in focus at the same time? It would be impossible to focus or distinguish what was pertinent versus irrelevant to the situation.

As you will learn in the Twelve Pillars of Mindful Leadership, the power of consciousness, the differing levels of consciousness and focus, and our ability to train our operating functions with practice are what allow us to achieve our conscious visions and goals while we reside in Presence and focus on what we are doing or who we are with at the moment. This is how we can live in the moment with Presence, with the people we are with, and in the environment we are in, and still achieve our personal, professional, and business goals.

Conclusion

In the Twelve Pillars of Mindful Leadership, you will learn to train yourself to consistently gain momentum toward activities that were determined as your stated vision and goals. It's not possible to multi-task with good focus on multiple activities, so you will learn to train yourself in activities most consistent with and according to your conscious objectives while focusing on the process, rather than the results. Your primary objective is Presence. Otherwise, your actions can occur randomly, or worse, possibly self-sabotage your conscious objectives.

Have you ever started a diet only to find yourself inexplicably digging in the refrigerator for a snack a few hours or days later? That type of thing happens frequently because of a disconnect with conscious objectives. Any areas of disconnect between your conscious objectives must be resolved and prioritized to achieve many of your stated goals and objectives.

Finally, we have only dipped our toe in the deep and evolving conversation of consciousness and Presence. I will further speculate on the meaning and possible implications of this discussion in the concluding chapter of the book. In the meantime, you now have enough background on Presence to make these theories actionable in your personal and professional life, and in the world of business.

Before we dive into transformation in the next chapter, let's recap what we've learned:

- *Presence* is used as a universal term to denote a class of nondual state in which you can recall or reflect on experiences.

- *Presence* is the primary purpose of life and business.

- Duality and nonduality are both critical concepts to live a meaningful life, in which you accomplish things in the material world and make a *Profit with Presence*.

- Analytic idealism proposes that we each create our own universe, and together create the universe.

- Training and practice are what allow us to reside in Presence and still accomplish our personal, professional, and business goals.

Chapter Takeaway

Presence is the primary purpose of life and business.

Chapter 2

TRANSFORMATION

When you *are* that life is empty and meaningless, and you're not making anything out of that, and you're not doing anything with it, and it's not a justification, and it's not an explanation, and there's no prescription, and it doesn't give you a prescription, then you're transformed.[1]

—WERNER ERHARD

In physics, transformation is defined as an induced or spontaneous change of one element into another by a nuclear process. In mindfulness, the equivalent is a change from being primarily identified with ego, thought, and form to being primarily identified with consciousness, or Presence. Form still exists in relative terms, but we choose to identify with consciousness, or Presence, in absolute terms.

Our goal is to transform from a world driven by ego, thought, and form (old) to a world driven by mindfulness and Presence (new). Admittedly, this is my interpretation, which I find empowering.

In my personal journey, transformation has been a combination of slow boils, such as daily practices of journaling, Yoga, meditation, prayer, affirmations, and gratitude; and transformational shocks, which are more dramatic experiences.

Let's begin the discussion with slow boils.

Jeff Olson describes simple, productive actions, repeated consistently over time, that make a massive difference to performance in life. He calls these "the slight edge."[2] The slight edge is relentless, and it cuts both ways: repeating simple errors in judgment over time leads to poor results. These practices are easy to do or easy not to do.

To illustrate, let's use a couple of simple examples. Walking one mile for one day may not amount to much physical benefit. But walking a mile each day, or 365 miles in a year, could make a difference to your health. The same goes for eating a doughnut every day for a year. The first one might have little impact, but eating a donut each day, or 365 donuts, may result in a serious health issue.

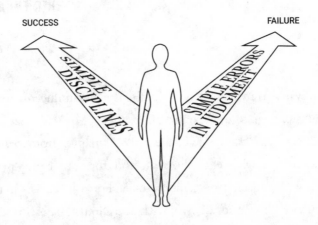

CHOOSE YOUR PATH IN LIFE

Used productively, the slight edge carries you up toward success in life. Used carelessly, it pulls you down toward failure. Olson says, "You can start with a million dollars, but if you don't understand the slight edge, you'll lose it all. You can start with nothing but a penny, yet if you understand the slight edge, you can go anywhere in the world you want to go."[3]

The slight edge approach, or slow boils, for our daily mindfulness practices such as prayer, gratitude, Yoga, and meditation keeps us open and fosters Presence.

These slow boil practices integrate transformational growth into our being over time, and they continually give us rewards. One day of meditation may not yield much in the way of results, but meditating every day for a year will bring noticeable effects. The slow boil practices I suggest are easy to do, and easy not to do. But when done consistently, they will open you up to new possibilities and new ways of being. These practices get us started, and we can add methods to accelerate transformation by directly providing the experience of pure consciousness. Once we experience consciousness, or Presence, slow boil practices help us maintain access to Presence in everyday life situations.

Let's delve into transformational shocks next. The basic tenet is that transformational shocks slow down the mind and allow you to experience a high level of Presence in a short period. Your first experience with Presence as the dominant way of being can be a shock, and you may not recognize it, other than the feeling of spaciousness or joy. A transformational shock is something that moves you directly into consciousness or Presence as the predominant state of being.

Michael Pollan's book *How to Change Your Mind* describes how psychedelics can cause a discovery of consciousness.[4] My experience with ayahuasca in Peru several years ago caused a transformational shock. Of psychedelic experiences, Steve Jobs said, "It was profound. It transformed me and many of my friends."[5]

I have also had transformational shocks in a variety of workshops, notably the Atlas Project* I mentioned in the preface, that created experiences in which there is no time or space to think and thus thrust participants into consciousness. Or the Landmark Forum† (formerly EST, made famous by Werner Erhard), which operates more linguistically, where over a weekend one mental construct after another was stripped away until all the participants had left was consciousness, leaving them to experience Presence directly.

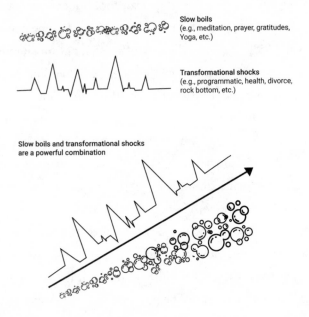

Slow boils
(e.g., meditation, prayer, gratitudes, Yoga, etc.)

Transformational shocks
(e.g., programmatic, health, divorce, rock bottom, etc.)

Slow boils and transformational shocks are a powerful combination

Some addicts find consciousness when they hit rock bottom because of their addiction, causing them to finally surrender, because everything is gone except consciousness. From there, they start a new life in sobriety. A heart attack, cancer, or a serious accident can also shock someone into Presence.

---

* https://atlasproject.org

† https://www.landmarkworldwide.com

I don't encourage anyone to take drugs, become an addict, or intentionally have a heart attack. I am not promoting attendance at an intense workshop unless someone is called to it, either. There are many avenues to experience Presence, but the larger question is, what makes a lasting difference? What allows someone to access consciousness in daily living? Once consciousness, or Presence, is experienced, the slow boils are what maintain it in daily living.

When I add a positive transformational shock to slow boil practices, the results produce a shift of profound growth that keeps getting better. I call that a permanent difference.

In my personal experience, and being involved in the transformation of many others, a transformational shock without some method of slow boil maintenance may be short lived. We close back up over time and lose our ability to maintain Presence.

Importantly, what works depends on what type of person you are. I am fairly intense and enjoy intense transformational shocks, and I have needed them to level up my Presence at different times. Also, I get bored easily, and they have kept me interested and engaged in my practice, which has basic slow boils but is also constantly evolving.

My wife, Tracy, is more mellow. She has tried transformational workshops, and they are not for her. She found a Course in Miracles[‡], and its more moderate approach works for her. She has found it transformational. I did a forty-day free trial and loved it, but I decided that I had enough different sources of practice. I support my wife's choice for individual practice, which I think she appreciates.

The main point is that what works is different for each individual. While the transformational shocks are optional, my experience is that the slow boils are not optional to establish a state of Presence in the long term, for reasons already stated. My advice is to start and maintain

‡   https://acim.org/

a slow boil, no matter what, and advance to mild to moderate transformational shocks when you see fit. Some slow boil practices are easier to establish and maintain than others.

While daily Yoga is an effective slow boil, deeper Yoga and pranayama practices can be completely transformational.[§] Some techniques, like advanced meditation or Yoga, can be both a slow boil and a transformational shock.

Over the years, I've worked with many people. For almost everyone, beginning, integrating, and sustaining a daily Yoga practice isn't as easy to do as the other practices I mentioned, such as meditation and gratitude.

Next to Yoga, meditation is the most challenging of the three to incorporate into a daily habit, in my opinion, and possibly the most rewarding slow boil of all. In fact, I find meditation to be essential to a long-lasting transformational experience. If I had to choose just one mindfulness practice, it would be meditation. But everybody is unique. What may shock one person into consciousness may not work for you. Some people are more or less predisposed to being conscious or even caring about their state of Presence. My mother walked each day on this earth with Presence and never practiced meditation a day in her life. The most important thing is to experience mindfulness as a "way of being" rather than an intellectual concept. We'll discuss "ways of being" extensively while describing the pillars.

Simple mindful meditation may transform some people eventually, especially if they start young and have sufficient time. My personal experience is that meditation kept me open to possibilities, but I would likely never have uncovered my blind spots without the variety of other

§   If you are intrigued, check out Swami Muktibodhananda's *Hatha Yoga Pradipika* (Bihar, India: Yoga Publications Trust, 2012). I learned of these practices in advanced training at the Kripalu Center for Yoga in Lenox, Massachusetts, www.kripalu.org. Doing these advanced practices without guidance and approval from your physician is not recommended.

practices and support that you are reading about. The other limiting factor may be how much practice you can accomplish daily, how deep, and for how long. For most of us, with all our responsibilities, time is limited, so transformational shocks can be added at whatever level works for you to accelerate the process. If you have Presence as the goal, discover what works for you and what you are willing to do, and do whatever it takes to realize Presence as a primary state.

Do you have to go to Peru, do LSD, or attend an intense workshop? Probably not, and I suggest you start with the slow boils and simple transformational shock techniques and see how it goes. I introduce simple transformational shock techniques in Pillar 2. Trust that you will know what other experiences you need when the time is right. "When the student is ready, the teacher will appear" is a famous Zen saying.[6]

Expectation

Lastly, a word on expectation, which is a strong belief of what is going to happen in the future; in this case, it's a strong expectation about what results you are going to experience from your mindfulness practice. Expectations keep us in the future and focused on results rather than being present in the moment and in the process.

Detaching from future results is key to being present. Also, specific expected results set us up for disappointment. Drop the expectations and be curious about the inner world you are about to enter. Trust the process, because if I can assure you of one thing, it's that achieving states of mindfulness and Presence is a process. You're not going to complete the process by next Tuesday. It's a process that is different for each and every one of us.

I wrote a poem about my personal journey of transformation, and I would like to share it with you.

TRANSFORMATION

I hear this word thrown around
Without really getting it
What it means and doesn't mean.

Webster is of little help
But a pointer of the way
Transformation to me is:

When I see that life of form
Has gotten me thus far
And now stalled my growth.

Now my life of Presence gets to kick in
And let a whole new life begin
One without the limits of form.

I get to see things as they are
It is what it is
Yet:

No limit on what it could be
And pure potentiality
And stop doing too just be.

Who am I?
Why am I here?
What is the source that moves in and through all things?

Nothing is stationary

Except the fixations of the mind.
Once I see that I am transformation.

Life is flow
I am not the same as I was
In the last instant.

Who I am cannot not be defined
When I stop trying
I am transformation.

The alchemy of life
Is the beauty
And is transformation.

It's not that I need to transform
It's that I get to see it, be aware of it, actually live it.
I always was transformation, just blinded by this or that.

Life is transcending one form to another
Death is transcending one form to another
Living a life of transformation is all that's available.

Unconsciousness to transformation and to life
Is optional, and thus
Transformation is the only certainty we have.

Who I am is transformation.
Neither I nor transformation can be described
Or denied.

- Slow boils are small daily practices.

- Transformational shocks shift you directly into Presence.

- Slow boils allow transformational shocks to make a permanent, lasting difference.

Chapter Takeaway

Transformation means the only thing that's permanent is your state of mind. Until you say otherwise.

Chapter 3

THE PRECESSION EFFECT

The Sun and the Earth are both bodies in motion. Despite the 180-degree gravitational pull of the in-motion Sun upon the in-motion Earth, precession makes Earth orbit around the Sun in a direction that is at ninety degrees—i.e., at a right angle—to the direction of the Sun's gravitational pull.[1]

—R. BUCKMINSTER FULLER

The precession effect was first theorized by the Greek astronomer Hipparchus as precession of the equinoxes, and then more fully explained by Isaac Newton.[2] Our interest is in the business applications first highlighted by R. Buckminster Fuller, who was an architect by trade, was Harvard educated, and lived from 1895 to 1983. I learned about the concept when discussing what I was experiencing in my life with one of my mentors Larry Kendall: Whenever I give of myself to worthy causes, the side effects are more business opportunities. How do I describe this to others? Larry pointed me to R. Buckminster Fuller and the precession effect.*

The Precession Effect

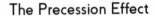

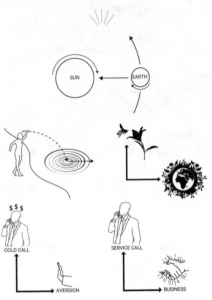

Fuller used the concept of an action that is at an angle to a body in motion to illustrate achievements made even though a purpose and goal are not aligned, but actually operate at ninety-degree angles like the early astronomers discovered. It's used in business to describe achieving a goal by moving at ninety degrees to the goal.[3]

Precession is important to understanding actions and the response, or karma. One of Fuller's famous examples is in the preceding quote about the Earth's rotation around the Sun at a ninety-degree angle. Another is the honeybee whose job it is to gather honey. In precession, the bee, whose pursuit is honey, gathers pollen from one flower for honey and accidently takes this pollen to the next flower, resulting in

---

* My appreciation to Larry Kendall, author of *Ninja Selling* (Austin, TX: Greenleaf Book Group, 2017), for referring me to the precession effect.

cross-pollination. This accidental event contributes immensely to life on Earth because a majority of the world's flowers requires cross-pollination, almost all done by bees. Another example is the ripples that appear when we throw a pebble into a pond.[4] Likewise, when the country goes to war with the intention of protecting its people, the economy often improves dramatically owing to military production and spending.

Albert Einstein said, "Nothing happens until something moves." In our context, action is necessary to set the precession effect in motion, and then, as Fuller theorized, what society rates as side effects are nature's main effects. I have found the side effects of providing community service work at the university and area nonprofits to be major business enhancers.[†]

It may be wise to notice the side effects (or precession effects) are the main event in many endeavors; they are not the reason to do it, but often provide a predictable and profitable indirect benefit. Additionally, we need to be aware of the consequences of our actions, both wanted and unwanted, and the applications are enormous. For instance, the internet was spawned by the US military to protect the country from adversaries. Then it transformed life, education, and business. Now the internet has evolved to include social media, which has recently been credited with the degradation of society,[‡] and ransomware, which is the antithesis of national security.

The Industrial Revolution dramatically improved the physical comfort and safety of the world. The precession effect of all the factories and automobiles and the built environment inadvertently led to climate change and its dramatic effects on weather systems. Earthquakes, tornados, fires, and glacial melting have all drastically decreased the physical

---

[†] Note: While I was paid for some, not all, of my time at the university, it was small compensation and paled in comparison to the time and financial gifts I provided to the same institution, thus in my view it was community service work.

[‡] For a study on the positive and negative effects of social media, see Waseem Akram and Rekesh Kuar, "The Positive and Negative Effects of Social Media on Society," *International Journal of Computer Sciences and Engineering* 5, no. 10 (2018): 351–354. Also see *Social Dilemma*, a documentary-drama hybrid from Netflix. Director Jeff Orlowski (2020).

comfort and safety of the same world the revolution was supposed to serve. The Industrial Revolution initially served to better the world; however, impacts such as pollution were not immediately known and, in the long run, these precessional effects also caused harm to the world. Leaders need to be aware of the "all in" cost of actions, both positive and negative.

How does this relate to business?

It seems that every time I give my time or money to a worthwhile cause, it comes back to me many times over. As Vin Bhalerao says of the precession effect: "The concept is all pervasive, and once you understand it, you will see it everywhere."[5] That's my experience of the precession effect; I see it everywhere.

The precession effect of a cold call will probably be the receiver avoiding the person making the call. Have you experienced a car warranty call lately? But genuine community service work with a nonprofit generates relationships with other leaders and may create business partnerships. This is not the primary reason to serve, but it's a predictable and profitable side effect of being out in the world with other leaders.

Infinite precessional effects emerge when practicing mindfulness. Listed here are just some of the effects of the Twelve Pillars of Mindful Leadership.

- Being mindful to promote peace and tranquility leads to better business decisions through awareness and detachment.

- Focusing on the breath calms the mind.

- Identifying your purpose in life dramatically improves motivation and presence, allowing business to thrive.

- Taking actions that don't provide an immediate reward—like community service work or a random act of kindness—may seem to be an unrelated use of time and energy to business, but "nothing happens until something moves," and positive actions establish positive reaction, or karma.

- Practicing compassion decreases negative judgment of others.

- Practicing nonjudgment increases understanding, awareness, acceptance, and performance.

- Caring and compassion for some people may seem to be a contradiction to profit motivation in the short run; however, improving relationships and serving a larger purpose is at the core of business performance in the long run.

- Making money creates the opportunity for you to make a bigger impact on humanity—affluence increases influence.

- Generosity and community service may seem like a money and time suck; however, by the precession effect, both can generate business as the side effect.

- Practicing acceptance creates the space for real change.

- Acknowledging we know very little absolutely may feel like admitting incompetence, when in reality it creates humility, credibility, and awareness, and improves performance.

The effects of mindfulness are enormous and often counterintuitive. It takes understanding and awareness to notice the precession effects that are everywhere but not obvious and often counterintuitive, like mindfulness improving the bottom line. If while reading this you find something counterintuitive to your understanding, step back and ask yourself, what are the side effects (or precession effects) of this action?

When we do nothing, we create nothing. We were born to take action with Presence. Mindful action creates mindful responses, including the precession effect, and establishes our karma, or the cause and effect of an action.

Finally, this is my recounting of my experience, and as you will read, it is my learned experience of how the world, and karma, works. Most all of it happened before I learned of the concept called the precession effect. I hope my experience, and the concept of the precession effect, inspires you to give of yourself in new ways so society and you can reap the predicable side effects.

- Bodies in motion operate at ninety-degree angles.

- Service work can create opportunities, as well as an enhanced mindset.

- Be aware of the total impact of your actions, both positive and negative.

Chapter Takeaway

The precession effect means the side effects of an intentional action are often the main event.

Now let's discuss spiritual cross-training and the secular approach to the Twelve Pillars of Mindful Leadership.

Chapter 4

SPIRITUAL CROSS-TRAINING

I think different religions are different doors into the same house. Sometimes I think the house exists, sometimes I don't. It's a great mystery.[1]

—STEVE JOBS

Spiritual cross-training denotes a secular and multidiscipline approach to transformation.

In this book, no dogma is proposed, or absolute truth espoused, and that is intentional. Hopefully, this work instead serves to give you greater access to spirituality and the ability to choose your own specific path, whether that be a formal religion, self-inquiry, study, or importantly, personal practice. Interestingly, many scholars and practitioners believe Buddhist practices can make you a better Christian. I have tried to steer clear of all religions, including Christianity and Buddhism, but a lot of what's been discovered in meditation started with Buddha, so it's impossible not to make certain references. My experience is that some business professionals raised in Christian traditions find the Buddhist history as a detriment to practicing mindfulness before they begin the practice; however, for those who do cross that bridge, their experience often results in a deepening of their Christian faith.

Here is a sampling of comments from Living in the Gap (LITG) Mindful Leadership participants, who are mostly Christians. These words document what I have experienced across the board:

> "My time in Living in the Gap gave me renewed awareness and a clearer mind, which allowed me to contemplate my faith. On Easter Sunday, 2022, I attended church in-person for the first time in around five years. During Mass, the priest spoke of how Easter is a time of renewal—it felt as though he was talking directly to me. Christ was truly with me during my time in LITG."
>
> **—ANDREW DRENNING**, Credenzio Studios

> "We are all sinners and searchers. LITG has blessed me with the tools and knowledge to love the process in pursuit and growth of my Christian faith."
>
> **—MATT HENRICHS**, CBRE

I look at the various methodologies introduced in this book as "spiritual cross-training" to allow access to Presence. What I do know of Christ is that he was Presence.

The slow boils of meditation, mindful movement, prayer, gratitude, visualization, and other spiritual practices will serve to open you to the possibility of Presence. Some of the material or exercises I describe may either slow boil or mildly "shock" you into Presence, and only you can know if and when this occurs. Noticing the occurrence of Presence is the key to mindfulness. Once the seeds of mindfulness are planted, they grow inside you in powerful ways. When it has occurred, you will certainly know it, however tepidly.

The point is that it takes what it takes, and each of our jobs is to keep digging until we find what works for us. Keep the teachings and exercises that work for you in your personal experience and discard the rest. The intention to be mindful and residing in Presence is paramount.

Don't think the knowledge you presently possess is changeless, absolute truth. Avoid being narrow-minded and bound to present views. Learn and practice nonattachment from views in order to be open to receive others' viewpoints.[2]

—THICH NHAT HANH

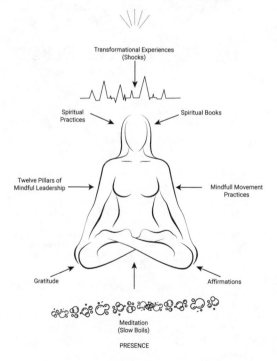

Spiritual Cross-Training

Transformational Experiences
(Shocks)

Spiritual Practices

Spiritual Books

Twelve Pillars of Mindful Leadership

Mindfull Movement Practices

Gratitude

Affirmations

Meditation
(Slow Boils)

PRESENCE

I encourage you to view all the teachings presented as "rafts" to get you to where you want to go. Once you reach the other shore, let the raft go and keep the essence of the teachings to foster your growth. None of the teachings, or even this book, matters in their own right; they only matter to the extent they make a difference for you. After that, put the book away for future reference. You can reread the book next year, or pull it out when you are struggling. I am not promising that if you follow and apply the exercises, practices, and principles outlined in the Twelve Pillars of Mindful Leadership, you won't continue to have ups and downs in your life—you are human. However, if you start a mindfulness practice—or already have—and follow these pillars, you will have a practice as the base, and tools to work with to help smooth out the lows and maintain the highs.

In a parable, the Buddha once asked what a man should do with his makeshift raft once he'd crossed the river. Should he drag it along with him or leave it behind? He should leave it, Buddha said.

The Teachings Are Rafts

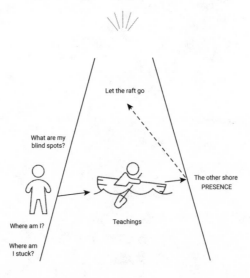

You are encouraged to take what is presented in the conceptual framework and the Twelve Pillars of Mindful Leadership, exercises, practices, and similar tools—and use them to achieve Presence, purpose, and vision, and establish a routine that works for you in your daily life that will make a lasting difference. Then, discard the rest.

- A secular and multidiscipline approach allows broader access to mindfulness.

- The teachings are rafts to be discarded when no longer useful.

- Take what works to achieve Presence and discard the rest.

Chapter Takeaway

These teachings are simply rafts to help you to achieve Presence
and should be released when no longer necessary.

You now have the background to fully embrace and understand the material presented in Part 2, "The Twelve Pillars of Mindful Leadership." There is always a deeper level, and I hope I have sparked your interest to explore these and other transformative concepts on your own.

PART 2

THE TWELVE PILLARS OF MINDFUL LEADERSHIP

PILLAR 1   Be Present and Practice Mindfulness

PILLAR 2   Identify Your Purpose in Life

PILLAR 3   Create Clarity, Vision, Intention, Commitment, and Habits

PILLAR 4   Success Is a Mindset of Be-Do-Have

PILLAR 5   Show Up, Take Action, and Detach from Results

PILLAR 6   Be Responsible, Practice Nonjudgment and Compassion

PILLAR 7   Foster Relationships with Your Word and Listening

PILLAR 8   Be in Flow, Create Affluence and Influence

PILLAR 9   Be Grateful, Give Generously, and Serve

PILLAR 10   Acceptance Means to Stop Resisting and Complaining

PILLAR 11   Take Everything Impersonally and Let Life Flow through You

PILLAR 12   Beginner's Mind Means to Know Nothing Absolutely and Be Curious

Reading, training, and practicing mindfulness over the last thirty years and being in business for over forty years has led me to create these pillars.

Any one pillar stands on its own, yet in the process of personal and professional transformation, they are set in a logical sequence. Additionally, the pillars are not meant to be one-and-done events. They are designed to be a continual process. Revisiting each pillar over time is key, because we are constantly changing and what we observe is different from one time to the next. It's a process. The deeper we get into our awareness practices, the more we notice, and the more we practice self-observation, the better we get at it.

There are detailed one-time or multiple-time exercises, and slow boil practices provided when relevant to a particular pillar. It's a book of practice and experience. The beginning mindfulness practices are designed so you can begin immediately, and practice as you finish reading this book. You will be more open, and get more from the discussion, if you do the exercises and practices while you read, rather than later on, even if that means taking a little longer to read the book. Alternatively, you can read the entire book and come back to do the practices in an orderly sequence, and they are repeated in Appendix 1 to give you this option as well. Some elements of the book may serve as a reference for further work when you are ready to go deeper.

Practice is how mindfulness and Presence bloom, and it generally means repetitive and regular practice—in other words, daily if possible. Move through the practices for the next pillar only when ready. If you are experienced with mindfulness, you will need to guide your own pace, possibly faster for things you are familiar with and slower for things foreign to you. Don't worry about that. They are suggestions, and the pace may and should vary for individual differences.

The most important thing is your intention to be mindful and your commitment to practice and form mindfulness habits. Also important is that you are willing to actually practice. This is not an intellectual pursuit; it is an experiential pursuit. As Steve Jobs said, "I began to realize that an intuitive understanding and consciousness was more significant than abstract thinking and intellectual logical analysis."[1] The research provided in this book is to help you overcome any skepticism and document the benefits, so you can earnestly commit to mindfulness practices. It's a balance I hope to have achieved.

Don't be discouraged if you don't experience instant results. Keep your commitment in the forefront of your mind. This is a process, and one that will be different for everyone. It's best to accept and trust the process. If in the end all you do is start a minimal mindfulness and/or meditation practice, then accept that and know that the rest of the process is there when you are ready for it.

Dan Harris, author of *10% Happier*, says meditation alone can make you 10 percent happier over time.[2] Another title for this book might have been "25% Happier," because if you follow all the possible practices described here, over time they will make a dramatic improvement in your life, guaranteed.

I have been at this practice for over thirty years and on my best days come in and out of Presence, which has different levels and depths. I hear and have read of instant enlightenment but have not had that experience myself. This is a book of gradual enlightenment with the opportunity for graduating levels of transformational shocks, and you can decide which work for you and which don't.

The first three pillars set the foundation, and the last nine pillars establish the mindful mindset for achieving presence. Discovering your purpose in life makes such a dramatic difference in how you show up with a deeper level of Presence that I have strategically placed it as the second pillar.

Don't be discouraged or believe that you have to go to the full depths of discovering your true purpose before you achieve results or move through the rest of the practices and Pillars. The balance of the pillars will help you experience your purpose, or Presence. Thinking you must experience and master your purpose, or Presence, in the next fifteen minutes is not productive or true. Be curious and realize that the process of discovering Presence as your true purpose is an adventure.

Most important is your intention and commitment to be mindful and to practice mindfulness. There is no wrong way to do it. I have laid out *a* way through the Twelve Pillars, not *the* way. I hope it's useful and you step on the path today.

Pillar 1

BE PRESENT AND PRACTICE MINDFULNESS

Pay attention to the gap . . . between two thoughts, the brief, silent space between words in a conversation, between notes of a piano . . . or the gap between the in-breath and out-breath. When you pay attention to those gaps, awareness of "something" becomes Awareness.[1]

—ECKHART TOLLE

T o "live in the gap" means to live in the space between our inner dialogue, the space between where one thought stops and another begins. This space is stillness, and the source of peace, joy, and happiness.

The voice inside your head

What? How does Eric know I have a voice inside my head?

Everyone has that little voice. The one that says, *What's the matter with him?* or *Why does she do that?* The little voice that creates an inner dialogue you hardly notice until you intentionally create a gap. The gap allows you to hear the voice and, more importantly, distinguish it from reality.

Unfortunately, the voice may be your reality until you create this gap.

You can think of the voice as an echo, typically repeating the most negative and debilitating conversations with ourselves: *You can't . . . You shouldn't . . . You won't . . .* These types of thoughts often stem from an underlying belief, such as *I am not enough.*

What's the voice echoing?

Our programming since birth—by parents, teachers, friends, society, and life's experiences. Oprah Winfrey says, "The outside world is constantly trying to convince you you're not enough. But you don't have to take the bait. Meditation helps you resist."[2]

Researchers have found we have some 6,000 thoughts per day.[3] Most of our thoughts are repetitive, and many are negative and not helpful—and importantly, stress and anxiety reside in thoughts. Descartes famously proposed, "I think, therefore I am," which most philosophers have since refuted. The relevant question is, "Am I my thoughts?" Or alternatively, "Do I have thoughts?" We have thoughts; we are not our thoughts. From that point of view, we can further ask, "Does who have thoughts?" What I am proposing is, "I am Presence, therefore I am."

In reality, we are not meant to be so identified with our thoughts. Years of unconsciously living within the tyranny of thought, without noticing or creating a gap or separation, lead many of us to believe we are our thoughts. We are so involved in our thoughts that we don't separate ourselves from the thoughts we habitually manufacture.

Why do we waste so much time and energy thinking with such little outcome?

Unfortunately, it's like a frog in water whose temperature increases by one degree per hour. The frog doesn't notice it is being boiled. Often, we don't notice we are consumed by habitual thinking. It can be exhausting. The main reason television has become so popular is that it replaces the internal voice with a new dialogue, so we don't notice the voice. Try an experiment the next time you watch your favorite TV show on a commercial channel: Notice changes in your internal dialogue when the next commercial comes on. You are observing a disruption when the internal dialogue switches back on from the TV show stream you were engrossed in.

When we first hear the internal dialogue, we don't distinguish it as an intrusion from someone who is not who we are. Worse, we listen to the voice and often believe it.

Are you listening to that voice, the one that echoes your worst fears and limitations?

Often, we aren't aware of the voice. When we first start noticing it, we frequently think it's real. In truth, we are the one who *hears* the voice; we are not the voice. As we develop awareness and create a gap, or space, around the voice, we realize listening to the voice is a choice. Awareness and the voice, or thoughts for that matter, can't exist in consciousness at the same time. We must grow our awareness if we want to quiet the voice and slow incessant thinking.

To my knowledge, it's not possible or desirable to stop thinking. But it is possible to reduce repetitive and unproductive thoughts. It is possible to create a gap between when one thought ends and another begins. Thus, it is possible to create peace, joy, and Presence.

I have not been able to eliminate the voice in my head, but I have been able to silence it substantially, create gaps in the voice, and make it a more positive force. As I mentioned in the preface, on my run that morning in San Francisco, when my inner voice asked, *Why don't you do something?* I answered with action. This has reduced my stress, improved my focus, increased my quality of sleep, and made me a better person.

Through practicing mindfulness, you can live in the gap too. One way to do this is to follow these pillars, beginning with practicing mindfulness, and possibly beginning a meditation practice.

Why mindfulness?

Mindfulness is the ability to be fully present and aware of where we are and what we are doing in a nonjudgmental state. Jon Kabat-Zinn says, "Mindfulness is awareness, cultivated by paying attention in a sustained and particular way: on purpose, in the present moment, and non-judgmentally."[4] It's also beneficial to think of what mindfulness is not: multitasking, distraction, less than full awareness of what you are doing, and judgment. Mindfulness is a natural state and possibly most easily accessed in nature. In the modern, fast-paced, online world, it can be difficult to access. Fortunately, there are practices that foster mindfulness. The most effective and portable practice is possibly meditation.

You can tame your thoughts through meditation by not paying attention to them and focusing on something else like your breath. This is a precession effect.

I know that sounds weird, but by focusing on something else, typically the breath or a mantra,* you notice a thought when it arises and can create a slight separation, or gap, between the thought and yourself. These gaps in the inner dialogue and gaps between thoughts create the stillness from which peace, joy, and happiness spring. Finding these

---

* A mantra is a word or sound repeated to aid concentration in meditation.

gaps in business is what motivated me to found the nonprofit company Living in the Gap and gave me the impetus to write this book.†

Meditation is a powerful practice to help you become aware of breath, thought, sensations, and Presence.

The good news is that it does not take months in a monastery or hours each day contorting into a pretzel. You can start sitting in a chair with as little as two minutes per day.

We can quiet the voice through meditation and learn what internal dialogues to pay attention to and which to let go of. Likewise, we can train what remains of the voice to be more positive and aligned with our life purpose and vision, and to be certain that we have them.

First, make the voice less prominent through meditation and then train the voice and thoughts to be more positive through following other practices that come in later pillars. Implement these after meditating for a time, so as not to overwhelm yourself. This is a process. Simply placing positive thoughts on top of a mind already lost in thought is not as effective as creating a clearing through meditation in which more productive thoughts can thrive.

Sorry, but mindfulness takes practice. It's up to you if you want to label it as work, but for me, finding the gap is finding the joy in life. Peace, joy, and happiness—all exist in the gap. Stress and anxiety exist in thoughts.

Other words for the gap are *now* or *Presence*. We cannot be in the present moment and in thought, or attending to the voice in our head, at the same time. By practicing being in the present moment, or being in the gap, you are reducing repetitive and unproductive thoughts *and* quieting the voice in your head. You can't stop thinking or stop the voice. Trying to stop either may cause them to amplify; what we resist persists.

† For more information, see https://www.Livinginthegap.org.

\\|//

Your inner dialogue may ask, *Do I have to meditate?* No, you don't. It's a personal choice, and there may be other ways, such as extended time in nature, that can accomplish the same result. Henry David Thoreau retreated to Walden Pond to experience Presence. I just haven't found an equivalent method to meditation that works in a busy professional world, and I feel meditation is the most direct and effective method. If it's not for you, find something that works for you and do that.

Everything of consequence in mindfulness involves practice, and this practice will improve your life in a positive way.

Meditation can improve your life

In *Psychology Today*, Emma Seppälä lists twenty reasons to start a meditation practice. Here are the most pertinent to our journey:

- It gives you perspective.

- It decreases depression, anxiety, stress, and loneliness.

- It increases positive emotions and emotional regulation, social connections, focus, attention, memory, and innovative thinking.[5]

In sum, meditation boosts your health, happiness, social life, self-control, brain function, productivity, and perspective. By observing your mind, you become free from learned limitations. There is additional research in Appendix 3 if you are interested.

Your mind may still swing into positive or negative states, but less dramatically, and it doesn't have to ruin your day.

We have daily hygiene routines that include showering and cleaning our teeth. We promote physical vitality by going to the gym or running outside, but what do we do for our minds? We mostly overlook it, despite it being so important.

Meditation is hygiene for the mind. It clears out unproductive thoughts, creates clarity, and helps you learn more about yourself.

HOW DOES MEDITATION ACCOMPLISH ALL THESE GREAT THINGS?

Meditation guides and organizes brain waves, which communicate between neurons within our brains.

I have studied brain waves for a long time. I got a master class on brain waves when I attended Dave Asprey's 40 Years of Zen program.‡ My brain waves were measured by detectors attached to my scalp. I sat in a pod and had my brain monitored while doing meditation and other activities.

Here is a small dose of the science of brain waves: There are five primary brain wave states, and we have a combination of these states in varying degrees at any given time. Brain waves range from high-amplitude, low-frequency delta to low-amplitude, high-frequency gamma.

Most forms of meditation cultivate alpha brain waves, which are midrange, varying from eight to twelve cycles per second. Alpha waves are associated with inner focus, a state where we are aware of our environment but not reacting to it. Alpha state is relaxing and restorative and generates peaceful, smooth, and calm feelings.

In the Zen lab, I could see the impact that over twenty years of meditation had on organizing my brain waves. I learned how to come in and out of the alpha state and other states at will. During that week, I

‡   For more information, see https://www.40YearsofZen.com.

also witnessed people very new to meditation make giant leaps in brain wave organization.

If you have the time and money, neurofeedback like that provided at the 40 Years of Zen lab can give you a jump start on receiving the benefits of meditation. If you don't have the time or money, you will still experience meditation's benefits from the simple practices outlined in this book with time and consistent practice.

In their 2017 publication *Altered Traits*, Daniel Goleman and Richard Davison document a science-based study that found that "beyond the pleasant states meditation can produce, the real payoffs are the lasting traits that can result."[6] An altered trait endures apart from the meditation session itself. Traits such as selflessness, equanimity, a loving Presence, and impartial compassion are all highly positive.

By observing the mind, you get to know yourself better and become more authentic, humble, grateful, compassionate, and real. You pay less attention to your stories and other people's stories and focus more on what's genuine. The more you meditate, the larger and more evident the benefits become.

Many of the assumptions about meditation—you have to have an empty mind; or you have to sit in the lotus position—are myths. They are false. Simply noticing a busy, full mind is quite beneficial. In fact, as soon as you notice you are distracted, you are in a state of Presence. Sitting in a chair works. Keeping an erect spine is the most critical aspect of your posture while meditating. What's more, sitting for as little as two minutes when starting is productive. Chanting mantras, dressing in robes, or adopting a new religion are unnecessary. If those things call to you, do them. If not, that's fine too.

I CAN'T MEDITATE BECAUSE
I CAN'T CLEAR MY MIND

If you notice you have a cluttered mind, you are present, which allows you to focus on an object of meditation such as your body, your breath, or a mantra.

Many people think meditation causes the calamity of the mind, but they later realize their minds were always like that; they just never noticed until they began to pay attention.

I DON'T HAVE TIME TO MEDITATE

What that often means is, "I don't have time to be present." Now just think about that statement. Gandhi is quoted as saying, "I'm so busy today that I'm going to meditate for two hours instead of one."[7]

You don't have to be like Gandhi. I have been meditating formally for over twenty years, and my practice is twenty minutes a day with longer stints during workshops or silent retreats when time allows. Keeping meditation sessions short when beginning can be the best strategy. Calmness will evolve, and then you can extend your sessions.

The first step is to be interested in mindfulness. If you are reading this book, you are probably interested. The second is to get started and know that consistency is more important than the length of the session.

The goal is to have a regular practice—that means daily or, at a minimum, regularly. I am sure three times per week is better than not at all, but I find practicing daily gives me consistency of practice that deepens the benefits of meditation. Do the best you can. The good news is that only two minutes of regular meditation practice to begin can make a substantial difference in your life. Everybody has two minutes. If your inner dialogue is blaring, *I don't*, then this practice is definitely for you. Some, such as Twitter founder Jack Dorsey, have more time: "Just finished a 10-day silent meditation. Wow, what a reset!"[8]

THE BREATH

It's hard to overstate the importance of the breath in mindfulness and Presence. The breath is not only constant and autonomous, but also observable and controllable within limits. By starting to observe the breath, you are being mindful and present. It's easier to start with your eyes closed and listen to the breath without contriving or controlling it; simply observe and listen to it. Then open your eyes with the same observation. This is an automatic way to be mindful, by just being present with the breath. Close your eyes again and notice how expansive and vast the inner world is, and that it is practically boundless.

This is an experience of consciousness itself, grounded in the breath coming in and out of the body. Opening and closing the eyes while focusing on the breath can demonstrate how our vision, as well as other outside distractions like noises, and internal distractions such as thoughts and emotions, overwhelm our subtle consciousness in the background and muffle its impact on our existence. The goal is to take this back, and reside in the background of consciousness, or Presence. The breath is possibly the most accessible, stable, and predictable entry to the state of Presence.

The breath also can either reflect or set the tone for the body. For instance, when we are anxious, the breath quickens. Interestingly, when we consciously slow the breath down, our anxiety lessens. Breathing techniques impact things like the vagus nerve, which impacts functions like sweating, heart rate, speech, and even digestion and inflammation in the body.[9] The vagus nerve's main contribution is to the parasympathetic nervous system. And the good news is, by controlling the breath, we can impact this important system and the anxiety and other factors that can help us become more relaxed and present. Here's a simple breathing exercise:

Breathing Exercise [10]:

Sit in a quiet place with few distractions, with your spine erect so the breath can flow without restriction, and you can notice the breath. Keep your eyes open with a softened gaze focused downward in front of you several feet. Relax your body and find a comfortable position, in which the body does not distract you. Take 3 deep breaths through your nostrils. Next, count to 5 on the inhale, hold your breath for a count of 3, and count to 6 as you exhale slowly through the nose. Do this several times and notice the movement of the belly and ribs as you breathe. Don't manipulate the movement, just observe the movements as you breathe. Do this for several minutes to positively activate the vagus nerve. The longer you can do the exercise, the more it will impact the vagus nerve, but I always suggest starting with short durations consistently, and increasing the time gradually as you become familiar and comfortable with the practice. This is a great preparation for the meditation practice that follows in the next section.

Breathing can be the doorway to transformation and Presence. Although we only introduce simple breathing techniques in this book, the world of breathwork is immense and practically limitless. We will focus on the breathwork that is particularly applicable to learning mindfulness and basic meditation practice.§

§   For a survey of breathwork practices, see Jesse Coomer, *A Practical Guide to Breathwork*, (Las Vegas, NV: Midwestern Method, LLC, 2022) or research Pranayama, the breathwork complement to Yoga.

THE BEST TIME TO MEDITATE

The best time to meditate is always now. Meditation is meant to make your life better off the cushion. It incorporates mindfulness into the rest of your day and makes your life better.

When first starting meditation, don't get too hung up on what time of day you have your sessions, but do try to be consistent.¶ Some days, I meditate for two minutes or maybe five. Sometimes at lunch rather than in the morning. I meditate on a plane or wherever I can fit it in, but I do not miss a day. In fact, I haven't missed a day of meditation in over seven years. But I did not start that way. I started the way everyone does, with one session, then a second, then a third, and so on. Following are simple instructions on how to meditate:

How to Meditate

If you are not already experienced in meditation, here is a simple breath meditation practice.** Find a quiet spot to sit where you won't be interrupted. Start in a chair or on a cushion. Rock back and forth a few times on your sit bones and find a comfortable position with your spine erect.

Next, set a timer or alarm for two minutes.

I suggest having your eyes closed to begin with, but if that makes you anxious or uncomfortable, keeping your eyes open

---

¶   Generally, the morning is regarded as the best time for meditation. It is for me. If you have the time, a second session later in the day or evening is beneficial but not essential, especially when beginning your practice.

**   If you have meditation experience, have beginner's mind, as discussed in Pillar 12. Also, this may be an ideal time to lengthen your sessions or add some of the other practices coming up in later pillars.

with a soft downward gaze two to three feet out in front of you is fine.†† Place your hands in a comfortable position in your lap or on top of your thighs.

Breathe through your nostrils. Start focusing on your breath, just noticing and listening to the in breath and out breath. Follow your breath in and out of your body. Notice your stomach rise on the inhale and contract on the exhale. Be aware of your breath as it enters and exits the body.

Notice when you are distracted by a thought, noise, emotion, or anything else. As soon as you notice, let the distraction go and return your attention to your breath. You are teaching yourself the skill of detachment, as well as how to be present in the moment by being one with the breath.

If your mind is particularly busy, that's normal; you are meditating, so don't change anything. Notice the distraction, then let it go and return your attention to your breath. Keep returning your attention to your breath until the alarm goes off. It's like training a puppy; be persistent and gentle.

When time is up, open your eyes and continue to focus on your breathing for a few breaths before getting up. This is how you bring your meditation to the outside world.

continued

†† Meditation instruction is split on whether to have eyes open or closed. I have found that when becoming inner focused, especially when first learning meditation or when first sitting down, eyes closed generates the best experience of the inner world. When becoming outer focused, or bringing my meditation out to the world, I find eyes open generates the best result. I recommend eyes closed when beginning to establish a meditation practice or when starting a session, even for advanced meditators. And when concluding the session, keeping eyes open while continuing to meditate for several minutes aids in bringing the meditative state into daily life. Nothing says you can't do both. It's also fine to meditate exclusively with closed eyes or open eyes if that's your preference. Feel free to experiment.

That's it. You have just completed your first meditation session. Commit to two minutes a day until it's a habit.

It's also okay to take a certain day of the week off if that's important to you.

Try to meditate at the same time and place each day.

If you miss your scheduled time, make it up later in the day. If you miss a day, don't miss the next day. Your goal is to do two minutes for twenty-one days straight. Then consider going to three to five minutes.

The most essential ingredient is consistency, so be as consistent as you can.

If focusing on your breath alone isn't working for you, counting can be helpful too. Instead of focusing on the breath, focus on the numbers while counting to 10 on the out breaths. Once you've reached 10, let the counting go and return to the breath. If you lose count, which is to be expected when beginning the practice, start over at 1. Once you can get to 10 easily, count backward from 10 to 1.

Even if you are very distracted, keep practicing. Noticing you are distracted, and returning to your breath, is meditation. As soon as you are aware you are distracted, you are present, which is something you can use all day long.

If you struggle to get in even two minutes of meditation, using a smartphone app is fine to get started. Apps should be viewed as training wheels, though. Once you have found balance in your practice, eliminate the app or use it for supplemental sessions.

The goal is to internally generate meditation so that you can eventually generate it organically at any time of the day or night. With time and practice, the experience of being with your breath will automatically appear in times of stress. But if apps help you to get started and keep you consistent, use them. Whatever it takes, do that.

Meditation is a very simple, formal mindfulness practice. It's not easy at first because we are not used to being present. If you want a guided meditation to start, check out an introductory meditation on our website (www.livinginthegap.org) under free resources, and check the resources page at the back of the book.

You can also practice mindfulness less formally throughout the day.

Less formal mindfulness practices

- Pay attention to your breath.

- Take a short walk, being very conscious of nature and your surroundings.

- Focus on your food and eat slowly. Chew each bite thoroughly.

- Wash the dishes or your hands, paying full attention to what you are doing.

There are many ways to practice mindfulness, and your brief meditation practice will help you find little ways to be mindful throughout the day. Even the intention to be mindful itself is quite powerful. A short book that I found helpful when beginning is *The Miracle of Mindfulness* by Thich Nhat Hanh, who passed away in January of 2022.[11]

THE INNER ENERGY BODY

Eckhart Tolle in *A New Earth* refers to "the inner body," and Yoga practitioners call it the "energy body."[12] I combine the two descriptions into "the inner energy body" for this discussion, to be clear as to what I am talking about. This is the inside world of subtle energy, similar to meridians and chi that acupuncture works with for energy healing. Our focus is to learn how to be aware of these subtle energies. If you are not paying attention to them, you may not notice the inner energy body at all. This is where we get our vitality and rigor (or *ojas* in Sanskrit). It's critical to mindfulness too.

The practice is to start paying attention and noticing the subtle energies and life forces in the body, which are not obvious when you are engrossed in thought or when your focus is external. The body is the first, best refuge from the tyranny of thought. When you place your focus in the body, thought ceases.

Additionally, the observer effect tells us that when we observe something with focus, it changes the object.[13] Focusing your attention on a part of my body allows it to change. As Deepak Chopra notes, "When you know how consciousness actually behaves, you find that something startling happens: You change with it."[14]

This makes consciousness, awareness, or Presence curative. According to Moshe Feldenkrais, "The nervous system has a fundamental characteristic: We cannot carry out an action and its opposite at the same time: At any single moment the whole system achieves a kind of general integration that the body will express at that moment."[15]

YOGA

Yoga with a capital Y means it is Yoga as the science of consciousness and represents the mind-body experience. Yoga is mindfulness and mediation with the body. Simple yoga postures, known as yoga asana, are represented with a lowercase *y*. I love Yoga, but many people are resistant to it, even when I have tried to convince them to practice. I found I had to invite them and show them options that work for them, not for myself. You will find some helpful options to Yoga coming up that will allow you to experience many of the benefits of Yoga without ever stepping on a yoga mat. I got you covered.

Yoga is more than simply stretching. When I hear someone describe their Yoga practice as "stretching," I know they are not really doing Yoga. A more accurate description would be "mindful stretching." Moreover, Yoga is the science of consciousness.[16]

Yoga involves stretching *and* placing your focus on the inner energy body. When we do that, we cannot think of other things at the same time. This practice proves that multitasking with focus is a myth. When we practice Yoga, we are being mindful and aware of our bodies, especially our inner energy bodies.

Yoga is mindfulness. Yoga is meditation with the body and was invented to prepare our bodies for sitting meditation. Only over the last 100 years or so has yoga asana (postures) dominated the practice. Sure, Yoga includes stretching, but it is much more than stretching. I understand Yoga is not for everyone, but I recommend that you find a way to experience being in your inner energy body. Barbara Stoler Miller describes the nature of Yoga with the following:

> This is the teaching of yoga.
> Yoga is the cessation of thought and the turnings of thought.
> When thought ceases, the spirit stands in its true
> identity as observer to the world.
> Otherwise, the observer identifies with the turnings of thought.[17]

I practice and teach Yoga. It is an area of my expertise, and my personal preference, but martial arts and tai chi are likely as beneficial to mindfulness as Yoga. Yoga also has infinite health benefits and is great for the joints. If you practice Yoga or are open to trying it, material in Appendix 2 gets you started and explains some of what this ancient practice is all about. Even if you don't want to practice Yoga, the material helps explain consciousness and could be a benefit to understanding Presence. But you don't have to do Yoga to practice mindfulness.

But the more pertinent question is, *What do you like to do, and how could you be* more *mindful and experience the inner energy body while doing it?* The following are some ideas.

MINDFUL WEIGHTLIFTING, PILATES, AND MORE

Awareness of our internal organic drives is the basis of man's self-knowledge. As Moshe Feldenkrais said, "Awareness of the relationship between these impulses and their origin in the formation of human culture offers man the potential means to direct his life, which few people have yet realized."[18]

I had always disliked weight training, but once I hit fifty, I had to lift weights to continue with an active sports schedule that included slalom waterskiing and (Heli) snow skiing. I never really enjoyed lifting weights, and my arrogance and ignorance told me it was because it wasn't mindful. I later learned it was because I wasn't mindful during these activities. According to Feldenkrais, to be mindful while weightlifting, you need to be aware of subtle differences:

"If I raise an iron bar, I shall not feel the difference if a fly either lights on it or leaves it. If, on the other hand, I am holding a feather, I shall feel a distinct difference if the fly were to settle on it."[19]

I had worked out with the same weightlifting trainer for twelve years, but with the disruption of the coronavirus pandemic, the trainer moved away and the gym closed. I messed around in the garage about once a month for two years before recently finding a new gym and trainer when things opened back up again. When I was lifting, she asked me to go slow and feel the muscle group we were working, and she even assisted this by touching muscles to get them to fire. Like Yoga, this was focusing my consciousness on my inner energy body. It was possible—with a little less weight, a few more reps, and a change of focus away from activating adrenaline and blowing out my muscles—to feel what was going on and pay attention to individual muscles firing. I now love weightlifting, as I am experiencing my inner energy body while lifting.

My experience with weightlifting is reflected by Feldenkrais: "To learn we need time, attention, and discrimination; to discriminate we must sense. This means that in order to learn we must sharpen our powers of sensing, and if we try to do most things by sheer force, we shall achieve precisely the opposite of what we need."[20]

The truth is that yoga can be either mindful or not mindful. It's much harder for me to be mindful in a power Yoga or an intense hot Yoga class—I am learning that I am part of that phenomenon. When adrenaline kicks in, it floods the brain to allow the body to go into overdrive, which we need from time to time. We need to notice when that is occurring and realize that when adrenaline is activated, it's quite difficult to be mindful at the same time.

The more aggressive the activity, the more adrenaline is released and the more difficult it is to be mindful in the activity. The main question for any activity you choose is, "Does this result in awareness of my inner energy body and the cessation of thought?" If no, keep paying attention to the subtle energies in the body until thought does cease. Noticing when you are in thought, or alternatively, present, is a practice for a lifetime. This is the practice of mindfulness and noticing Presence.

For weightlifting, if you still need to do some power lifting, during which it is not as easy to be mindful, my suggestion is to start with some mindful stretching and then use less weight and more reps, with a focus of experiencing being in your body for the first thirty minutes. Then go back to your normal routine for the rest of the hour. Importantly, notice the difference. Noticing makes all the difference in being mindful—noticing when we can experience being in our body and when we cannot. This simple practice can be transformative. Feldenkrais tells us, "To recognize small changes in effort, the effort itself must first be reduced. More delicate and improved control of movement is possible only through the increase of sensitivity, through a greater ability to sense differences."[21]

I had the same experience with Pilates as I did with weights. I switched to an instructor whose gentle and slow approach was different from the previous more aggressive one. And she specialized in hands-on adjustments and muscle activation. I could feel more and focus my consciousness into the body part being worked. Pilates has become much more like a Yoga experience, despite having a different breath sequence and focus. Now I can be mindful doing Pilates, when before I loved the physical results from Pilates (and weights) but did not enjoy doing it and didn't get the same mindful benefits as I did from Yoga.

I still believe Yoga, as the science of consciousness, is the best form of mindful movement practice, but I have learned, through the disruption from the pandemic, that other forms of exercise, done slowly and gently, can provide the benefits of experiencing being in your body rather than your head.

One activity in Yoga that translates to other pursuits you may prefer is that of practicing balance. It's impossible to balance while you are in thought. You will fall down. Balance requires a focus on the inner energy body, which calms thought and brings stability. Try simply standing on one foot and thinking about something that's distracting.

Once you are stable in your inner body, what also helps balance is to focus on a small object or spot several feet in front of you, which brings focus and stability. This demonstrates that balance (and the zone, or Presence) is an experience of the inside world of the inner energy body and outside material world at the same time. If you don't believe it, try closing your eyes while trying to balance and see how destabilizing it is.

MINDFUL ATHLETICS

I am an athlete and love sports of all types. I used to love playing football and basketball, but now I spectate these sports. I still love to participate in water and snow skiing and golf. Experiencing being in my body doing these sports has increased my enjoyment and my performance. It's so rewarding to be improving performance and enjoyment in these activities in my sixties.

Being in your body and in the activity at the same time is being in the zone, which is being in the flow of optimal experience discussed in Pillar 8. It is the experience of Presence. I believe sports often draw people because they experience Presence while they play, something they don't get anywhere else. The goal is to experience Presence, when it's there and when it's not, and bring that into the rest of your life, where you spend a lot more time. Moshe Feldenkrais says, "If a man does not feel he cannot sense differences, and of course he will not be able to distinguish between one action and another. Without the ability to differentiate there can be no learning, and certainly no increase in the ability to learn."[22]

Golf has been a laboratory for my mindfulness practice. I didn't take up golf until I was in my thirties, and the first time I started meditating, I said, "This is golf!" After discovering Joe Parent and *Zen Golf,* I attended several of his workshops and worked directly with Joe for a couple of years. I recommend his book.[23]

Joe introduced me to the golf school run by Fred Shoemaker and Jo Hardy. I spent over fifteen years with them, and they remain close personal friends. I relate several stories in this book of how golf catalyzed change in my life. Fred wrote the book *Extraordinary Golf* with his brother Pete, and if you are a golfer, I recommend it.[24] If you are a golfer or interested in beginning, the book and approach might lead to a transformation of your entire life. Golf has gone from frustrating to liberating for me.

George Mumford, a mindfulness coach, wrote *The Mindful Athlete*. In it he discusses working with leading basketball athletes like Michael Jordan and Kobe Bryant in their championship runs under the coaching legend Phil Jackson, who was a mindful coach.[25] It's a good read, as is Jackson's first book, *Sacred Hoops*.[26] The point being, try to incorporate mindfulness in the activities you love to do and notice when you are mindful, or present, and when you are not.

The point isn't to meditate or do Yoga; the point is to be present. I believe it's harder to notice Presence in more aggressive activities than in gentle Yoga, but it's not impossible. You should not have to do Yoga to be mindful and should be able to mindfully do what you like to do. Consider doing slow and gentle Yoga for a month or so to get the feeling of being in your body, then take that feeling to your favorite activity.

We introduce Yoga as a mindfulness practice in our workshops. Although I have introduced Yoga to hundreds of professionals, many take it up as a regular activity afterward, and many are also resistant to Yoga. So I have decided to start asking people to try Yoga for a month and do their best to truly feel themselves being in their bodies. If after that they don't want to do Yoga, they can take that experience, and feeling, to their exercise of choice and do their best to experience themselves in their bodies.

A trial effort of mindful movement such as Yoga would be much better than having no experience of the inner energy body, as it's essential to mindfulness in my experience. What I resist persists, meaning acceptance of an issue can bring space, clarity, and change, so I am trying something new. Try Yoga and if it doesn't work for you, take this approach to your exercise of choice.

There are Yoga resources in Appendix 2 for learning more and possibly incorporating this practice into your daily life. The wealth of information about the body, breathing, energy, and so on in this ancient practice is amazing. You will learn a lot about being human from the material even if you never do the physical postures of Yoga, called asana. If you have a home Yoga practice you do enjoy, I also recommend attending a weekly Yoga class at a studio or selecting from the many options online to keep learning and to meet others who can support your practice and you theirs.

If you don't want to do Yoga, don't. If you are willing to try it, find a slow and gentle practice for starters. Living in the Gap offers a free simple standing Yoga/mindful stretching routine on our website.‡‡ Find other ways to experience being in your body to slow your thoughts and to prepare for meditation. The following exercise presents a visualization practice called a body scan to experience the inner energy body that is phenomenal.

Body Scan Exercise

A body scan is a way to place your consciousness in your body while sitting still. It takes only a few minutes.

Find a comfortable chair or cushion and sit with your back straight and eyes closed.

‡‡ https://livinginthegap. org/free-resources/

continued

Place your awareness in your feet. Notice that you can direct your conscious attention where you choose in the body. Start with the soles of your feet, slowly move on to your toes, and then to the tops of your feet. Spend several moments at each body part before moving to the next.

Now, carefully place your awareness in your ankles, shins, and then calves. Slowly continue up to your knees, thighs, and hamstrings. Gradually, move the focus of your awareness to your buttocks, genitals, and midsection.

Slowly become aware of your solar plexus, ribs, and lower spine. Move up to the heart area and upper spine. Become aware of your shoulders, biceps, forearms, wrists, and hands. Reverse the sequence and move awareness from your hands to wrists, elbows, biceps, and back to shoulders. Gently and slowly move your awareness to your neck, cheeks, ears, nose, eyes, brow, forehead, and the top of your head.

At this point, flood your entire body, from the top of your head to your toes, with awareness. Notice any tension in your body and place your attention in those areas. Notice your ability to place awareness in your body and the lack of extraneous thoughts when you do so.

This is being in your inner energy body as a refuge from the mind, an exploration of consciousness and an accessing of your intuition, or gut.

Recognize how you can place your consciousness in different areas with the body scan exercise. This can be empowering, and that ability improves with practice.

The body scan is good preparation for meditation or useful on its own. This practice can also be a great aid to falling asleep at night when you have difficulty quieting the mind. A formal practice called Yoga Nidra also helps if you have trouble falling asleep. If you want to experience a guided body scan, check out the free resources on our website.[§§]

Among other useful activities, massage can give you an inner body experience if you actively focus on the part of the body being massaged. Don't let your mind just go away; focus and stay present to the working of the muscles as it's happening. It can be delightful.

Acupuncture is an energy body practice that activates the meridians in the body and can be an effective alternative to Western health care. I have found that it's a practice that works if you surrender to it and stay aware. It's important to be aware of the subtle energies of the inner energy body while receiving the treatment. Alternatively, if you don't believe in acupuncture, you may not reap its rewards if you have overridden the subtle effects with your negative mindset.

Tools I use to experience being in my body are a flex belt stomach massager (great for the abs too), massage gun, and power plate, which shakes the entire body. The power plate is pricey. I call the power plate a thought shaker and use it to experience life flowing through me as described in Pillar 11. Don't worry if this sounds weird; it probably is, but it's effective for me. Find what is effective for you to experience your inner energy body and do that.

Everything can become a mindfulness activity. Even washing the dishes, laundry, or the car; brushing your teeth, flossing, or taking a shower

[§§] https://livinginthegap.org/free-resources/

can be mindful activities. It's your mindset that matters, your conscious intention to be mindful and aware of what you're doing, rather than the particular activity that you perform while going through the motions.

Being mindful and present is not an all-the-time state. In other words, we come in and out of Presence even at our best. It is practiced by noticing when you are not present and returning to the present moment. Improving this, in my experience, is most readily accomplished by regular meditation and mindful movement practices, such as Yoga, or your favorite activities, such as spending time in nature.

Successful professionals and celebrities and notable CEOs, such as Jack Dorsey, Ray Dalio, Naval Ravikant, Marc Benioff, Andrew Cherng, Bill George, Ramani Ayer, Jeff Weiner, Bill Gates, Bob Stiller, Oprah Winfrey, Alak Vasa, Jonathan Tang, Archana Patchiranjan, Russell Simons, Rick Goings, and Chirag Patel, have been reported to have established mindfulness and meditation practices.[27] You can establish yours too; just start small and be consistent.

Finally, I would be remiss to not mention the ethics of mindfulness. I believe practicing mindfulness automatically makes someone more ethical, but having a focused intention on the ethical component leads to another level.

The ethics of mindfulness

One must adhere to a certain ethical foundation of mindfulness. Professionals learning powers of mindfulness should not omit important features, such as nonjudgment and compassion, and should learn to discover the roots of suffering and not stop at the symptomatic relief that mindfulness can bring.

The core of the ethics of mindfulness involves purifying ourselves of greed, hatred, and delusion. Most of the ethical foundations come from Buddhism, and I have chosen to embed them in the Twelve Pillars more secularly.¶¶ At the heart of the ethics of mindfulness is the right livelihood, or finding your purpose in life, the topic of Pillar 2.

PILLAR 1

- Practice mindfulness.

- Be present.

- If possible, meditate regularly.

- Use less formal practices of mindfulness while performing mundane tasks.

- Make physical activity mindful by noticing the inner energy body.

- Adopt the body scan and other tools to gain awareness of the inner energy body.

Chapter Takeaway

Practice mindfulness as if your life depended on it.

¶¶ For more on this, see Jon Kabat-Zinn, "Too Early to Tell: The Potential Impact and Challenges—Ethical and Otherwise—Inherent in the Mainstreaming of Dharma in an Increasingly Dystopian World," *Mindfulness* 8, no. 5 (2017): 1125–1135.

Exercises

Try a body scan, mindful massage, or acupuncture and be open to feeling the inner energy body.

Pick your exercise of choice and go as slow and gently as you can to feel and notice the inner energy body. If you haven't yet, consider trying gentle Yoga for thirty days to get the feeling of the inner energy body. Then continue if you like it, or take that experience to your exercise of choice.

A note on practices: Perform practices regularly, daily if possible. Record the practices in the Practice Journal that follows or your own journal. This will heighten your awareness of what you are doing and track how regularly you do them. Try to do these practices while you continue to read this book for the maximum benefit of both.

- Read ten pages per day from an inspirational book, starting with *Profit with Presence*.

- Journal your dreams and whatever is coming up or bothering you.

- Gratitude: Journal three things you are grateful for and why.

- Breathwork sequence (5-3-6): 1 minute

- Body scan: 3 minutes

- Mindful movement: 5 minutes (activity of your choice)

- Meditation: 2 minutes

- Estimated duration: less than 30 minutes

Practice Journal

Date: ___ / ___ / ___   Woke: ___ : ___   Bed: ___ : ___

Any dreams?

_____

_____

_____

_____

_____

What are you grateful for?

1. _____

_____

_____

Why?

_____

_____

_____

2. _____

_____

_____

Why?

_____

_____

_____

continued

3. _____

_____

_____

Why?

_____

_____

_____

Breathwork sequence? Yes____ No____

Body scan? Yes____ No____

Meditation: _____ minutes

Yoga or mindful movement of choice: _____

Minutes: _____

Reading

Book: _____ Pages: ____

Minutes: _____

Notes: _____

_____

_____

_____

_____

_____

_____

Pillar 2

IDENTIFY YOUR PURPOSE IN LIFE

It is better to do your own duty badly than to perfectly do another's; when you do your duty you are naturally free from sin.[1]

—THE BHAGAVAD GITA

When I hear people say, "I can't get motivated" or supervisors say, "I can't get them motivated," I wonder whether these people are aligned with their purpose or whether they have even considered what their purpose in life is. I believe we are born to take action—why else have body and breath? So, whenever someone does not take action and they don't know why, I ask them to look at their purpose in life. Is the task aligned with their purpose?

Their innate and learned skill sets? I believe actions are born from purpose. I believe leaders are born from purpose. In my experience, when someone finds their purpose in life, motivation and leadership cease to be issues.

As I discussed in the introduction to Part 2, this pillar may be the most challenging in the book, but it is also one of the most rewarding and it can be as simple as adopting mindfulness, Presence, or awakening as your purpose. As we discussed in chapter 1, Presence and mindfulness are essential to finding and maintaining Purpose. If you become bogged down or overwhelmed in what follows, feel free to simply adopt your intention to be more mindful, or fostering Presence as your inner purpose for now, and move on to Pillar 3 at any point. You can come back to go deeper into Pillar 2 if and when you are ready. I positioned identifying your purpose as Pillar 2, but it is also important to revisit after completing all twelve pillars, as each pillar helps you go deeper in purpose and Presence. Once you establish your purpose as Presence, either by the process that follows or by a powerful choice, you will live a much more mindful and meaningful life, and increase your joy, happiness, and success.

For everybody, identifying purpose and experiencing Presence is a process. This pillar is designed for you to read the conceptual context of purpose and do the one-time exercises to get the experience of purpose and Presence, get what you get, and move on to Pillar 3. Understanding the conceptual context is often what allows us to experience something, as we pursue what we start to believe at least as a possibility. As your practice deepens, so will your experience of Presence, and thus your feeling of living with purpose. You matter, and you are in charge of your own journey and process. Let's begin.

Discovering your true purpose in life

As humans, our primary biological purpose is survival. Once survival is established, most people start searching for a higher purpose. Eckhart Tolle in *A New Earth* describes life as having an inner purpose and an outer purpose.[2] Inner purpose is an experience, a state of being, and is primary. Discovering who you truly are is awakening to your inner purpose. You are Presence itself.

Bringing your inner purpose, Presence, to what you are doing in the moment is the goal. Outer purpose is a state of doing and is secondary to Presence. Outer purpose is what you do and the roles you play, such as CEO, athlete, or parent.

Inner purpose establishes who you really are. Presence is why you do things or your purpose and how you do things in a qualitative sense, and inner purpose relates to "being." Outer purpose establishes what you do or your roles, and where you do things, and relates to "doing." Some may question why it's so important to establish inner purpose, and it's simply because your best self shows up with Presence, and that's an inside job that happens when our inner and outer purposes are aligned. Let's discuss some potentially competing inner purposes.

Inner purpose

The three broad categories of inner purpose each have subcategories.

1. Biological and genetic, and cross-cultural

   a. Survival: food, shelter, clothing

   b. Family: protection, sex

2. Egotistical and learned, and cultural

a. Survival: control, domination, good appearance to others

b. Survival: fear-based

c. Family or culturally imposed purposes

3. Spiritual and cross-cultural

a. Awakening into consciousness, awareness, or Presence

b. Love and connection

c. Serving a higher power (and others)

The first of these categories is consistent with Maslow's hierarchy of needs and comes before self-actualization or spiritual growth. If you are hungry, the search for a spiritual or cross-cultural inner purpose is secondary to the subcategory of survival. The other subcategory is family. Providing for and protecting your family are of paramount importance and are hardwired into our biology.

There is an interesting catch here, as pointed out by David Deida in *The Way of the Superior Man*. If a man's deepest purpose is outside of his family, and he never discovers his deepest purpose, or if he continually uses his family as an excuse to compromise it, then his core becomes weakened and he loses depth and Presence. A man should, of course, be a full participant in caring for his children and the household. But if he gives up his deepest purpose to do so, ultimately, everyone suffers.[3] Deida's book is focused on men, but the same concept should hold true for women.

Having an inner purpose to survive and protect your family is also biological, and its importance is undeniable. To become aware and acknowledge this innate purpose is powerful, and even though it's biological, it exists to varying degrees in each of us. We all know people who never want to have kids, and others who make their kids their whole life. I don't know the reason for this, other than that our personal experiences affect this as well as genetics and biology. What's important is that you explore and acknowledge your innate purpose.

We have a biological drive to promote the survival of the species, which is displayed strongly in those who want to have a family. But many who don't want a family also have a strong desire to have sex for its own sake. Accordingly, we must tread with caution when it comes to sex, because much sexual activity is driven by desire. I am not making a value judgment but simply want to point out that sex has the potential to be a threat to transformation and growth. How can this be? Napoleon Hill, author of *Think and Grow Rich*, also focused on men and asked why men generally start to succeed only from age forty or fifty. He found that younger men's tendency to dissipate their energies through overindulgence in the physical expression of sex lessens as they gain perspective with age.[4]

I know when I found the love of my life and got married at thirty-three, I began thinking of broader societal issues. Something was released, and something new was born. I began teaching and doing service work, and my business blossomed too. Before that, I was all about me.

MINDFUL SEX

Because sex has been identified as something that can inhibit business success, a discussion of mindful sex in a book promoting mindfulness to business professionals is appropriate. Furthermore, the prescription outlined in this book is to be mindful in all your affairs (no pun intended), especially a primary purpose such as sex. It is a slight but worthwhile diversion, and this brief discussion is applicable to men and women.

What is mindful sex? Studies in spirituality and health have identified three rules for mindful sex:

- Be present.

- Let go of goals.

- Listen with the body.

Recall Pillar 1 and the inner energy body, and that being present (this requires letting go of goals) and listening to the body are both extremely important and not easy to do given the adrenaline associated with sex for many people. The good news for those readers who enjoy sex is that this is going to take practice, with the intention of slowing down and feeling what is going on with the inner energy body. For those readers who don't enjoy sex, maybe mindfulness during sex will make a difference for you.

Psychology Today defines "spectatoring" as the mind wandering during sex, most typically to thoughts about the way you look or your sexual performance.[5] But it could also wander almost anywhere, even to an email you forgot to respond to, and cause a lack of Presence to the event. In contrast, you reside in physical sensations in your body during mindful sex.

Mindfulness is a practice that slows down the brain or even turns your brain to off mode, which leads to better sex. And "during an orgasm . . . part of the conscious mind turns off, and this is exactly what mindfulness helps you do. Having an orgasm requires letting go . . . and not thinking at all."[6]

Now that I have piqued your attention, I will leave this important topic with a final teaser from Emily Nagoski, who wrote *Come as You Are*, a good resource for mindful sex: "Well. The frustrating reality is we've been lied to—not deliberately, it's no one's fault, but still. We were told the wrong story."[7] It appears the cultural lie regarding sex is that men and women's sexual experiences and desire should be similar, but in reality, many times they are not similar at all: "In reality men and women are different."[8] Nagoski points out that we have been trained to think of sex in terms of behavior itself, rather than what's beneath the behavior and how the behavior came to be. How and when we experience arousal, desire, and orgasm can vary dramatically depending on the why and the how of what's underlying the behavior, which varies for men and women, and individually. Those most interested in researching this area can consult Nagoski's book. Let's continue our discovery of inner purpose.

EGOTISTICAL LEARNED AND CULTURAL PURPOSES

The second category of inner purpose is drawn from egotistical learned and social sources. Ego and external considerations are not actual inner purposes and cannot be a solid basis for transformation. They are listed as inner purposes because our culture and upbringings convince many of us that these purposes are really the purpose of life. Understanding that this is myth can be key to being mindful and finding your true inner purpose.

Families, schools, churches, friends, media, social media, employers, culture, and society have embedded their purpose within us almost since we were born. While this isn't necessarily bad, because we have to start somewhere, it can be liberating to break from external opinions and judgments and look inside to search for, find, and declare your own inner purpose.

Additionally, some things are taken to mean survival when they're simply cultural norms we've been led to believe are much more important than they really are. Let's say having a car is essential to getting to work. That is valid and tied to survival, as we have discussed. Having a Mercedes or Porsche, however, is not linked to survival. It's possibly about culturally imposed desire.*

The desire to look good or dominate are not valid internal purposes but rather driven by ego or a subpersonality, as I'll describe later. Similarly, purposes imposed on us by our family are not proper inner purposes unless we have contemplated and adopted them as our own. Each one of us needs to explore these and decide whether we want to adopt these familial purposes as permanently ours. Once we are aware of their impact, it's a choice.

The third category of inner purpose is spiritual and cross-cultural. This is primarily what I am referring to when describing inner purpose from this point forward in the book. We proceed with the premise that biological and family needs must be met before self-actualizing into spiritual and cross-cultural inner purpose.

FINDING YOUR (SPIRITUAL AND CROSS-CULTURAL) INNER PURPOSE

Inner purpose is most readily revealed in a state of stillness and silence, when your innermost self is noticeable. When sitting in stillness and silence, we are in the world of "I am" versus the world of "I am this" or "I am that," meaning we have become aware of our being, aware that we are aware, and aware of our simple existence. From this place of silence and stillness, we become aware of our awareness, consciousness, or Presence, without which there is no perception, no thought, and

---

* I am not denying that a difference in quality may be a valid reason to upgrade your car.

ultimately no world. Of course, you can experience your outer world whether or not you are consciously aware of it, but this points to the qualitative difference Presence offers.

How do you find your inner purpose? The answer is another question: How do you discover the awareness, consciousness, or Presence of who you really are?

Discovery typically occurs first by the intellectual understanding of Presence introduced in chapter 1 and the beginning of this pillar, which establishes the importance and, in a way, gives permission to explore your experience of Presence. Next is to experience Presence, possibly starting with the mindfulness practices outlined in Pillar 1 and allowing some time for them to affect your brain waves and for you to begin to experience a separation between thought and who is noticing the thoughts: Presence.

Third is possibly to set the intention to experience Presence as your highest calling and begin to look inside and notice how different reality is from what we "thought" it was. For instance, it seems we often have things back to front, like believing that we have a life when we *are* life. That we have consciousness when we *are* consciousness. Eckhart Tolle says, "Life is the dancer; you are the dance."[9] When living in Presence, you observe life playing out like a movie. No matter what happens in the movie, the screen isn't affected; it is there before, during, and after the movie. You are the screen; life is the movie playing out.[†]

---

†   Thanks to Rupert Spira for this analogy. For a phenomenal deep dive in this area, see his *You Are the Happiness You Seek: Uncovering the Awareness of Being* (Oakland, CA: Sahaja, 2022).

Fourth, the entry to Presence is to be curious and examine your inner world through meditation and/or other mindfulness practice. I suggest starting a series of practices with slow boils and graduating to various levels of transformational shocks. This is where it gets messy, because everyone is different, both in what it takes and in what they are willing to do. I am not making a claim that this is a clear and set process, and it's definitely not an exhaustive list. What I am doing is showing you a graduated path and giving you an idea of what's involved. Once you start, only you can tell how far to go, what you are or are not willing to do, or what you have time to do. Critically, some practices are more effective for some and less effective for others. Experience is the only way to know for sure what's most effective for you. The key ingredients are a willingness to explore and the intent to be mindful.

It can be difficult to initially differentiate when you are residing in Presence and when you are not. There are methodologies to get you to experience Presence firsthand. In ancient times yogis worked with a guru who guided them through the process, which was often extreme. I am not a guru, nor am I proposing you do anything extreme. The practices I recommend and describe can definitely give you access to Presence, or who you really are, if you are diligent, patient, and persistent. One of my personal slogans is "Constant, pleasant persistence in all things," and I will add, especially when identifying your inner purpose of Presence.

The first of these practices involves meditation, with the inquiry, "Who am I?"

WHO AM I?

We have at least two identities. One is in the world of form, relative to other forms. You are a person, with a name, height, weight, family, occupation, and so on. This is the ego's identity, that which identi-fies with form. Or, as Eckhart Tolle defines it, "Ego is identification with form."[10]

Form, or the body, is the "little you" that's limited in many ways.‡ It's the you that compares yourself with everyone else and seems to always lack something and never be quite enough. While this little you is important, it's secondary. The second identity is the "big you," or BIG YOU for emphasis, who knows that you see, hear, smell, taste, and are aware and, ultimately, is aware that it's aware. It experiences form through the senses but is beyond sensing. BIG YOU is Presence. It observes the breath as it enters and leaves the body.

Sri Ramana Maharshi, a Hindu sage (1879–1950), proposed that the most important question anyone could ask is, "Who am I?" According to Maharshi,

> I am not; the five cognitive . . . senses . . . I am not; the five cog-nitive sense organs . . . I am not; the five vital airs . . . I am not; even the mind which thinks, I am not; the nescience . . .
>
> If I am none of these, then who am I?
>
> After negating all of those mentioned above . . . it's Awareness [Presence] alone which remains—that is your "I am."[11]

Similarly, Lanza, author of *Biocentrism*, and others postulate that we are simply Presence. They propose that consciousness is the basis of the universe; we are consciousness itself; thus, we are also the basis of the universe, and nothing exists outside of our conscious perception. We are ultimately Presence.

---

‡ The terms *little you* and *big you* are adopted from Doug Harding, *Face to No-Face* (Carlsbad, CA: Inner Directions, 2000).

Holy crap! As highlighted in chapter 1, this is a really big deal. Our inner purpose must be to awaken and explore and experience Presence, the basis of ourselves and the universe.

Exercise 1. How to explore the inquiry "Who am I?"

Once you have established your meditation practice, you can find your way with a meditation that changes the focus from breath to the question "Who am I?" Repeat the question silently and expect no answer during the session.

I typically do it for a few minutes and just let the question hang. Keep asking yourself, "Who am I?" silently on the out breath. It could be done for hours if you have the time and patience. As you sit with the question, you are in meditation or Presence itself. Allow Presence to fill the space of the inquiry. Keep practicing this until you identify yourself as Presence.

TRANSFORMATIONAL SHOCKS

Transformational shocks, introduced in chapter 2, have been proved to help many people discover Presence. The exercises just outlined for finding your inner purpose can be repeated until you experience Presence, and you can use it to distinguish when you are Present and when you are not.

The biggest question, which is framed well by Doug Harding in *Face to No-Face*, is: "Have you ever looked within for anything? If not, how would you go about it?" Consider that, for your entire life, you've been staring into the enormousness of another human and reduced them to a face. You've viewed yourself similarly, and you just haven't been aware of the enormity of who they or you really are: Presence. When you look at your partner, you have their icon, but the reality is that the very same consciousness is on that person's end, too, waiting to be seen. True love is seeing the Presence, and enormousness, of another.

Buddhists describe this as seeing your original face, or the face before your mother was born, and it's who you really are, your authentic self, your I am, or simply Presence. Seeing it isn't hard, or something you can do wrong, but it is something that can take some time practicing mindfulness to recognize. I find residing in Presence to be empowering and limitless, because from this vantage point, I am eternal and will never die. My body, or skin bag, will simply be discarded. Many believe that God is this consciousness, but I'll leave that exploration up to you.[§]

If you would like to experience what Presence feels like, please try the boxed exercises.

Exercises to Experience Presence:

Exercise 2

Point Finger[12]. Sit in a chair at least ten feet from the wall. Point your index finger at the ceiling and look at your finger and the ceiling. Next, point your finger to the wall and just look.

Now, point your finger to the floor and look. Notice how the ceiling, wall, and floor are "out there."

continued

§   If this interests you, check out Michio Kaku, *The God Equation* (New York: Doubleday, 2021); Peter Russell, *From Science to God* (Novato, CA: New World Library, 2002); or Bernardo Kastrup, *Brief Peaks Beyond* (Hampshier, UK: Iff, 2015).

Continue by pointing your finger at your foot, then at your knee, then at your stomach.

Then move to point your finger at your eyes. Does anything shift?

You see your finger, but who is seeing the finger? Is it "little you" (i.e., your material body) within the eyes, or is there a "BIG YOU" (i.e., Presence) behind the eyes? Notice what's looking at your finger. Could it possibly be bigger than your eyes? Possibly even bigger than your face or body?

Ask yourself, "Who or what is looking?" Consider that it is your true essence or who you really are: Awareness, Consciousness, or Presence.

Exercise 3

Inner World. Find a quiet spot and sit with your spine erect and your eyes closed. Focus on listening to your breath for several rounds, then let the focus on your breath go. Dive deep within your inner self and sit in the darkness. Notice the space of the inner self. Let your body disappear in the vastness and notice the enormity of the space; in reality, the space is as large as the universe. Once you notice the enormity of the space, open your eyes, and notice the space shrink to fit within your visual landscape. Close your eyes again and regain the enormity of the inner space. Open your eyes and see if you can gain the awareness and spaciousness your noticed with your eyes closed, with your eyes open.¶ This enormous black hole of your inner world points to the universe and Presence.

Exercise 4

Constricted Space. Stand in the middle of a quiet room with an open doorway in sight. Try to expand your vision as wide as possible and see as much of the room as you can with your peripheral vision. This is known as *wide angle vision*, and it slows down your brain waves. Close your eyes and notice the vastness and enormity of the space within the darkness. Open your eyes and try to gain as much of the feeling and sense of vastness and enormity as you can and keep your vision within as wide an angle as possible. Next, slowly walk toward the doorway and notice the space shrink as you approach the doorway. Stand in

continued

¶   It's much harder to experience the feeling of vastness and the enormity of Presence with your eyes open, so don't be discouraged if you can't. Just close your eyes and regain the spaciousness. Possibly try this exercise again when you have completed the book; it's repeated in Appendix 1. We do some more advanced practices to experience Presence in our workshops. Presence is a process, so be patient with yourself.

the doorway and notice the space contract. Close your eyes and notice the vastness and enormity return.

Open your eyes. What difference do you notice? Your vision constricts your felt awareness or Presence; that's its job and allows you to focus.

This is the experience of Presence. Seeing this void of nature, seeing into the vast nothing of consciousness; this is the true seeing. This seeing is seeing the eternal. Your Presence is eternal.

You are experiencing your own consciousness and Presence. Our visual, external activities and internal mental distractions tend to drown out Presence, or overwhelm our own consciousness, so you have to practice to gain the feeling of Presence. When you feel it, it may be so foreign as to be a mild transformational shock. The goal is to rest in Presence, this vast and enormous field of consciousness, as you conduct your day. Your life experiences can unfold within your field of Presence, like a movie playing on a movie screen. While the movie or experiences change, the movie screen and Presence contain whatever plays out without being impacted.

My experience is that when I can reside in Presence, everything changes. Nothing is as dramatic or disturbing, and I know that I can handle whatever comes up in my field of Presence. It's a knowing, a calmness, and pure joy or bliss, even in the middle of activity. Experiencing Presence can be harder in the middle of activity; however, when it's accomplished it's known as "the zone" in sports. The inner state and the outer world melt together, and there is a flow of an activity without a doer. It's an amazing feeling, and one worth mastering in our lives. You will hear more about flow and being in the zone in Pillar 8.

In my experience, with intention and the proper environment, noticing Presence is the easy part. The hard part is trusting Presence. Especially as we go back into our lives and the culture of enormous and constant distractions, and never-having-enough mentality. Trust that you, or Presence, are enough. If you can learn to trust Presence, your chances of happiness and success become limitless. Practice being your authentic self and living from who you really are, Presence. Your life will take on a new simplicity and purpose when you can reside in and trust Presence.

Once you understand the importance of Presence, have experienced it, and have learned to trust it, by these exercises or otherwise, it's much easier to reside in Presence with the ultimate accomplishment of being aware of being aware. The lifetime practice is to be aware of when you are Present and when you are not. On my best days, I come in and out of Presence. As soon as you notice you are not present, you are present again. Simply noticing is enough.

Once you've experienced Presence, adopting Presence as your inner purpose and learning to trust it ultimately becomes a choice.

As Viktor Frankl describes in *Man's Search for Meaning*, "That which was ultimately responsible for the state of a prisoner's inner self was not so much the enumerated psychophysical causes as it was the result of a free decision."[13] It's an important choice, so please choose wisely.

I've adopted the term Presence to refer to who I really am, refer to who you really are, and to describe inner purpose because I find it's true for me intellectually, in my personal experience, and because it's simple and empowering. I find it is as complicated, or as simple, as you want to make it. If you have a different word for Presence that works better for you, please use it, provided that it aligns with your spiritual, cross-cultural inner purpose.

Similarly, once you recognize the foundational inner purpose of Presence, you may choose to personalize your inner purpose—for instance, to serve your higher power or to share love and compassion with the world—but it starts with awakening into Presence and learning to trust it. The goal is to bring who you are (Presence) to what you do, rather than bringing what you do to who you are. You are not your job; you are Presence, and you have a job. When I show up with Presence to a task, I show up in a powerful and persuasive way. And we accomplish showing up this way to our outer purposes through the Soul.

Consider "Who Am I" is a choice

WHO AM I? Self

CHOOSE TO COME FROM ESSENCE:
Presence

WHO AM I NOT? self

CHOOSE NOT TO IDENTIFY WITH FORM:
Body, job, possessions, etc.
The world of suffering

SOUL

Soul is the spiritual, or immaterial, part of a human being or animal, regarded as immortal, including the emotional and intellectual energy. In my experience, my Soul is the life force where Presence and form, or my body and the material world, meet consciousness. Soul is how I translate Presence into action. I was born into a body and given breath so I could take action.

In Greek, *Soul* is *psyche*, or life force. The Soul resides within the body as a collective of all aspects that make up a person and what connects them to the universe and earth. Soul is the essence of your being. If the term *Soul* doesn't resonate with you, find a word that does, such as "essence," "being," or "psyche," that can point to your essence and connects to Presence.

When you can identify with your Soul's life force, it changes everything. It becomes evident in your enthusiasm for your outer purpose. It can change your life from one spent in activities running amok to a Soul-driven life, in which your Presence captains the ship of your outer purpose. The Soul is what makes Presence actionable.

INNER PURPOSE ⟶ PRESENCE ⟶ SOUL ⟶ OUTER PURPOSE

OUTER PURPOSE

Outer purpose is simply what you do or what you're doing in the moment. It encompasses all the roles you assume in your life. The goal is to bring Presence to what you do. Your outer purpose, what you do, may or may not change once you identify and align your outer purpose with your inner purpose and Soul. However, the essence of who you are being while doing your outer purpose will change forever. That's because your Soul won't tolerate inconsistency between your inner and outer purpose. If that happens, your psyche will suffer severe consequences. Once you align your inner and outer purposes, through the Soul, you become unstoppable.

You should be present and aware while engaged in any role you are fulfilling at the moment. This is harder for outer purposes that don't fit our innate and learned skills or for roles we are not passionate about (which likely don't align with our purpose). Most of us have driven by our exit ramp on the highway, completely lost in thought or other distractions. When we're present and aware, we don't miss our exit ramp.

Suppose you're CEO of a Fortune 500 company, mother of two, avid golfer, and president of the school board. These are all outer purposes. The primary question is whether you can fulfill your inner purpose of Presence while engaged in these outer doings.

As CEO, are you present during your meetings? Or are you checking your phone or emails while others talk? Do you truly listen to an employee, shareholder, or director who isn't happy with the company's current state? Or are you so caught up in thinking about what you're going to say in response you barely hear what they're communicating? (This was me.) Are you genuinely compassionate to an employee diagnosed with a terminal illness who has to quit the company, leaving the person without insurance or income while battling illness? Or is that just business or just the breaks? Compassion doesn't mean you have to solve every issue, but you should be aware and concerned. When you are present, you are more compassionate because you are connected to others (rather than disconnected).

As a mother of two, are you present when you are with your children despite the enormous demands of your job? Or are you constantly checking email and social media for critical information? When playing golf, are you present for your fellow golfers, helping them find their misplaced drive? Or are you so distracted by your own performance or your cell phone dinging with messages that you hardly know others are playing? (This was me.)

As president of the school board, do you have compassion for the students who have a harsh or nonexistent home life? Do you consider making opportunities for the less fortunate as meaningful as those available for the gifted, and vice versa?

To be aligned with Presence, I taught at the university while maintaining my real estate profession. More recently, I felt Presence change my direction through my Soul, and I shifted my responsibilities. I left the university and started training professionals in mindfulness and to be more service oriented. I've found ways to fulfill my inner purpose of Presence and to share the concept of Presence with others. I've found many ways to fulfill my inner purpose without leaving my real estate business. When I am engaged in real estate, I endeavor to remain present, compassionate, and grateful. I am connected to others and know they are important too.

What happens when you are already in a job and you discover it does not align with your inner purpose? For instance, if your inner purpose of Presence is further refined to serving others and your job (or outer purpose) is to foreclose on single mothers who are behind in their mortgage payments, what then? You may be able to come to terms with that role by feeling compassion and a way of being that's of service to these mothers. Perhaps you start listening to them with compassion or help them find an alternative place to live. If you can't come to terms with the role, you may find you need to change jobs to deliver on your inner purpose. Trust Presence and you will know.

If you're a real estate broker who's discovered your Presence, you may find an entirely new connection with clients and need to modify your role to be of genuine service. You might need to change jobs or locations to be fulfilled, because inner and outer purposes need to be aligned. In fact, if you are truly living in Presence, they have to be aligned. In other words, what you do needs to support who you are, and what you do may need to change. That is, how you show up needs to change to showing up with Presence.

The outer purpose of service, applied to various positions, is consistent with most valid inner purposes and becomes quite inspiring. Showing up with Presence is much easier to accomplish when your outer purpose is something you are both passionate about and good at doing.

FIND YOUR ELEMENT

You probably already have a good idea of your passions and what you're good at doing. Ken Robinson defined where passion and ability merge as "the Element."

Human intelligence, which is you, is diverse and multifaceted and includes the following:

- Analytic intelligence

- Creative intelligence

- Practical intelligence

- Emotional intelligence

Robinson says to ask, "How am I intelligent?"[14] Where do your passions and skills merge?

For example, I loved to sing as a young boy, but I couldn't carry a tune in a bucket, so I got cut from the band (that I started!). It was not my

Element. I loved teaching students at the university but struggled with the bureaucracy. It was not my Element. I love Yoga, so I opened a yoga studio, which drove me crazy. Doing Yoga is my Element, but owning a studio was not. I love real estate and am very good at it. It's my Element.

Robinson also points out that we overvalue IQ tests and college performance. Some years ago, a former dean of the College of Business at Colorado State University, who was my good friend and colleague, and I were going to make an ask of a billionaire to support the real estate program. As we were driving to meet the billionaire, I turned to the dean and said, "Isn't it ironic this person only spent twelve weeks in college before dropping out?"

"Yeah," the dean commented. "He started his own business and look at him now."

"The other successful real estate company in this area is run by two college dropouts. They may well be billionaires one day. Look at Bill Gates, Mark Zuckerberg, and others who have quit college. They've redefined what business is all about," I replied. He gave me a nod.

I shook my head. "And we're asking this billionaire to support something that didn't serve him."

The dean acknowledged my point.

We knew real estate education was important to the university, but we were not sure it would be important to the billionaire we were asking to support the program. Thankfully, the person did support the program and we were able to establish a minor in real estate.

Similarly, consider that Tiger Woods didn't finish college, and the members of The Beatles never attended formal music training. Time and again, we find the most successful people often skirted the very systems put in place to provide an avenue to success for the rest of us.

The Element is valuable as well in our exploration into mindfulness to identify things we do to cause us to be the most present in our lives. For me, that's snow skiing. For my wife, Tracy, it's painting.

When are you most present in your life now? Where do what you are really good at (aptitude) and what you love to do (passion) meet? This is your Element. When you discover it, you may say, "I get it! I love it! I want it!"[15] In the meantime, be aware and search for your Element. I'm pretty sure you'll find it. In practice, finding your Element is actively seeking opportunities to explore your aptitude in different areas. Residing in Presence is key to finding your Element; finding your Element is key to finding and aligning your inner and outer purposes through your Soul.

Finding your professional Element will help you be on the right side of the Pareto Principal:[16] 20 percent of the people do 80 percent of the business. These people are in their Element, and that's why they perform so well.

The work of finding your inner and outer purposes will help your career. You will find ways to align your inner purpose with your current position. You may add duties or activities to your current schedule that align with your Presence, or you may change positions or start a new company or nonprofit organization.

SELF-SOUL-SPIRIT MODEL

In our workshops, we introduce Dr. Roger Strachan's Self-Soul-Spirit model, which has its roots in Gestalt therapy. This model proposes that we have multiple subpersonalities that are parts of who we are as a whole person and can be discovered by examining our lived experience. Have you ever said, "A part of me wants to do it . . . and another part of me doesn't"? We all have. Where does this come from?

This powerful model allows us to work with different subpersonalities to gain awareness and control of ourselves and our actions. Also, it treats things like depression as possibly arising from one or multiple subpersonalities and whose treatment is to strategize with other subpersonalities, rather than always a disease to be treated with a prescription.** The Self-Soul-Spirit model is actually an alternative form of therapy.

The model is based on genetics and experience, or nature and nurture. "What am I going to do about my genetics at this point?" you may ask. The good news for meditators is the emerging new science of epigenetics, or how ingrained traits can evolve with their environment. Meditation can be a main influence even on the level of altering ingrained traits, and we can actually change to embody mindfulness characteristics, such as compassion and listening.[17] In epigenetics, even our genes can be modified.

Interestingly, Bernardo Kastrup has posited that subpersonalities, or as he defines them more generically, "alters," are disassociated with each other.[18] The Self-Soul-Spirit model reconciles this phenomenon with awareness of the various subpersonalities and organization through the Soul.

The Self-Soul-Spirit model aims for you to live a Soul-driven life in which the Soul directs the individual parts. The Soul is the essence of our being and totality. We revisit and further describe the Self-Soul-Spirit model in the concluding chapter of the book, and I give my personal experience at the end of that chapter.††

I have found that knowing what you are not good at is as important as knowing what you are good at. Filling that void is equally important. For instance, I am a ready-fire-aim guy, and create things

---

** I am not saying there aren't times when this is warranted, and I have done some of this myself, but the Self-Soul-Spirit model may be a powerful option to explore.

†† The most effective way to learn the Self-Soul-Spirit model is to work with a facilitator trained in the model, which we provide in our workshops, or you can visit the website for the Center for Creative Choice to find a facilitator or to explore. The website for The Center for Creative Choice (CCC) was undergoing a revamp at the time of this publication. Please send an email to info@livingingthegap.org or go to RyanHolsappleGuide.com for more information; and you may check the CCC website too.

like buildings, programs, and opportunities that would often not exist if not for me. But I am no manager. At LC Real Estate, Blaine Rappé cleans up my messes and makes sure all the management duties are performed with excellence and on time. He makes up for my deficits, and I try to make up for his. Know your Element and know what's not your Element and find a partner or employee who has an Element in those areas. This allows for both of you and for organizations to succeed long term with Presence.

The Element is what Joseph Campbell meant by follow your bliss: "I do know what bliss is: that deep sense of being present, of doing what you absolutely must do to be yourself. . . . So what I have told my students is this: follow your bliss."[19]

THE JOURNEY INTO YOUR INNERMOST SELF

For those who have come this far on the journey into the self, know that this journey is what Campbell called a hero's journey and what the *Star Wars* movies were based on. As it applies to this journey:

> You have ventured into your innermost self and the world of the spirit to discover your inner purpose. The miraculous force of Presence was discovered and a decisive victory won: You have come back from this adventure with the power to bestow Presence on your fellow man and woman. Once you return to the real world with the spirit of Presence for the benefit of your fellow man and woman, you are transformed with the wisdom of both the material and spiritual worlds.
>
> Importantly, when you return to complete the adventure, you must survive the impact of the material world without

losing the Presence you gained from the spiritual adventure and share the wisdom you gained with the rest of the world. For you need to achieve balance between the material and spiritual worlds, no matter how many times you have to return to the process of exploring the dimensions of the inner self in the search for the inner purpose of Presence, or the separation from your known world and material self.[20]

In other words, after you have gained Presence and go back out into the material world with its lack of mindfulness, you need to share Presence to help shift this world to be more mindful. Additionally, you may need to repeat the process of discovering your inner purpose of Presence until you have reached a maintainable balance between the material world of the householder and the spiritual world of Presence. The discovery and maintenance of Presence as a primary state is a process, and it takes what it takes.

Summary

By identifying your inner purpose as Presence and aligning it with your outer purpose, you are using your innate abilities and personal skills to make the most out of your life. What can you do to awaken into your inner purpose of Presence? Practice awareness and use the mindfulness tools available as if your life depended on it. That should be enough, but if more is necessary or possible, you'll see it and pursue it with Presence. That's how Presence works when it is cultivated and nurtured. Presence is curative. Presence is everything. You are Presence and the seed of Presence, and it must be nurtured to grow.

Profit with Presence simply means right livelihood or making your living by being who you truly are.

Once you've identified your inner purpose of Presence and aligned it with your outer purpose through your Soul, life force, or essence, you have determined who you are is Presence, why you're doing something is your purpose, and how you do things is with Presence. After you've confirmed or determined the outer purposes that align with Presence, you have determined your roles, or what you do and where you do it.

The next step is to create clarity, vision, intention, commitment, and habits.

PILLAR 2

- Your inner purpose is Presence.

- Soul connects our inner and outer purposes.

- Outer purpose is your various roles.

- Find your Element.

- The Self-Soul-Spirit model.

- The journey into your innermost self is a continuous process.

Chapter Takeaway

Your inner purpose is Presence.

Before we move to the next pillar, I would like to share a poem I wrote about leadership.

LEADERSHIP

Leadership is underrated,
Being who you truly are
Unabashedly, unashamed, unstoppable
To be completely free.

Finding who you truly are
Who you were meant to be
And who you aren't
Is leadership to me.

Once there
actions that were once unthinkable
are natural, spontaneous, and free
Freedom to simply be.

Leadership is
Finding Purpose
Setting Intention, Vision, and Commitment
Showing up.

Being change
Being responsible
Being your word
taking action, again, again, and again
regardless of the outcome.

Leadership is being
full of other
and empty of self

Admitting you don't know.
Anything,

Except who you are and what you stand for.

Accepting yourself and others,
Accepting what is
Aiming for what's possible
And be willing to go there.
Is true leadership.

It takes courage
It takes hard work
It takes awareness
It takes being willing to follow
To truly lead.

You can do it
Once you know the way
To your true self
It's who you were born to be.
The leader of your life.

Pillar 3

CREATE CLARITY, VISION, INTENTION, COMMITMENT, AND HABITS

A university professor went to visit a famous Zen master. While the master quietly served tea, the professor talked about Zen. The master poured the visitor's cup to the brim and then kept pouring. The professor watched the overflowing cup until he could no longer restrain himself. "It's full! No more will go in!" the professor blurted. "This is you," the master replied, "How can I show you Zen unless you first empty your cup?"*

* Various sources often attribute the story to a famous conversation between the scholar Tokusan (782–865) and Zen Master Ryutan (760–840), https://www.learnreligions.com/empty-your-cup-3976934

I am a real estate developer and create things that often weren't going to happen without me. I learned that creating a vision and relating that vision in a way to inspire clarity, intention, and commitment was the key to success. I had material success but was not satisfied with my life. I learned that the same process was true for personal development as was true for shopping centers—that creating a personal vision, focused intention, with commitment and enrolling others in my vision being the keys to my personal success and happiness. Later, I learned the importance of habits in maintaining Presence in my daily life.

This pillar is about clearly seeing your current situation, stating your vision, establishing your intention, and committing to practices and habits that support your vision.

This process is guided by the law of attraction, which states that what you send out into the universe is what you'll get back. Send out positive vibrations, and that's what you'll receive in return. Conversely, send out negative vibrations, and that's what will rebound back to you. The law of attraction further states that nature abhors a vacuum and that removing negative thoughts, feelings, or emotions from your life makes space for more positive things. Basically, it's impossible to have an entirely empty space and impossible to simultaneously house opposites. Take, for example, love and fear. Both thoughts and ideas are made of energy, but positive energy attracts positive energy. So which would you choose?

Although the scientific community for years was skeptical of the concept of positive attracting positive in personal transformational work, recent research into its aspects has added to its credibility. My analysis shows that scientific research already cited or further developed in this pillar supports the law of attraction in areas such as mirror neurons, the reticular activating system, neuroplasticity, visual motor rehearsal or visualization, gratitude, and even the placebo effect, which simply affirms that what you believe matters.

Despite the recent scientific support, there are still many skeptics and critics of the law of attraction. When I look deeply inside myself and to my direct experience, I know that these things have worked for me and for many others I know. I have used the law of attraction to create shopping centers. For instance, I typically start with a hand sketch of what I see as possible on a parcel of well-located land, then have a site plan and a rendering made by an architect. I stand on the site with the site plan and rendering, visualize the shopping center as fully developed, and it sends me the signals for what actions are necessary. I used to have a detailed checklist with goals to develop a shopping center, but now all I need is a picture or a rendering, which activates my reticular activating system. Then, I am neurologically wired to know exactly whom to call when and the sequence of what to do when.

Admittedly, I can also rely on my partner Blaine to have a detailed checklist.

After over a forty-year career of using visualization tools in real estate, I need less prompting than I did when I started. The same will be true for you as you gain experience in using these tools, but initially I suggest using specific details, checklists, and goals.

Importantly, the context is critical to the prescription. For the skeptics of these practices, I point out there is a difference between renunciants sitting on a hill in India and professionals running businesses in the United States who need to take intentional actions to move their world. Do you know many successful businesses that don't set goals? This book is for professionals creating things in the material world through establishing a vision and goals, and manifesting them such that they materialize, and hopefully result in profit. As Peter Drucker said, "The best way to predict the future is to create it."

I also wonder, how many skeptics have tried these practices, believing they work? Or as Herbert Spencer said, "There is a principle which is a bar against all information, which is proof against all arguments, and which cannot fail to keep a man in everlasting ignorance—that principle is contempt prior to investigation."[1]

I have found that another major detriment to residing in Presence is intellectualism: I understand the concept, so I get it. Intellectualism is an important aspect of allowing yourself to experience something new, and in this instance, allowing you to practice the concepts with the belief that they work. However, practice itself is where experience is gained and where the benefits reside, not in intellectualism. Successful businesspeople can't just sit there. This work prescribes intentional action toward meaningful goals, like in business.

One of the benefits of being in this work for a while is that I rely much more on my personal experience than on what I hear or read. The following is what I believe and what has worked for me. I am not claiming all of it is proven scientific fact, but neither is consciousness itself, despite its undeniability.

If you want to experience the benefits of this pillar, set your skepticism aside and actually try the practices and trust the process. If your internal dialogue is telling you *poppy cock*, and you can't set that aside to give it a legitimate effort, then I suggest you simply move on to Pillar 4 for now, because you need to believe in the power of the tools for them to work.

As with the last pillar on purpose, you may want to revisit this pillar later, after practicing mindfulness for a while. It might come more easily after you have been practicing for a while and, after you have established Presence as your purpose in life. If at that point you have genuinely tried for a reasonable period while truly residing in Presence but don't see results, then set this material aside and come back if and when you are called to return. Let's continue.

The reticular activating system (RAS) sits at the base of the brain and connects to the spinal cord. It's part of the brain that stands guard to filter sensory input to the brain. Furthermore, it determines what we notice or are focused on perceiving and what we are not focused on perceiving. The RAS is like our own personal search algorithm. When we create a clear picture of what we want and focus on it, the brain doesn't stop looking until it finds it, and the RAS filters it to our conscious attention. In other words, it's our focus that determines what is filtered and to where. The RAS, mirror neurons, and the like are why life lists, vision boards, and business plans are so important: We see what we are searching for, and what we don't focus on (i.e., everything else) is left in the brain, which records and stores everything.

Some take the law of attraction to an extreme to say, "You can accomplish anything," but I don't take it that far. I'm even more skeptical of those who say the law of attraction is all BS. That's because I've seen it work in my own life and in the lives of so many others. I also believe in karma, the law of cause and effect. I have experienced it firsthand when what I give of myself is returned to me in beneficial ways. When I do something kind for another person, it immediately makes me feel better. It sends a positive signal to the universe, which triggers a positive, energetic response. If I smile at someone, they smile back thanks to mirror neurons. As I practice gratitude, I feel better every time.

The laws governing subatomic particles also govern our thoughts, ideas, feelings, relationships, careers, and material successes. And that's great news for us because we are practicing mindfulness, creating positive thoughts to improve our relationships and mindset.

But why do we need to stabilize the mind and clear out unproductive thoughts?

To create a clear vision.

Why do we need a clear vision?

To be sure it's your unique personal vision, and because we want to attract it.

How do we attract our vision?

By cultivating the vision with the positive energy you're looking to receive.

How do we send out positive energy?

With practices that train the mind, such as meditation, gratitude, affirmations, and visioning.

Let's get started.

Clarity

Everything you've been reading up to this point has been about creating clarity. Mindfulness creates clarity. Shakespeare writes, "There is nothing either good or bad, but thinking makes it so."[2] This is true for thoughts. Thoughts are neither good nor bad, but thinking makes them so.

I've been quite critical of thoughts, but humans couldn't function without thought. The real problem is the habituation of thought, the lack of awareness around thoughts, and the unrecognition of the impact negative thoughts often have on performance. That results in a lack of clarity. Clarity is the quality of being coherent and intelligible, of transparency or purity. Tibetan Buddhists call the epitome of this clarity *Ringpa*, or "clear light mind." I love that phrase.

Humans have around 6,000 thoughts a day. I don't know about you, but not all my thoughts are empowering or even helpful. Some are negative, self-sabotaging thoughts that I would prefer not to manifest into ideas or reality. Thoughts create ideas that can produce material reality, but I certainly cannot and do not want to foster every thought, especially those negative ones.

Around 95 percent of human activities are generated without conscious focus—that is, we're not focused on them at that moment or able to recollect or recall the experiences. These actions often create frustration and "blind spots" that can narrow our vision.[3]

The top ten leadership blind spots by leaders, according to *Inc.*, are the following:

1. Going it alone (being afraid to ask for help)

2. Being insensitive of your behavior on others

3. Having an "I know" attitude

4. Avoiding conflict

5. Blaming others or refusing responsibility

6. Not honoring the other person's time

7. Being driven by a personal agenda

8. Withholding emotional commitment

9. Not taking a stand

10. Tolerating low performance[4]

These blind spots and others could be holding you and your organization back. Our inability to see the truth due to blind spots affects our clarity.

What leaders identify in themselves as needing work rarely overlaps with what their peers and key colleagues see as areas that need improvement. The most common leadership traits identified as needing improvement included emotional intelligence, time management, listening, delegation, communication, team and leadership development, accountability, prioritization, executive Presence, and vision and strategy. And the data show a 96 percent probability that leaders have a blind spot toward being perceived as ivory-tower executives who don't provide adequate clarity on the company's strategy.[5]

My experience is that employees often don't give the CEO accurate feedback, implying it may be necessary to get outside feedback to identify our blind spots from employees, such as a 360-degree confidential performance review. Sometimes there are clues if we're listening. About fifteen years ago, I heard one of my partners, Nathan Klein, say to someone, "You can't talk to Eric." Wow, that struck me, especially when I realized it was true. I started working on being someone who was approachable and listened. In other words, I became present. I doubt that Nathan would say the same thing today. I was grateful to receive his feedback because I knew that accurate feedback is essential to discover blind spots and grow.

Mindfulness makes us more aware of our actions and more open to candid feedback. It might not expose us to every action we perform, and feedback can be essential. The vastness of brain activity, combined with our limited ability to focus, means clarity can be a somewhat daunting task without mindfulness tools.

Another area that can cause issues is our limiting underlying beliefs. An underlying belief that you can do anything or that you're supported will help you succeed. More commonly, underlying beliefs are in the areas of self-sabotage, fears, critic, anger, jealousy, procrastination, and negative thinking.

You might not even realize how dearly these underlying beliefs are costing you. Years ago, I was at a conference and one of my fellow participants asked, "Eric, what are you so mad about?" I had no idea I was angry. With awareness of the behavior, I learned my family and business were being dramatically affected by others' fear of my anger. This wasn't acceptable to me.

After much soul-searching, I recognized I'd adopted a belief of righteousness, and I later learned that I have a righteous subpersonality, believing I was better than others and deserved particular treatment. When someone acted below my standards or did something, like ignore me, I unleashed anger to get my way. This examination moved the pattern into my focus. Once there, I started witnessing the pattern, and only then could I gradually change the dynamic through awareness that originated with candid feedback.

Do you know what your limiting underlying beliefs are? It's essential to place your focus on these beliefs because they're likely holding you, your family, and your business back. The hardest part is overcoming the resistance to our flaws and having the courage to be brutally honest with ourselves. Often, a part of ourselves resists change and doesn't want to acknowledge its unfavorable conclusion. For instance, I notice that when I am on a diet and losing weight, I check the scale regularly. Yet when I'm over my target weight and not making progress, I walk past the scale for weeks. It's like I don't want the bad news. It requires a commitment and awareness to step on the scale every day and honestly assess what it reports, which increases my awareness of my weight and what I eat. Walking past the scale leaves the issue out of my conscious focus. When I step on the scale and acknowledge what it reports, it brings the issue into focus.

This is a night-and-day phenomenon, because when the light of Presence shines on an issue, it starts to change. Presence is curative.

I've noticed a similar phenomenon in business. We avoid talking about the underperforming division or assets, even when evaluating them and taking action is the only way they have a chance of being turned around. It's easier to look at the best-performing division or assets, which typically need less attention. Accordingly, we need to candidly assess each situation. Am I twenty-five pounds overweight? Do I have high cholesterol or blood sugar? Is a division losing money each quarter or does it have extremely high employee turnover? Time spent uncovering blind spots and limiting underlying beliefs is time well spent.

Everything starts with a thought, and as Wallace Wattles says in *The Science of Getting Rich*, "THOUGHT is the only power which can produce tangible riches from the Formless Substance. The stuff from which all things are made is a substance which thinks, and a thought of form in this substance produces the form."[6]

John Assaraf and Murray Smith say in *The Answer*, "Thought is the most powerful force in the universe. Our thoughts are the controlling factor in what we manifest and create in our lives. The idea precedes the thing."[7]

Thoughts are matter, all matter comes from energy, and energy is composed of consciousness. I want to distinguish between thought, which occurs in the mind unabated, and an idea that is fostered with focused attention and contemplation. Thoughts can be random; ideas are not. Thoughts are the seeds for ideas, and ideas are seeds for creation.

Meditation can be instrumental in letting less productive thoughts go. Letting go helps you create space and clarify the ideas you want to foster and to become reality. You need to place your focus on the thoughts you want to turn into ideas. If you are not immediately aware of thoughts, you may be inadvertently fostering thoughts that are not productive. Meditation teaches us to notice our thoughts by focusing on the breath. By focusing elsewhere, thought activity becomes more evident, and it slows down. When we notice thought distractions and return our attention to the breath, we're learning not to be attached to thoughts. Using a baseball analogy, learn how to take a pitch. You don't have to swing at every pitch or follow every thought, and that's good news.

But how do you hold on to and foster the thoughts you would like to manifest? By choosing to focus on these thoughts and forwarding them into action through your RAS. It's vital and necessary to train yourself to be in sync with your conscious vision and objectives to improve performance.

You've discovered your empowering inner purpose of Presence and created clarity; now you can create a vision for your life that's empowering. This vision is critically yours. Not your parents', family's, society's, or any other external influence. The other practices I recommend, such as reading inspirational books or practicing gratitude, affirmations, and visualization, plant seeds that will generate ideas that are consistent with and support your vision while also training your mind and RAS to fulfill your vision and goals.

What works for me is to practice gratitude each morning by journaling three things I'm grateful for and why. I also practice affirmations like "I am Presence" by writing it twenty-five times each morning. Then I read at least ten pages from an inspirational book. Afterward, I visualize accomplishing my vision and use my conscious vision to create positive visual images that guide my intentional activity.

In other words, create a clearing or clarity through meditation and practices to place yourself in Presence and, from this place, create your empowering vision for the future (rather than society's vision for you). Place your attention on creating this vision and train yourself through these practices to work toward fostering this vision. That is to say, train yourself to work nonstop on your objectives or vision, even in deep, dreamless sleep. If you are fully aligned with your established vision and responsible for delivering on the vision, your attention can be focused on Presence. It requires you to trust your operating system to deliver on your objectives, just like it keeps you breathing and your heart beating.

The critical practice is to reside in Presence and notice when you are not. You cannot focus on your vision of the future and be present in the moment at the same time. Thus, training yourself and the RAS to search for those things that fulfill your vision, and filter other things out, is key to living a life of Presence and achieving your goals at the same time. It is possible to do both, just not possible to focus on everything at the same time. This is a key element of *Profit with Presence*.

Vision

Vision is the ability to think about or plan the future with imagination and wisdom. You are probably very familiar with corporate vision statements, which are similarly critical, and this is the similar process with a different focus. Here we're talking about your personal vision. Ideally, your personal vision will guide you when revisiting the company's vision statement or, at a minimum, ensuring your personal vision and the company's vision are in sync. In this visioning process, we create clarity, set a vision for the world, create a "life list," create a vision board, and create a comprehensive personal vision and plan for ourselves, and eventually for our business. Lynne McTaggart writes,

> We can improve our health, enhance our performance . . . and possibly even affect the future by consciously using intention. The intention should be a highly specific aim . . . which you should visualize in your mind's eye as having already occurred while you are in a state of . . . hyper-awareness. . . . Engage all five senses to visualize it in detail.[8]

Thoughts and ideas are tangible energy, and intention is a focused energy force that can shape and influence our vision. Once we have an idea backed with intention, which is solidly visualized, it sets our future into action and sets off the momentum to carry it forward.

As a real estate developer, visioning is a critical element of real estate development. In 1997, I had an idea to develop a shopping center. I found land for the potential development and then hand sketched how the shopping center would look on the land. Then we selected an architect and had a site plan and colored rendering of the completed shopping center drawn. With this vision created, I went to work with my partner Don Marostica, completing feasibility, purchasing the property, and developing the shopping center, which opened in 1999.†

Personal visions are manifested similarly. You have already started the most essential part of the visioning process. You've created clarity, or a clearing from which a fresh vision can spring, free from the tyranny of thought. Your vision comes from your inner self and through your Soul.

A few years back, I participated in a vision quest. It took place in the wilderness, and I had to set up a ten-foot circle that I couldn't leave, except to go to the bathroom or retrieve more water. All I had with me were the clothes on my back, water, and a tarp. The vision quest originates from American Indian culture, and the concept is to fast and clear away all distractions, to look inward to create a new vision. Fasting brings distinct clarity by the biological need to find food—you are sharper when you are hungry. The current craze of intermittent

---

† Neighborhood residents were not in favor of the project. We also had the architect create a model of the planned shopping center, which showed how it laid out in scale in relation to their personal residences. The model removed the neighbors' objections, and the project was overwhelmingly approved. Vision is critical to personal development, and communication of vision is critical to business development.

fasting creates some of this focus, and the more intense vision quest also helps with discovering personal vision. Vision quests typically last for about four days, with preparation and integration time on either end. A quest is intense and can lead to transformational shock. If you have the time and inclination, a vision quest can be life changing.[‡]

But you can discover a powerful vision through a different process of mindfulness while you stay in the comfort of your home. For instance, researchers have found almost similar success in visualizing shooting basketball free throws as from physically practicing free throws. One study had two groups of participants: one practiced basketball free throws and the other visualized making free throws. The visualization group made a 23 percent improvement in their free throws, almost the same as the group that physically practiced, who experienced a 24 percent increase.[9]

Another study by Karin Hinshaw found: "Mental practice has some distinct advantages over physical practice that provide a strong case for widespread utilization . . . the mental 'picture' can closely mirror actual performance conditions."[10] Her study concludes that "the findings of the present meta-analysis confirm the effectiveness of mental practice on motor skill performance."

I can also confirm to you from my experience that visioning works similarly in both personal and business settings. You will find detailed instructions to create a life list, vision board, and a visualization technique at the end of this pillar. You can begin to experience the effects of visualization for yourself. Here is a graphic that represents the process:

[‡] For more on this, check out Tom Brown Jr., *The Vision* (New York: Berkley, 1988), or Dave Asprey, *Fast This Way* (New York: HarperCollins, 2021). Some form of fasting may be beneficial to setting your vision, but that is beyond the scope of this book. You should research carefully and consult your physician before you attempt any intense fasting program.

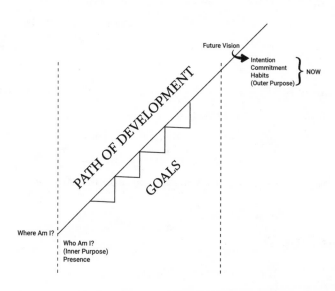

It's best to complete these exercises to manifest your own vision for your life again after you have clearly identified, established, and learned to trust Presence, and have been practicing mindfulness with meditation for at least several months.

Intention

Thoughts that are fostered become ideas; reasonable ideas that are fostered by intention become reality. Intention involves mental planning and forethought. It's a mental state that represents a commitment to actions in the future.

In 2015, I spent nine months commuting from Colorado to Lennox, Massachusetts, participating in the Yoga and Shamanism Program in Lennox with Ray Crist and the Jaguar Path.§ I learned the powerful

---

§   For more information, see the Jaguar Path website, https://www.jaguarpath.com.

impact of intent through shamanism—an ancient approach to energy healing. In shamanism, intention is paramount and includes creating the will for a specific outcome. In business, focused intention is essential to improve performance.

Intention sends a specific energy signal to the universe, signaling a precise desired result. With your intent, you are asking the universe for exactly what you want and being open to receiving it. Vision gives the RAS a target. Intention puts the RAS in overdrive.

To get your desired results, you must be committed to your intention.

Commitment

Do you know anyone who has trouble keeping their commitments? Do you know someone who doesn't? If you answered yes to the latter, this is someone you want to associate with more often.

Commitment is the state of being dedicated to a cause, activity, or anything that matters to you. Commitments are closely related to habits and training the brain. A habit is a regular practice, especially one that's hard to give up. It's an acquired behavior pattern regularly followed until it becomes almost involuntary. Almost all actions we are not consciously focused upon are driven by habit. Habits are how you train your actions to align with your conscious objectives. The best way to keep a commitment is to create a habit around it.

Fred Shoemaker, author and founder of Extraordinary Golf, once said to me, "Life gets good when you can keep your commitments." Throughout my life, I've found that statement to be true.¶ Who says golf can't be useful?

¶   My brother Kevin is an Episcopal priest, and he officiated for Tracy's and my wedding over thirty years ago. I'll never forget his sermon for the service: "Love Is a Commitment; Marriage Is a Commitment."

A surefire way to break a commitment is to make one your habits contradict. A typical case may be smoking. I made a verbal commitment to quit and tried a thousand times before I quit for good. The commitment stuck over thirty years ago, when I had a health scare (a transformational shock). I combined smoking cessation with quitting drinking for a period, losing forty pounds, and instituting a serious exercise routine. I had a clear vision and intention to improve my health and was finally able to remove my internal inconsistencies and to quit smoking.

Commitments are a matter of your word, the topic of Pillar 7, and the ones we're most interested in currently relate to your commitments made to realize your vision. They are related to daily practices to support your clarity, vision, and intention. These are commitments specifically needed to form habits and train your actions.

Habits

According to James Clear in *Atomic Habits*, a habit is a behavior that is repeated enough times to become automatic, and the ultimate purpose of habits is to solve the problems of life with as little energy and effort as possible.[11]

There is a process. It starts with a thought. *I should meditate.* When fostered by attention and contemplation, it becomes an idea. *I am going to try meditation.* Then it becomes a commitment. *I am going to meditate for two minutes every day.* After practicing for some time, meditation becomes a habit. Commitments don't require a habit, but ones that become habits are more likely to stand the test of time.

I realize that, despite our best intentions, things like holidays, vacations, illness, and other demands on your time (like writing a book) happen to disrupt our habits. First, we miss a day, then a week, then a month, until we no longer have a habit. It's commitment that keeps us in the game to reestablish the habit, again, again, and again. Habits are easier to reestablish than to establish the first time around. Commitment and habits support each other when they are aligned.

In *Meditation: Now or Never,* Steve Hagen says consistency is the most important factor in maintaining a meditation practice.[12] Repeated actions carve new and deeper neural pathways because of neural plasticity. Repetition makes the action easier. In fact, after an extended period of practice, it's easier to perform the activity than to neglect it. Our commitment causes us to keep going until the habit is formed. And it's our commitment that keeps us going when our lives are disrupted and habits are in jeopardy. Consistency eventually overcomes our resistance to activities such as meditation.

The habits of mindfulness and visualization support our clarity and vision. Our intention and commitment to form these habits and keeping our word to ourselves are what hold it together. A support system of other committed individuals can be a great help too.

We may need to break certain habits to make room for the new ones we are creating. To be present, new habits are implemented while breaking the habit of not being present.

James Clear's book *Atomic Habits* is one of the best resources to understand habits. An atomic habit is a regular practice or routine that is small and easy to do but also the source of incredible power, promoting compound growth. Clear identifies three layers of behavior change relevant to habits:

1. Changing outcomes or results, such as weight loss

2. Changing the process through habits and systems

3. Changing your identity, beliefs, worldview, image, and judgments about yourself[13]

The key to establishing the habit of mindfulness is to build identity-based habits about who you are, such as "I am mindful." What you do may or may not change, but who you are while you are doing it will change forever. Established habits become part of your identity, and true behavior change becomes part of who you are. Your behaviors and habits are part of your identity.

This is a key point. The more deeply actions are tied to your identity, the stronger the habit becomes. A major barrier to establishing habits is identity conflict. The goal is to become mindful, or to meditate. The belief that I am mindful, or I am a meditator, supports the habit of mindfulness and meditation. A belief that I can't meditate will work against the habits of mindfulness and meditation. The underlying reason you don't stick with a habit may be that your self-image gets in the way. To establish meaningful habits requires upgrading beliefs and self-image to match the habits you wish to establish. In other words, your habits are how you embody your identity. Your habits are who you are; the habits of mindfulness ensure you are Presence.

Fundamentally, habits are not about having something but about being someone. You become your habits. Habits are that important; they get you better results because they change your belief about yourself. Importantly, habits establish your default way of being. Establish the habit of being mindful and your default way of being is mindful.

How many times must an action or behavior need repeating to make it automatic? It depends on the complexity of the action *and* the alignment of underlying beliefs with the action. It also depends on whether your environment is supportive of the behavior, or not. The purpose of habits is to solve problems or create opportunities with minimal energy and effort. I would give mindfulness practices at least a year to ripen into a habit.

Clear describes a feedback loop of cues, cravings, responses, and rewards. He lists four laws of behavior change in establishing habits, which are to make it obvious, attractive, easy, and satisfying. The reverse is true when breaking bad or undesirable habits, meaning make them inconvenient and less obvious.

Clear identifies the greatest threat to success to be boredom, not failure. Ironically, he finds that people who are doing well wish for a change as much as those struggling. "At some point, everyone faces the same challenge on the journey of self-improvement: you have to fall in love with boredom."[14]

A word about affirmations

Affirmations train the mind. The repetition, however boring, records the statement in memory and your inner dialogue, and they can be quite effective. Your affirmations should be bold, clear, positive, and stated in the present tense. Avoid using negative statements because this may be committed to memory. Here are some examples:

I am Presence.
I am enough.
I create a miracle each morning.
I am free and clear.
I accept myself.
I accept what happens.

Another powerful approach that works for many people is to perform affirmations as a question—for instance, "Am I Presence?" You'll have to try it to see if it works for you. Use affirmations that are meaningful to you. Keep them simple and in the present tense. A good practice is to write down your affirmations each day, typically twenty-five times, for a minimum of thirty days. I typically write them for a longer period, ninety days or so, and then write the old ones one time each day to keep them fresh in my memory. I have over twenty-five prior affirmations that I rewrite one time each in my daily journal to keep them fresh. It works for me. Try it for a while and see what works for you.

Summary

Creating clarity, vision, intention, commitment, and habits are key components to creating or manifesting things you want in your life. Without clarity, we can be confused about what our purpose and vision is and what has been instilled by culture, and so on. Vision allows you to create a new reality and start to put it into action. Intention is focused awareness desiring a specific outcome. Commitment is what allows you to take action and begin to form habits. Once established, habits help you keep your commitments. Commitments and habits form a positive feedback loop.

PILLAR 3

Create:

- Clarity

- Vision

- Intention

- Commitment

- Habits

Chapter Takeaway

Your habits are who you are—make Presence a habit.

Pillar 3 Exercises for Vision

Steps to Creating Your Vision

Creating our future is communicated through language. Future-based language transforms how situations occur to us and others. The default future is a projection based on the past and told through descriptive language. What we resist persists. Future-based language transforms or literally replaces the default future, like Martin Luther King Jr.'s "I Have a Dream" speech, which put listeners in the future world without discrimination. State your vision using positive phrases, similar to affirmations.

1. Create clarity through mindfulness and discover your inner purpose and your Soul.

2. Go big and bold. Set your "vision for the world." This vision is overarching and personal. It could be for world peace, opportunities for all, equality, or a world where art is fully appreciated. It's your distinct vision for the world.

   Mine is "world transformation starts with me." I found mindfulness to be missing in much of the business world. From this vision, I created Living in the Gap Workshops and this book.

What's important to you? Hunger? Education? Peace? Don't be shy. What matters to you? Notice any resignation or skepticism, and LET IT GO! Come back to your breath to create your personal vision for the world. To be honest, when I first attempted this, I couldn't sleep because I saw the world in such disarray, as I described in the preface.

3. Make a "life list" by setting out what you want to accomplish in important areas of your life. I suggest focusing on four main categories.

   - To Learn

   - To Be

   - To Do

   - To Have**

4. Create a vision board.

   - What is your vision for your life? Ask yourself, "How can I 'move the needle' on my vision for the world through the vision for my life?" (For instance, you don't have to solve world hunger, but you might join your local food bank.)

continued

** For more detailed guidance, check out famous explorer and adventurer John Goddard's life list: https://johngoddard.info/index.htm.

- Make a 2' x 3' (poster size) color vision board that represents your life vision. Use magazine and online images or draw your own in color. Use as few words as possible.

The emphasis is on your life list and demonstrating Presence. Keep materialistic images to a minimum. But if you need a house, a house should be on your vision board. Being secure in a home may foster Presence. Also display what ways of being the house will provide, whether that is a close-knit family space, your sanctuary, or a haven for relatives. It is important that you place the vision board where you will see it daily. This will help you continually download your vision to your memory and RAS (reticular activating system).

In our workshops, attendees also complete the extensive personal vision and plan exercise to include family, professional, financial, health, spiritual, relationships, service, hobbies, and more. You can write about these areas on your own; we set aside an entire day to draft it.

Once you complete your vision, you will have two points: 1) where you are, or "what is"; and 2) where you want to go, or "the vision." Having these points established, you can then chart your "path of development"—how to get from point 1) "what is" to point 2) "the vision."

Vision is critically important to create a future to live into and to be present. The clearer your vision is, the greater your ability to detach from it and be present. Training and practicing your morning or daily routine are key to achieving your vision and goals with Presence.

A promising future allows us to be present in the *now*, although it takes mindfulness practice, and specifically detachment, to accomplish it.

Visualization

Now that we have a vision, we need to visualize. Visualization is a practice of internally creating the vision to be as authentic and real as possible. Look at your vision board.

Close your eyes, and picture yourself achieving one aspect of your vision in minute detail.

Consider the steps and process necessary to fulfill this vision in minute detail. Highlight the journey, celebrating 10 percent, 25 percent, 50 percent, 75 percent, 90 percent, and the most difficult, final 10 percent of the journey. Then celebrate achieving 100 percent of the goal!

Pick one word that best describes your feeling of accomplishment. Embody this felt emotion as it lifts you toward achieving the goal.

Consider how you will feel once you accomplish 100 percent of your vision and feel that emotion. Are you safe, secure, fulfilled, loved? Who are you with? Who will you call to share your accomplishment? Pick one word that best describes your feeling of accomplishment.

Embody this felt emotion as it lifts you toward achieving the goal.

Embody that feeling in Presence as you prepare for the day ahead.

Take a few minutes each morning to look at your vision

continued

board and visualize, with emotions, making it as real as possible. When complete, review the steps you visualized and write them in your journal. Your intention will lead you to what the appropriate actions are to achieve your vision and goals. What actions can you take today?

Pillar 4

SUCCESS IS A MINDSET OF BE-DO-HAVE

We become more successful when we are happier and more positive.[1]

—SHAWN ARCHOR

Approaching fifty, I had "everything" but was not satisfied or happy. I had bought into the cultural model of working hard and delaying personal gratification until a future date. The problem was that, by always chasing goals for future satisfaction, I had formed the habit of not being present. My meditation practice helped, but I still had a blind spot.

I attended the Landmark Forum around this time, as well as reading a ton of mindfulness books in Eastern traditions, and books like *The Answer* by John Assaraf and Murry Smith, that explained how the metaphysical world related to business. When I learned that happiness and satisfaction were states of mind, it gave me the freedom to focus on being present in my daily life. The result was even greater financial success, this time coupled with being present, satisfied, and happy.

Do-have-be model

As I highlighted earlier, culture has taught us to *do* certain things, such as get a good job and work hard so we can *have* a nice home, provide for our families, and take vacations. Once you've accomplished all that, you will *be* successful, happy, secure, and content.

This do-have-be model postpones being present until we've accomplished everything on the list. In my experience, before everything on the list is accomplished, more things are put on the list. It's a model that promotes producing things, growing GDP, corporate growth and profits, and consuming things that grow the economy, but it lacks Presence and purpose.

Success, happiness, security, and contentment aren't things you can become; they are things you embody in the moment.

Presence is a habit that needs to be generated through the practice of mindfulness. It requires breaking the habit of not being present, which most of us have worked our whole lives to accomplish. So all we've accomplished is working hard and accumulating stuff. Committing to being mindful and present is a start. But ultimately, you still have to overcome the habit of not being present. Unfortunately, if you're waiting to be successful, your underlying belief is you're not successful enough right now. If you're waiting to be happy, at least a part of you is unhappy. Likewise, if you're waiting to be secure, you are insecure, and if you're waiting to be content, you are discontent.

These underlying beliefs are possible blind spots. We are shining the light of Presence and logic on those beliefs. Because success is defined as the accomplishment of an aim or purpose, and now that you've adopted an inner purpose of Presence, then success is being present, and you can be successful only *now*. I know, I tricked you. I have a subpersonality that is a manipulator, but I have trained myself to (mainly) use it only for good.

Of course, we want nice things for ourselves and our families, but we don't have to wait to be successful, happy, or content to have nice things. From the studies of visual-motor rehearsal, or visualization, we cited in the last pillar, we know that you can not only generate feelings but also mimic the results of actually doing physical tasks.

Let me demonstrate what I mean by utilizing a visualization technique in the following exercise.

Visualization Exercise

Select a professional or personal goal that is important to you, that you feel is reasonably achievable, but you haven't achieved yet. Keep it simple; there will be time to stretch later on.

Now let's turn the goal into a vision. For vision, we need to visualize. Visualization is a practice of internally creating the vision as authentically as possible. When you have some time and space to complete this exercise, find a quiet place and, while seated, do the following:

1. Close your eyes and focus internally, possibly after meditating or practicing breathwork, at least briefly.

2. Call forth your goal with the intention to make it a reality, to complete it now.

continued

3. Picture yourself achieving each aspect of your goal and envision it in minute detail. Picture yourself achieving each step in the process as you slowly progress through 10, 20, 30, 40, 50, 60, 70, 80, 90, and finally 100 percent of goal achievement, and notice how you feel, and what emotions are felt, at each step.

4. Take several minutes to mentally create each step you know has to be completed to achieve this goal and vision.

5. See yourself after completing 100 percent of the goal: Who are you with? Who do you tell? What emotions do you feel? Are you safe, secure, fulfilled, loved?

6. Consider all these feelings or emotions and pick one word that best describes the feeling of having accomplished your goal and vision.

7. Open your eyes and write down your word.

What was the one word? I have done this in all kinds of workshops and events and the participants have listed amazing things they have felt: unstoppable, invincible, free, successful, happy, joy, content, satisfied—the list goes on and on.

Next question: Is this feeling you wrote down real? I mean, come on, all you did was sit there. Did you really feel happy? How could you? You didn't achieve the goal! That's the point. You have possibly been withholding happiness from yourself until some future event, rather than deciding, choosing, and allowing yourself to be happy (or unstoppable, invincible, etc.) now. Presence and happiness are choices you can make now.

Yes, it's that simple. And the good news is that having this improved mindset will make it even more likely you will accomplish this goal and the bigger ones coming up after you have been in this work for a while.

Journal this experience. Repeat the exercise after meditation for the next week. See what you notice. Do it when you feel down or are trying to accomplish something that's not going well. The more you practice visualization, the harder the tasks you can take on through this technique. Success begets success.

We do this exercise in our workshops and the results are phenomenal. You can absolutely create your own happiness, once you give yourself permission to be happy now. It's almost as if we are punishing ourselves for not achieving society's goals for us yet. The best part is that if you generate the feelings of happiness and success now, it greatly enhances your chances of taking the necessary actions to achieve your vision and goals. Harvard researcher Shawn Archor confirms that "new research in psychology and neuroscience shows it works the other way around: We become more successful when we are happier and more positive."[2]

Put your effort into being happy now. Generate feelings of success, happiness, security, and contentment by visualizing accomplishing your vision. Give yourself permission to feel successful, happy, secure, and content now. You don't have to wait. Creating these internal feelings and beliefs will make you even more successful. There's nothing wrong with having stuff. The mistake is to think having more of something we already have plenty of will make us feel better.

Be-do-have model*

A be-do-have model means that you separate your way of being from results, meaning happiness, success, contentment, and so on, are inside jobs that in fact make you more successful. So rather than waiting for happiness to occur after some result, we become happy now and that same happiness will increase our likelihood of success.

Who do you want to deal with or be with more? You have choices:

- Someone who is successful, or someone who's waiting to be successful (i.e., unsuccessful)?

- Someone who is happy, or someone who's waiting to be happy (i.e., unhappy)?

- Someone who is secure, or someone who's waiting to be secure (i.e., insecure)?

- Someone who is content, or someone who's waiting to be content (i.e., discontent)?

Which group is likely to take appropriate risks and actions? Which group is more likely to take care of themselves and others along the way? Which group is likely to speak their truth in difficult situations?

Who is more likely to prosper? Someone who's present, successful, happy, secure, and content, or someone who's waiting to have these things? You now know that you don't have to wait to be happy, successful, secure, or content *if* you choose to be those things now.

Most people in the world can't even dream of reaching the level of affluence professional ranks in the West have achieved. You can make

---

* I learned this model in several transformational workshops, and it was introduced to the mainstream in Stephen R. Covey's bestselling book *The 7 Habits of Highly Effective People* (New York: Simon & Schuster, 2004).

this powerful choice and influence others in a positive way. I'm not saying the change will be immediate or easy. It's a choice. These false beliefs are buried deep in the mind, so we need to train ourselves to support the choice to feel that we have enough now.

- Practice gratitude for all you already have.

- Visualize being happy right now, as we hope to be when we fulfill our vision.

- Write affirmations that support these positive feelings, such as "I am successful," "I am happy," "I am secure," or "I am content."

- Look into the mirror and say, "I accept myself" and "I am enough" until that little voice in your head doesn't offer resistance by saying, "No, you're not."

Do whatever it takes, because if you don't feel successful, happy, secure, or content now, chances are you'll never achieve these feelings. In all likelihood, your conditioning will cause you to desire more, like buying a sports car or taking a trip into space. Maybe that will do it? Maybe then you'll be satisfied?

You have everything you need to be happy right here, right now. What's the downside to feeling successful, happy, secure, and content now? Do you believe you'll just stop generating or being productive at work if you are happy, satisfied, and content? My experience is that you'll generate more *and* make a more significant difference along the way by being present, generating a powerful vision for the future, and focusing on the process rather than the results. And if I'm wrong, you're still successful, happy, secure, and content because they are mindsets. If that's the downside, I'm okay with being wrong.

Adopt daily practices that train yourself to believe and trust you are successful, happy, secure, and content. Practice mindfulness and these supporting practices as if your life depends on it.

The mindset of being rich

Merriam-Webster dictionary defines *rich* as "having abundant possessions and especially material wealth; having high value or quality; well supplied or endowed."[3]

Back in 1910, Wallace D. Wattles published *The Science of Getting Rich*, which is still relevant today. It is a recipe book to generate material wealth. Despite his effective recipe, we all know people who are rich with material wealth but not very happy or positively affecting the world. They have material wealth but live in a world of fear and scarcity, often resulting in a paranoia, needing more wealth rather than allowing them to enjoy the wealth they have.

Being rich means having a mindset of fullness and abundance, which may or may not include having a lot of money or material wealth. Being rich means you can have it all—money, wealth, happiness, success, relationships, and love—and be a leader who makes a positive impact on the world. Being rich is a mindset and a habit that can be learned, fostered, and shared. You can have the mindset right now, in this moment. Being rich is a mindset of abundance, in which you already are enough.

Many billionaires are insecure and unhappy. A good friend of mine, an icon in the real estate industry, retired young with tremendous material success, only to commit suicide, a shocking action that was devastating for his family and the community. I know many happy people who have little material wealth.

What is the purpose of wealth if not to bring joy and happiness to ourselves and our loved ones?

Being rich offers another path in which success, happiness, and security are assured. All it requires is that we create the mindset first and use it in all aspects of our lives. This means we can have a job we love, more wealth, and better relationships and still make the world a better place in which to live. It's a be-do-have model. Being rich is a mindset of abundance in everything we do (job, family, hobbies, service work, etc.) without attachment to the material wealth we've obtained. It's not that we don't care about what material wealth offers; it's just that we know that money doesn't buy love, happiness, or success. They are mindsets.

This is a mindset of affluence increasing influence. Not using money to control others, but to influence positive outcomes by supporting them. It's a subtle, but important difference of choosing what to support versus controlling some result.

Wealth can help make a bigger difference in your life and the world. Having a purpose bigger than yourself is the path to liberation, while allowing you to enjoy the fruits of material wealth along the way.

- You can have it all.

- Success and happiness are states of being, not destinations.

- Success is a mindset of be-do-have.

- Train the mind so that you can live in Presence and still accomplish you vision and goals.

- Foster the mindset of being rich and of abundance.

Chapter Takeaway

Be happy and successful now and achieve your
vision and goals with Presence.

Pillar 5

SHOW UP, TAKE ACTION, AND DETACH FROM RESULTS

Without concern for results, perform the necessary action; surrendering all attachments, accomplish life's highest good.[1]

—THE BHAGAVAD GITA

Have you noticed some people show up, ready to go, and others you must constantly remind to show up? Or worse, their bodies show up, but they are distracted and not present. Most truly successful people show up, are present, and are aware of what they are doing in the moment rather than having complete focus on the result. I believe we were given a body and breath to take mindful action with Presence. Mindful action with Presence sets our karma, and training our mind allows it to deliver on the details. Detaching from results is what allows us to be present in the moment.

Show up

Showing up is a matter of motivation or purpose, prioritization, and Presence. Motivation is why people initiate, continue, or terminate a particular behavior or action at a specific time. Motivation is a force that acts within a person and creates a disposition to engage in goal-directed behavior.

In my experience, the most essential ingredient in motivation is purpose. If you can't seem to get motivated, explore the alignment of your inner purpose and outer purpose, as we discussed in Pillar 2. If an inner purpose isn't aligned with the outer purpose, it may manifest as a lack of motivation. Ensure they are aligned, and motivation should no longer be an issue.*

Your morning routine is the surest way to show up and show up with Presence. Try starting your morning with reading ten pages from an inspirational book, meditating, mindful stretching, expressing gratitude, writing meaningful affirmations, and visualizing accomplishing your vision. This will get you into flow and ensure you're ready to meet the day. You will show up.

How can you balance various priorities and get everything done?

I created a system from a baseball analogy.

---

* There may of course be deeper psychological or health issues causing the disconnect.

Balancing priorities

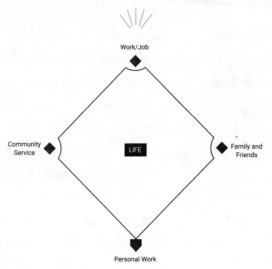

Balancing Priorities
Don't Miss a Base

Work/Job

Community Service

LIFE

Family and Friends

Personal Work

Getting up to bat at home plate: First priority is to get personal work done and establish your mindset for the day.

Meditation, spirituality, health, and wellness are all in this category.

If you're not healthy and centered, you won't be much use to anyone else. The airplane air mask instruction is right on here. Put your mask on yourself and then help others.

There are limits to your time, and you need to prioritize your mindset to be present for your family and friends, work, and community. Getting up early to make sure personal work is done for the day is recommended. A workout at the gym might come at lunch or after the workday, because there are limits on time commitments. But take care of personal work to make sure you are centered and present. If you are mindful and present, you will take better care of all your bodily needs, such as diet and exercise, guaranteed.

First base: Second priority is family and friends.

If you are centered and present, it will help your entire family. Take care of family and friends before starting professional work when possible. Do your family and friends have what they need for the day? You can have the most incredible job in the world, but if your family is a mess, it won't matter in the least. If your employer insists on coming before your personal health or your family, it may be time to get another job, or create your own. And if you go to work before taking care of your family and friends, you get thrown out for missing first base.

Second base: Third priority is work.

A job is there to support yourself and your family. With them taken care of, you can go to work and give it 100 percent of your effort without distractions from health and family obligations. How many people are constantly checking their phones and social media rather than focusing on work? Prioritization allows you to focus on the task at hand, which is currently your job. If you go out to save the world before taking care of your job responsibilities, you'll get thrown out for missing second base.

Third base: Community and service work; saving the world.

There's still time for community service work, especially if it's part of your professional strategy. It needs to come after personal work, family, and your job. Of course, there are times when you must place a service commitment ahead of another priority, but generally you won't be much use to the service organization if you lose your job or your family situation is volatile.

If you aren't healthy and present, your family isn't satisfied, or your job isn't done satisfactorily, you can't save anyone else. I believe that service and community work are hugely important, but only after you've touched all the other bases.

Home run: If you prioritize correctly . . .

Forming healthy habits, prioritizing, and taking care of personal work, family, job, and community and contributing to the world—it's a *home run*.

That's how I do it. Give it a try and see if it helps you prioritize your day. If you're an employer, consider letting your employees know you expect them to prioritize their health, wellness, and family ahead of their job. In fact, it's unreasonable to expect someone to prioritize their job ahead of these things. Do you actually think long-term, successful, and healthy employees prioritize their jobs ahead of their families? Do you think that's wise?

Let your employees know you care about them. Of course, you expect them to complete their work assignments promptly, too. You'll have healthier and more productive employees when they sense you truly care for them.

One question every mindful leader should ask: What can only I do?

Why? So you can make space to be mindful and to connect with the members on your team more mindfully. To gain clarity to answer the question, identify everything you do, and highlight both the things only you can do and the things you genuinely enjoy doing. Omit the things you do just to be busy or to look like you're busy.

You need to create space, so what are the things only you can do? Hiring or firing those on the executive team, setting vision and strategy, running the board meetings, handling the big problems that no one else can, and the like. Then look at the things you enjoy doing, those that put you in flow. If you can keep those things, keep them; if you are too busy, even some things you enjoy doing may have to go, at least for a while.

What about everything else? Dump it or delegate it. Handing off responsibilities can be a gift to someone looking to grow in the organization. By delegating, you're being mindful. Presence blossoms with stillness and space, so give yourself some space. Mindful leaders need to be more, meaning exhibit Presence, and do less so they have time and space to be present for others.

I hope that my baseball analogy shows you how to balance multiple priorities and make sure you have the space to lead mindfully.

Take action

There are two approaches to action: Either we approach the world promoting performance with a simple yes or no, or we obfuscate by promoting reasons, complications, fears, and irreverent meaning. Mindful leaders take the former approach, promoting performance without the need to provide reasons, complications, fears, and meaning. Those who play the victim often approach the world by promoting reasons, complications, fears, and meaning.

Mindful leaders take action. To take action, you need to show up with Presence and have your mind clear of distractions from unfinished commitments. Taking action is having your inner purpose aligned with outer purpose, being adequately motivated to take action. Remember, it's memory that inhibits or invokes action, so generating Presence is the key to unlocking *appropriate* action. Action is critical because it establishes karma. Our memory is where our habits and karmic seeds are stored. In fact, karma means action, and is based on cause and effect. There are four basic types of karma:

- Proximate karma, or the state of mind or mindset;

- Habitual karma, or the force of our ordinary habits;

- Heavy karma, or the force from major events; and

- Random karma, which arises when the other three types of karma are not dominant.[2]

Establishing a new mindset is proximate karma. Establishing new daily habits is habitual karma. These are essential ingredients to keep the forces of heavy and random karma at bay.

If we send positive energy into the universe, karma returns the favor. If I want to take desired actions and receive the benefits of precession effects, then establishing proximate and habitual karma are of paramount importance. In other words, prior action establishes karma that affects current action.

Karma is about being the captain of your own life.

According to Sadhguru,

In the East, we simply say "Your life is your karma." . . . How much karma you can take into your hands depends on how much of you has become conscious. If you have mastery over your physical body, fifteen to twenty percent of your life and destiny will be in your hands. If you have mastery over your psychological process, fifty to sixty percent of your life and destiny will be in your hands. If you have mastery over your life energies, a hundred percent of your life and destiny could be in your hands.[3]

Finally, karma is not about right and wrong or good and evil. It's about cause and effect, or the type of energy you're sending out through your actions. Pay attention to the precession effects of your actions to understand the karmic effects. Karma refers to taking responsibility for your life and taking appropriate actions.

Detach from results

You have a right to your actions, but never to the fruits of your actions. Act for action's sake. . . . Be self-possessed and resolute, and act without a thought of results, remaining open to success or failure.[4]

—THE BHAGAVAD GITA

Take the actions you're committed to taking and leave the results up to a power greater than yourself or your karma. You control your actions because they are your duty, but you don't control the results.

Attachment means we bond to something, and when we bond to results, we bond to some future event. Detaching from results allows us to be present in our activities. It's not removing our care about results. We still want good results; it's just not our purpose or primary focus. We focus on what we're doing in the moment and check in on the results from time to time, making appropriate modifications to our actions.

While meditating, we practice detachment from thought. As we focus on our breath, we notice a thought, and we let it go without attaching to it and return our attention to the breath. When involved in an activity and the thought of the result comes up, which it will, let it go and return to being present in the activity. For instance, if I'm playing golf and my focus is on breaking 80, there's no way I can be present for the shot at hand. I let the score go and turn my focus to the shot. The same is true in business when we hyperfocus on short-term profits and share price at the expense of Presence.

It may seem counterintuitive, but detaching from results allows us to be present in action. Being present means you prioritize your inner purpose and Presence more than the outcome. Setting goals and working diligently toward achieving the goals while staying present to the process, rather than hyperfocusing on the result, is essential for Mindful Leadership. Despite our best efforts and actions, the results aren't totally up to us. Detachment from results acknowledges many forces at play and allows us to take responsible actions. As quoted from *The Bhagavad Gita*: "The wise man lets go of all results, whether good or bad, and is focused on the action alone."[5]

Thomas Sterner writes extensively about the topic of detachment in *The Practicing Mind*. He summarizes letting go of the attachment to results: "Focus on the process, not the product that the process was meant to achieve. It's a paradox. When you focus on the process, the desired product takes care of itself with fluid ease."[6]

You can't be both attached to results and present in the moment. You have to choose, and to be consistent with your inner purpose, that choice must be to be Presence. Fortunately, our mind works 24/7 on our vision if it's trained to do so by our mindfulness practices. While it takes some practice and trust, the rewards are worth it.

- Align your inner and outer purpose to assure motivation.

- Showing up starts by having a morning routine.

- Prioritize your duties, using the baseball analogy.

- Mindful leaders ask, "What can only I do?"

- Detach from results so you can be present.

- Train and practice to deliver your vision, so you can be present.

Chapter Takeaway

Detach from results and be present in the process.

Exercise

Notice when you show up and take action and when you don't, and then journal about what you notice about the experience and how you felt.

Pillar 6

BE RESPONSIBLE, PRACTICE NONJUDGMENT AND COMPASSION

Responsibility is not blame or guilt or fault. When I say I'm responsible, I'm not saying I did it, or I am to blame or I'm guilty. When I say I'm responsible, what I mean is that I stand for being cause in the matter. Not I caused it. It's a stand for being cause in the matter.[1]

—WERNER ERHARD

Being responsible is a statement of confidence: I got this. Nonjudgment means I am willing to examine, explore, and listen rather than judge and stereotype. Compassion means I am Presence and thus connected with all through consciousness rather than disconnected, and realize our separation is only a relative concept. Compassion is an antidote for judgment.

Be responsible

Being responsible means being dependable, keeping our word, and honoring our commitments. It is accepting the consequences of our actions and our words. People who are responsible don't make excuses or blame others when things go wrong. It also means developing our potential. These are all things we have discussed in previous pillars. Additionally, being responsible means being the source and the cause in the matter of our own lives and being the cause in the matter of the issues facing the world.

It seems like many of us are waiting for someone else to solve the issues facing the world. The day may come when more of us decide it's up to us to take on issues and problems, to be the cause in the matter of creating solutions. It's unlikely any one of us will solve world hunger or world peace by ourselves; however, what if each of us committed to moving the needle a little bit toward the ultimate solution?

If everyone chipped in rather than waiting for others to take action, the world's problems would be much easier to solve. Being responsible means taking the actions you are capable of taking, regardless of the actions or inactions of others. Being responsible means continuing to take actions we know are our duty and detaching from the results.

None of us had a perfect upbringing. You may have been more or less blessed with your environment, but the simple truth is, at some point, each of us needs to own who we have become, the good, the bad, and the ugly.

As long as we say the problem is "out there," we will live in a world of complications, reasons, justifications, and fear. This is playing the victim, blaming others, and making an excuse for everything. It's not whether you were treated fairly or got what you deserved; the simple fact is that it is disempowering to blame others for our current situation. You don't have to agree with what happened or didn't happen in the past; you need to own who you are right now in this moment.

Mindful leaders own their situation, take charge, and chart the course for the future. Mindful leaders do their part regardless of the actions of others and regardless of how hopeless the situation. If we all did our part, very few situations would actually be hopeless. We are the only ones we can control, and it's our own actions—and inactions—we need to take responsibility for, starting now.

Have a look in the mirror and own who you see. Are you ready to take responsibility for your life?

I have rarely struggled with being responsible, although I have worked with lots of people who have. Where my struggle has been is in judging others and myself, and it was amazing to learn how judgments held me back. Judgment closes the mind and leaves no room for awareness and growth. Judgment is efficient and limiting at the same time. If I can observe without judgment, I have room to be aware and grow.

Practice nonjudgment

When we judge, we label and put something in a neat category. We stop listening or evaluating because we already know. Judging closes the mind and the conversation. It's incredibly efficient and incredibly limiting. When we judge, we're not present or inclusive. We're setting ourselves apart from the person, place, or thing we focus on. The same happens when we judge and splinter ourselves, rather than accepting ourselves, despite our imperfections, and becoming whole.

It's not that we don't want to improve; of course we do. But judging doesn't lead to improvement. It just closes the door to consideration.

If we can be aware of a problem without judging, it allows space for improvement without dismissing the present moment as unacceptable. Steve Hagen, in *Meditation: Now or Never*, says, "But if we just come back, look honestly at what we're doing, and let the judging go, if we learn to come back and come back and come back. Eventually, our judgmental mind will lose its strength."[2]

With our judgmental mind, we label. And labeling organizes things into neat known categories: Democrat, Republican, socialist, racist, car salesman. We can stop listening because we know everything that falls under the label we placed on them. In meditation, we sometimes label to eliminate. When a thought distracts us, we give it the label "thinking" and return to the breath. The label is the signal to not consider the thoughts.*

We judge almost constantly, so we must practice to stop, to observe, and to shine the light of awareness on people, places, and things and simply be present. Be careful not to judge your judging: *There I go again, dummy.* Just notice you judged and let it go and return to the present moment. You cannot judge and be in the present moment at the same time. Be patient with yourself and just observe. If judging is a big issue, it can be helpful to carry a journal and write down when you judge to increase your awareness.

The world is in a precarious place, with political division, disagreements about handling the pandemic, climate change, the economy—the list is endless. We need to stop judging and start listening and seeing each other. When we judge, we label, and when we label, we dismiss. We can disagree without dismissing others. In fact, we have to, and it begins with each of us personally. It can begin right here and right now if you choose to raise your awareness. It turns out an antidote to judgment is compassion.

---

* Try this in your next meditation session. When the first thought arises, label it "thinking," then let it go and return to your breath. See what you notice.

Compassion

Some say compassion is our deepest nature, and I must admit compassion is something I really had to work at. It came after many years of practicing mindfulness.

I feel compassion may be difficult for many businesspeople to comprehend because it sounds soft and enabling. After all, can't you just pull yourself up by your bootstraps (like I did), dust yourself off, and get going? And what about compassion for ourselves? More crap, just suck it up.

Compassion is to have sympathy and concern for the sufferings and misfortunes of others. Compassion requires a quiet mind and an open heart. I have found it also takes some trust in human nature, in believing that most people want to contribute and do well on their own but sometimes can't, due to circumstances. Compassion comes from our interconnection with one another—for instance, almost everyone is compassionate with a baby, even someone else's (unless the baby is in the plane seat in front of you). To feel this compassion for one another more generally, and even with plants, animals, and the planet, may take having the experience of a consciousness in which we are connected with all things. Consciousness is the basis of compassion, and compassion is a natural occurrence of a growth in consciousness and Presence.

Neurologically, compassion is felt through mirror neurons, where we actually feel the emotions, feelings, and suffering of others. Being more conscious allows us to sense the signals the mirror neurons are sending versus not noticing these signals. The signals are there either way; however, it takes Presence to recognize these feelings. More conscious people are generally more compassionate. Some people are just more compassionate naturally, and I am not disputing that.

Furthermore, compassion for ourselves opens us up to feel compassion for others. This may seem at odds with taking responsibility, but it's not. I am not saying compassion means not taking action—quite the contrary, I am saying to take compassionate action. Compassion is part of the ethical foundation of mindfulness, and compassion is an antidote to judgment.

In summary, being responsible, practicing nonjudgment, and having compassion are critical skills of a mindful leader and essential to Presence. The practices within the Twelve Pillars of Mindful Leadership will allow you to live in the world without worry that you have let things go undone or be incomplete, to live freely to observe and accept the world you live in, and to share love and consciousness with others.

- Be responsible; you got this.

- Practice nonjudgment and start seeing people as people.

- Practice compassion; be connected rather than disconnected.

Chapter Takeaway

An antidote for judging others is compassion.

Meditation on Compassion Exercise

Meditation on compassion.[3] For the next month, at the end of your meditation session, repeat the following phrases to yourself:

First verse

May you be held in compassion.

May your pain and sorrow be eased.

May you be at peace.

Second verse

May I be held in compassion.

May my pain and sorrow be eased.

May I be at peace.

Work on detaching from results and being present in all activities. Notice when you are attached to outcomes and journal about it for the next month as you meditate on compassion.

Pillar 7

FOSTER RELATIONSHIPS WITH YOUR WORD AND LISTENING

Human interaction can be hell. Or it can be a great spiritual practice.[1]

—ECKHART TOLLE

F inancial knowledge and marketing prowess are necessary ingredients for business success. These things came easy for me. The biggest job I have each day is to get over myself, slow down enough to see people as people, and listen. I have found, after surviving at least four major downturns in my career, that the most important element in business is relationships. Fostering them by being able to give and keep my word and by listening has been critical to my success.

Fostering relationships means we must encourage and promote being connected with others. We've discussed one problem with personal interactions—not being present, being on mobile devices or distracted while in a conversation. Another issue we may face is viewing others as irrelevant or as an obstacle or possibly as a means to get what we want.

In that case, we tend to see ourselves as either better (more important) or worse than whomever we're dealing with at the moment.[2] There's a simple fix, but it's not easy. Be present and see everyone as someone equal to you in essence.

You might say, "But they are not equal. I'm the CEO" or "I'm the parent, and this is my child." You can, I hope, see through this trap, but these interpretations are from ego or a subpersonality and the world of form. In the world of essence, your real identity and the other person's real identity are equal. Even if you are more conscious than someone else, your consciousness is not superior. If you have any inkling that you are better or worse than someone else or deserve better or worse treatment, you should immediately recognize you are not present but stuck in a thought or judgment.

Can you imagine how it makes a subordinate, or worse a child or spouse, feel to know you believe you're superior and he or she is inferior? It's not to say that you don't have a higher level of responsibility or authority, but does that distinction make you superior? If you believe you are superior or inferior, then you can kiss a good relationship good-bye. Relationships are formed on seeing each other's essence, on seeing the other as equal. This is the basis of relationships that work long term.

Consider your station in life as temporary. You might be CEO for twenty years, but that's temporary, and when your body is gone, the universe isn't even going to blink. If you have children, you are the authority for a while, but fast-forward twenty or fifty years, and they may be acting as your parent, and they may even be giving you care and feeding one day.

Everyone is equal in essence, which is what really matters. All else comes and goes. Remember the phrase "This too shall pass." Forget seeing people as a means to an end and start seeing them as individuals who have the same concerns, desires, and fears that all people have. It's not something you can fake; people know when you believe you're superior and when you believe they're your equal. Be real. Be present. Be in relationship *with* others rather than in command of them. You will see, an amazing thing will happen. You will experience love and affinity. It's okay to love the people you work with. They are people just like you, your family, and your friends.

Part of this process may be setting aside your self-importance and gaining some humility. Eckhart Tolle's words are insightful: "In the eyes of the Ego, self-esteem and humility are contradictory. In truth, they are one and the same."[3] The most confident leaders, who have the most self-esteem, are the ones who operate with humility. I often say, "The biggest job I have each day is to get over myself."

An ego fueled by fears and desires, taking things too personally, defensiveness, arrogance, or being controlling prevents a healthy relationship. According to Melinda Fouts in a recent *Forbes* article, four key mindfulness practices can enhance relationships:

- Give your fullest attention to the person without judgment (Pillar 7).

- Accept yourself and others (Pillar 10).

- Appreciate the person and give a high level of trust and respect when warranted (Pillar 8).

- Allow yourself and others to be who they are, making it safe to be transparent and to share ideas (Pillar 2).[4]

In the end, relationships are all we have. If you are up to big things, you'll find quickly that what you can do by yourself is quite limited, and you will need to move others to get big things accomplished. Relationship is the key to moving others in a mindful way, versus command and control, which a mindful leader tries to avoid. I have found two particular practices or skills critical to fostering relationships, which are your word and listening. Sometimes it's said as "being your word," which might sound a little weird, but it makes the point that your word is who you are being. People who are being their word can be trusted and respected. Giving your fullest attention to the person without judgment is the practice of deep listening. Let's discuss each of these practices or skills in more depth.

Your word

When you consider your word deeply, it's all you really have to offer yourself, another human being, your company, your community, and the world. If you can't give and keep your word, you're not much value to anyone. If you can give and keep your word, then anything is possible.

There's nothing more critical to your success than being able to give and keep your word. If others can depend on what you say, they will trust and follow you. Conversely, if they question your word, they'll protect themselves from your lack of integrity, and performance will be critically impaired. Think about how you depend on those who give and keep their word, and how you silently protect yourself from those who don't. You probably check on them or ask multiple people to do the same thing. It's a recipe for inefficiency and distrust.

Giving and keeping your word is the key to the kingdom. When you say something, it magically appears because of your integrity. This is power. Give and keep your word and surround yourself with others who do the same. It's a key ingredient to leadership and getting anything of value accomplished. When you find yourself not keeping your word, you need to clean up the damage you have done, and recommit: "I know I didn't complete what I said by Friday, but it will be done by Tuesday." If you're up to a big game, you'll be committing to big things, and sometimes they don't happen when you say they will. Communicate that to keep your integrity. I have found that everything—how you dress, your posture, your tone, and even a non-response—communicates something; and that everything works with good communication.

Be aware when you give your word and be impeccable about keeping it. If you find this difficult to do, journaling when you give your word and ensuring you clean up the damage when you aren't able to keep your word are beneficial practices. Cleaning up your mess usually takes more time than keeping your word, and it's uncomfortable. This trains you to keep your word, or your conscious self will make you clean up the aftermath. Your consciousness makes the promise; your practice, training, and awareness keep it or don't keep it. Training, practice, and awareness will help you fulfill those promises and provide you with more influence.

Remember, you are listening to yourself as well. Keeping your word to yourself is key to your personal and professional transformation. You matter too.

Listening

Giving and keeping your word is crucial to others trusting and depending on you. Listening to others is also key to building relationships. Listening is possibly the greatest gift you can give another human being. When you find someone incessantly talking, perhaps it's because no one has stopped to listen to them. You've experienced not being listened to. We all have. It doesn't make us feel valued or essential to the person who isn't listening. Regrettably, we don't listen most to those closest to us, typically not because they don't matter to us, but rather because we believe we already know what they're going to say. I violate this with my wife more often than I wish to admit and continue to work on it.

To listen is to give attention to sound or action through a complex cognitive-behavioral process. Listening is paying attention to what others are saying and trying to understand what it means. Despite being a critical function of effective communication, listening is a tricky task without Presence. What some call listening is often reacting, filtering, translating, comparing, evaluating, or judging. It's from stillness and silence that we can truly hear someone else, and we need to be able to focus and set aside everything else.

Even our inner dialogue and incessant thinking make listening to someone else a challenge. The practice is to begin to notice this inner dialogue, set it aside, and truly be Present to listen. Listening requires conscious attention to the speaker. It's the same attention we've been training to do while meditating or focusing on various body parts during a body scan. Listening takes conscious attention and practice. This is the next level of focus.

Garry Lester, one of my mentors from Extraordinary Golf, puts it this way:

> Listening arises from suspending what we're in the middle of in service of being here for another fully. It's about acknowledging who's speaking along with getting what they're saying, feeling, and experiencing, without adding anything. . . . When truly present, relatedness, appreciation, affinity, respect, compassion and love show themselves as a greater ground for listening.*

Presence and placing our attention on another with the intention of hearing and embracing their feelings create the silence necessary for listening.

---

* Garry communicated this at a corporate workshop in 2015.

Listening involves placing our attention and quiet mind on the other person with the intent of hearing them and giving them the experience of being heard. We place our conscious attention on the person and the words and truly listen. We can make sure we understood the person and that he or she feels heard by reflecting back what we got from the person's words, asking him or her to concur or clarify.

Here's an example.

Husband: How was your day?

Wife: Oh my, Johnny wasn't feeling well and didn't go to school, and I spent the day caring for him. He was sick all over the bathroom, and I had to take him to the clinic. I didn't get anything done. I missed two appointments for myself and didn't get my work for the office done, so I need to do it tonight.

Husband: That sounds like a tough day. It must have been frustrating between Johnny being sick, the mess, and not getting your own work done. Now you're stressed because you need to do the work you'd planned for the office this evening. Is that right?

Wife: Yes, you got it. Thanks for listening.

Notice that the husband didn't solve the issues; his wife just wanted to be listened to. The next step, once the person is heard with Presence, could well be the following:

Husband: How about I cook dinner and put Johnny to bed tonight so you can finish your work project?

Though Presence and listening, we'll know the right thing to say and do. If we're not present and don't hear them, we won't have the sense for the appropriate action. My experience is that these generous gestures do not come from thought, they come from Presence.

Sometimes just listening is enough. As I've been told many times, "I don't need you to fix it. I just needed you to listen." You'll sense that too, through Presence. Your efforts to be mindful and present are not selfish activities. They are gifts to your family, friends, work associates, and all you meet. Being present and listening is an act of extreme generosity. Who knows, maybe more people will start listening to you if you start listening to others. It's simply how mirror neurons work.

To start, we need to drop our attachment to the result of any pay-back and get totally engaged in the process of listening. Or as my cousin Steve Wiley of the Lincoln Leadership Institute says, "Listen until it hurts." Do you want to foster relationships? Start listening.

Ordinary Listening

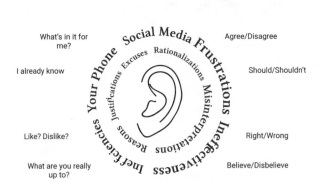

Consider the little voice(s) inside your head

Deep Listening

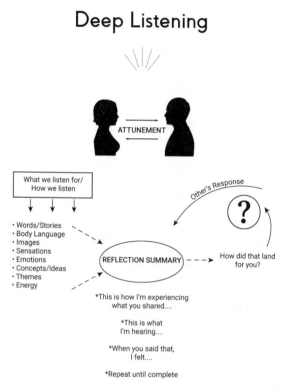

You'll find a deep listening exercise at the end of this pillar. Practice it for instant results.

Fostering Presence through forgiveness

Another aspect of relationships is when they go wrong, and negative emotions and energy sabotage Presence. Lasting resentments from old relationships can sabotage new ones too. It's important to clear any and every blockage of energy, even if it means forgiving someone who you don't feel deserves to be forgiven. Forgiving is an intentional process of releasing feelings, attitudes, emotions, and resentments regarding an offense by another person.

While we may and possibly should have empathy for the other person, the main beneficiary of forgiveness is you, the one who is forgiving. The benefit comes from the generosity of forgiveness, by changing from a negative mindset to a positive mindset. Forgiveness doesn't mean you need to agree with what someone did or even that you're open to restoring the relationship. It just means you're done placing your energy on the negativity associated with what you perceive they did to you.

It may be perfectly appropriate to have boundaries around the relationship or break ties with the person altogether. Through Presence, you'll know what to do. Forgiveness allows more Presence because negative energy can pass through you, making space for positive energy, attitudes, and emotions.

You'll be amazed how relieving it is to forgive someone, and you don't even have to let them know you forgave them unless you want them to know. Try the forgiveness exercise below and notice what you experience.

Forgiveness Exercise

The Forgiveness Process. Visualize a setting that's familiar and empowering to you, like a nature setting; somewhere neutral for you and the person you wish to forgive.

Meditate for several minutes, following the breath. Visualize yourself as a person of great wisdom and compassion. Call forth an intention to resolve all conflicts in the world. Given your wisdom, you know that the process must start with you and the person who you feel needs to be forgiven. Call forth the intention to forgive this person genuinely, so you can both move on in peace.

You are not agreeing to bring the person back into your life unless you want to. You are free to set any boundary around forgiveness you wish, including never seeing or speaking to the person again. It also works with people you are in regular communication with.

You are forgiving the person to clear the air, to remove the negative energy in your system, and to be the first step in moving the needle toward world peace. It's that important.

Then picture the person you wish to forgive in the scene with you. Quietly, confidently, and nonemotionally, state what the person did to you that has caused negative feelings, attitudes, emotions, and possible resentment toward the person. This can be done silently or out loud; however you feel most comfortable. Take your time and re-create the feelings and resentment as if the person is there and continuing the behavior. Stay in that state until it feels as real as possible.

Next, close your eyes and look within. Search for any and every positive experience you had with this person, no matter how small. Try to remember anything the person ever did for you, perhaps doing good things for you or being a close friend. Maybe you still love the person even though the relationship is toxic. Everybody has redeeming qualities; find them. Maybe the acts committed made you see something about yourself that is fuel for personal growth. Look deeply until you find any positives you received from this person and what they did.

Ask what positives have or could come from it. Were any blind spots uncovered? Did it make you more self-reliant?

continued

Next, return to meditation with your eyes open so you can read. Take a few breaths to reestablish the meditative state. Then recite these lines, either to yourself or out loud, whichever you prefer:

May you be held in compassion.
May your pain and sorrow be healed.
May you be at peace.[5]

Keep your eyes open so you can read the next piece:

There are many ways that I have been harmed by you.
I have carried this pain in my heart for too long.
I offer you forgiveness.
I forgive you.[6]

Now, through compassion and love, forgive the person for what they did. Actually say the words out loud again with emphasis: "I forgive you."

This part can be challenging, but it's worthwhile. We start to expel the negative emotions by filling ourselves with love. When we're full of love, we have no room for negative emotions. Feel love and be released from negativity. Feel the positive energy flow into you as negative energy flows out.

When you feel a new energy in yourself, check in with your highest self and ask if you are complete.

Depending on what the person did, this can take some time and several attempts. Even if you feel complete, later resentments may creep back into your psyche. Your highest self will know if you're complete or need to repeat the practice to thoroughly forgive and receive the energy shift. Listen to your highest self until it gives you an indication that you are complete. If you try twice and are still not complete, then you may need other methods to achieve forgiveness or more time to pass. The statements "Time heals all wounds eventually" and "This too shall pass" may be helpful.

If you do feel complete, you can decide after this session whether you want to let the person know of your forgiveness or not. That's totally up to you. One effective way is to send a short, friendly letter. My suggestion is not to go into detail or tell a story, just say something like the following:

"I don't appreciate how you treated me, but I have decided to move on through forgiveness. I am still not wanting to see or hear from you; it just hurts too much. But I do forgive you. Love or Sincerely, _____." Sign it with your name.

You can write it and never mail it, or you can mail it. It's your process. Just don't feel as if you have to let the person back into your life unless you want to. If you are not positive you want to send the letter, or you don't want to give the person an opening to return to your life, don't send it. Put it away in a

continued

safe place, burn it, or throw it away. Time to move on to bigger and better things.

If this is a business relationship, know that I have found it never pays to burn a bridge. You don't need to burn the bridge; just don't do business with the person again. Businesspeople can resurface when you least expect it, or you need something you never expected to need. Just shut your mouth, close your email, and move on. That's my advice after many years in (mindful) business. As always, of course, it's totally up to you (and your highest self).

Forgiveness Exercise

Setting & Meditation   Bring the Person   State the Offense   Feel the Emotion

Find the Positive   Meditate on Compassion and Forgiveness   Forgive through Compassion, Forgiveness, and Love   Check with your Higher Self: "Am I complete?" (Acknowledging you may repeat at any future date)

WHEN FORGIVENESS IS NOT ENOUGH

Sometimes our neural pathways and inner energy body, pain body, or in the Sanskrit language, *samskaras*, have such a significant impression that forgiveness practices aren't enough.[†]

Another option is to reset your electromagnetic field. This is a shamanic practice that can release deep impressions. Energy lines known as cords attach from one person to another. When a relationship is alive and healthy, the cords help us communicate with and feel one another. We feel each other deeply because the exchange of energy is visceral. When a relationship is over or perhaps changed—as when a child matures and separates from a parent—the push and pull sensations transmitted via cords can be stressful and unhealthy.

If that is interesting to you, Appendix 2 goes into more depth. Even if that's not of interest, it's useful to know that electromagnetism is responsible for practically all the phenomena encountered in daily life. It governs the orbiting electrons in an atom. The electromagnetic field of the heart chakra (see the following image, the silhouette on the right) is reported to be 5,000 times bigger than the energy field around the brain.[7]

[†]   Pain body is a term you can find in Eckhart Tolle's *A New Earth*. Samskaras are explained in detail in Appendix 2, "Yoga Is the Science of Consciousness."

You will find one more method, referred to as "The Work" in Pillar 12, that you can try on troubling relationship situations. Letting a little time pass while you continue reading may be a good thing, but if you can't wait, feel free to jump to Pillar 12 and come back to finish reading this pillar. I also find the Self-Soul-Spirit model helpful in resolving my own relationship issues, and you can learn more about that in the concluding chapter of the book. There are always conventional therapy options. The point is, don't let anything fester. Deal with it so you have a clear space and no energy blockages so you can move on with Presence.

Relationships are the most incredible and important thing in life. Being present, keeping your word, listening, and forgiving are the keys to fostering meaningful relationships.

Next, let's review an example of how relationships that formed while providing community service work can affect your success. This will lay the groundwork for the next several pillars.

Remember the financial crisis of 2008? Relationships are essential to long-term success

I would like to share with you the impact the relationships I and others at my company gained through being in flow, being generous, and being of service to the community. These are personal stories and examples of the precession effect.

Many people asked me how LC Real Estate Group navigated the financial crisis of 2008, and even grew while others shrank or went out of business. Amid the Great Recession, we developed a shopping center anchored by a national retailer on the north end of Fort Collins, Colorado, and launched a building company that built upward of 100 homes annually.

How did we do it? It's simple, and I can describe it as the precession effect and the resulting relationships we made providing community service work (Pillar 9). During that time, we curated relationships with key people, banks, and nonprofit groups. I served on the board of our regional economic development corporation with Ralph, a local real estate broker who was very involved in community service. After a meeting one day in 2005, he said, "You know, North College Avenue [in Fort Collins] needs a developer like you. I love what you guys have done with CSU and the community. I know you develop shopping centers. You should go meet the head of the North Fort Collins Business Association and get involved up there."

I contacted the head person, and my business partner Nathan Klein and I had lunch with him. He wanted a major shopping center that would drive customer traffic to and support the urban renewal efforts the association was spearheading. We searched all the properties in north Fort Collins and came up with one land parcel large enough for a substantial shopping center. It was owned by someone whom I knew through my connections with the university. But we learned the land was under contract to be sold to a Denver developer. There wasn't another feasible location available at the time, and the Denver developer planned a center that may have met the need, so we put the idea on hold for the time being.

Two years later, I ran into the owner and learned the property had recently fallen out of contract, and he wanted to sell. We set up a meeting with an anchor tenant whom we had worked with before and who also had an interest in the Fort Collins area. At the same time, the Denver developer had reinvigorated their interest, but the owner agreed to go under contract with us to develop the site. Why? Because we were a local company and had a personal relationship with him. He knew, liked, and trusted us.[8]

In 2008, it wasn't easy to get financing. Land was a four-letter word to banks. As a result, all the banks we approached to finance our project turned us down. I called a former student of mine who was a classmate and friend of Nathan's, Dan Spoelma, who worked at a local community bank. Dan loved the project and knew, liked, and trusted us. He got the land financed for us while we worked out the details with the City of Fort Collins. Dan pulled through when no one else could, providing the critical financing we needed to close on the land. We got our agreements signed with the city and the anchor tenant. This was a critical project for LC Real Estate Group at a tough economic time, and it was the catalyst for the redevelopment of north Fort Collins that allowed that part of town to prosper.

How about LC Home? The bottom dropped out of the building market several years before the crash in the commercial market, and in 2006 we were in the middle of a residential subdivision called Boise Village North. At the time, we only delivered lots to builders and didn't build homes ourselves. When the home building market stopped, the builders couldn't close on the lots, and we weren't going to be able to repay the bank development loans. The interest carry on the remaining lots wasn't sustainable, not to mention property taxes, insurance, maintenance, and other costs. All this while, the market was nonexistent for alternative builders to step in and purchase the lots. We had to pay down the loans using other asset sales to survive as we headed into the Great Recession.

Mike Kendall, who currently works at CBRE in Denver, was a sales intern with LC Real Estate when he was a CSU student. He wanted to live and work in Denver, so I connected him with a large Denver brokerage firm, who offered Mike a job upon graduation. Mike represented a national bank and brought that bank in to purchase a non-listed land parcel in one of our shopping centers.‡ Mike knew about it because his office had been there during his internship. The sale to the national bank gave us a critical $1 million to go with other asset sales to pay down the bank loans in our subdivision.

My partner Don Marostica and I built several affordable housing communities in Loveland. We had great relationships with the Loveland Housing Authority and Habitat for Humanity. Because I had served on the local Habitat board, had already helped provide lots for thirty homes with Habitat, and we had donated money to relocate their thrift store, people there knew, liked, and trusted us.

Habitat's business plan was to build ten homes per year in Loveland. Many developers wouldn't sell Habitat building lots because of the low-price stigma it might have placed on the subdivision. Habitat was one of few builders in a position to purchase lots during the recession.

To make these Habitat homes indistinguishable from other homes in the neighborhood, I worked with the Habitat executive director to create covenants for the homes requiring accents of stone and other architectural features so they would fit in with the neighborhood.§ While doing so, we made a discounted sale of twenty lots to Habitat, raising another $1 million to pay down bank debt on the subdivision and reduce our lot inventory and related holding costs, which helped us survive.

We were then in the worst of the recession, and we couldn't find any other home builders willing to build. My partner Blaine Rappé and I decided to form LC Home and build homes ourselves because it was easier to sell a house than to sell a lot at that time. Good staff were easy

‡   A non-listed land parcel is one the owner has not put up for sale or at least has not hired a real estate agent to list it for sale. Also known in the business as a "pocket listing."

§   A covenant is a legal document that restricts or requires certain features on a home so one neighbor's house doesn't degrade the value of a neighborhood.

to find due to the layoffs from the recession. We lost $10,000 to $20,000 per home when starting, but by detaching from those results, we were able to recognize that we were not only surviving, but also possibly creating a profit-making organization for the future.

While we had eighty building sites remaining in our inventory that we had gotten back from builders who couldn't continue through the recession, we still needed to obtain a loan to build the homes. Because of our previous borrowing relationship with our lead bank and our presence in the community on boards, commissions, and the university, they were people who knew, liked, and trusted us. The bank agreed to loan us money to build forty homes when no one else would even talk with us, because the bank regulators were clamping down on real estate loans. We had to put up an abundance of collateral, but that was acceptable in the circumstances.

Subsequently, LC Home constructed upward of 100 homes per year until we closed the division because of lack of profitability, risk, and the coronavirus pandemic. We had made back our losses from the Great Recession and then some. It was hard to close the division, but we did so mindfully and compassionately, and we are still friends and in contact with most of the people who left. Even being mindful and compassionate, it's still business and sometimes tough decisions have to be made.

The Precession Effect: The mindful relationships fostered while teaching, running the Everitt Real Estate Center at CSU, serving on various community boards, and having a history and reputation of being a responsible developer were critical to our survival and contributed to the growth and expansion of our portfolio and brand during the Great Recession.

While it wasn't the reason I taught at CSU for twenty years, or the reason to have served on numerous community boards, the relationships and connections others at my company and I gained have been instrumental in our business success.

When I look at our company today, I see how we have all grown, benefited, and continue to contribute to the communities through service on numerous boards and committees. For example, Nathan Klein is currently the immediate past chair of the Food Bank for Larimer County, the vice chair of UC Health Northern Colorado Hospital Foundation Board, and a board member of the CSU Everitt Real Estate Center. Nathan recently received the Titan award for community service from the regional commercial brokerage association.

Rollin Goering is on the board of the Food Bank of Larimer County, and he is a board member and immediate past chair of the Loveland Chamber of Commerce. Nick Galluzzo is the former chair of the Northern Colorado Commercial Association of Realtors, formerly on the advisory committee of No Barriers USA, and serves as a member of Northern Colorado United for Youth. Blaine Rappé is chairman of the City of Loveland Construction Advisory Board, treasurer of the Loveland Development Fund, and on the HBA board. Rico Devlin serves on the Loveland Planning Commission, on the Northern Colorado Commercial Association for Realtors Board, and is chairman of Loveland Satellite Rotary Club. Our junior partners are all in service too, and that's how they grow. These nonprofits give them valuable experience in how to make things happen.

In addition, we all learned from Don Marostica, my former partner who is now retired but who was a state representative and ran the Colorado Office of Economic Development and International Trade after his real estate career. He continues to serve on numerous nonprofit boards and commissions all over the state of Colorado.

Service is a valid business strategy. LC Real Estate is walking the walk of its vision statement of Mindfully Creating Community.

To me, the significance of these stories about the Great Recession is that we give to give and serve to serve; however, the relationships we gain through giving and service are stronger than ordinary, transactional business relationships. There's a level of trust and genuineness based on service and giving.

Our relationships are often informal, made while getting coffee or having lunch. My experience confirms the bond formed when providing service is stronger than traditional business relationships typically generate, and the incredible power of the precession effect.

Abundance comes to those who give. Relationships fostered and developed over time, and especially when giving of ourselves in service, are often the ones that contribute most to our long-term success. And if such genuine contribution and connection is made to any cause and the people surrounding it, the business significance cannot be overstated. I encourage you to seek to give back to the community in which you work, whether it's local, regional, national, or international, not because a direct business impact will follow, but because it's the right thing to do. Then just be aware of the action's possible cause and effects. "All things being equal, people do business with and refer business to those people they know, like, and trust."[9]

- Giving and keeping your word is the key to being trusted and having influence.

- Listening is the key to relationships.

- Forgiveness is important to clearing away negative energy.

Chapter Takeaway

Mastering relationships with Presence
is the key to life and business.

Deep Listening Exercise

For this exercise, you will need a partner.

Center yourselves with several 5-3-6 breaths as described in Pillar 1's exercises. Select a partner A and a partner B. Share with your selected partner the following:

Consider that listening is best done from a state of silence and stillness. Listen for this silence and stillness and listen until it hurts. If thoughts come up, or you start thinking about what you want to say, try to set that aside and listen. While the other person is talking, don't say anything, even internally to yourself. Set aside whatever you are in the middle of and just listen for the next several minutes.

Once you both feel present, look into each other's eyes. When you each have this felt sense of connection, proceed with the following:

Partner A: Share when you haven't listened to someone else and when you haven't been listened to. Explain how it felt and how you think it made the other person feel.

Partner B: Listen and ask yourself, "How does the experience of listening impact me? How does the person occur to me? What images come up for me?"

Next, partner B, reflect back what you heard, without personalizing (e.g., I always do that!) or modifying the content.

continued

Partner B, then ask partner A, "Did I get it?" or "Do you feel like I heard you?" If your partner hasn't felt heard, ask which part, re-create it, and reflect it back until your partner feels the experience of being heard by another human. When this point is attained, switch. Partner B talks and partner A listens until partner B feels heard.

You will find ways to do this less formally in your conversations. I find this process invaluable in important business meetings when it may take quite an effort to get people back together again. My wife also appreciates when I am present enough to listen.

Practice listening less formally until you can fully hear others, as you were doing in the exercise. Then try this less formally, just by deep listening, and re-creating by simple statements like "Is that what you mean?" for the next month, and hopefully adopt it as a permanent practice.

Your Word Exercise

If you have any trouble with giving and keeping your word, keep a journal of when you give your word for *anything*, big or small, to yourself or to anyone else, for the next thirty days.

Note when you kept your word and when you didn't. When you don't keep your word exactly as you promised to someone else, clean up the situation by going back and correcting it with the person. This trains you that it's less effort and less embarrassing to keep your word than to have to clean it up. For promises to yourself, just be aware of them and recommit to yourself; awareness is curative, and you are listening.

Pillar 8

BE IN FLOW, CREATE AFFLUENCE AND INFLUENCE

When it comes to customers, you create value by being likable and trustworthy, solving their problems, and making them feel good. You'll also need to be in what we call flow with them.[1]

—LARRY KENDALL

For years I was stuck in my mindfulness practice because what I read said I needed to renounce my possessions to obtain enlightenment. Later I learned that pennilessness was not a prerequisite; in fact, I could make a bigger difference if I was successful as long as I was willing to serve and work with others. I also learned that I get to define enlightenment for myself, so it must be achievable on my terms.

Be in flow

There are two crucial aspects of Flow. One refers to an internal state of being, and the other to the frequency and methods of external connectedness, especially with significant people, such as customers or other leaders who could affect your success. Both types of flow are highly relevant and important, and I use a capital *F* for Flow when representing both of these concepts simultaneously.

Mihaly Csikszentmihalyi's book *Flow: The Psychology of Optimal Experience* describes the internal state and how "People who learn to control their inner experience will be able to determine the quality of their lives, which is as close as you can get to being happy."[2] Csikszentmihalyi calls the state "optimal experience," "enjoyment," or simply "flow." As noted previously, flow also means being in the zone, living in the gap, and Presence. For this section, all terms will be represented by flow, which is also a synonym for Presence as we define it, unless otherwise noted.

Csikszentmihalyi's book *Flow* describes eight major components of flow:

- Performing tasks we are capable of completing,

- Being able to concentrate on what we are doing,

- Having clear goals,

- Receiving immediate feedback,

- Sustaining deep, effortless involvement that removes worry or frustration,

- Having a sense of control over one's actions,

- Feeling that the sense of self disappears during the experience, and

- Experiencing a loss of the sense of time.

The combination of these eight components causes a sense of deep enjoyment that motivates people to put forward a great deal of effort to have the optimal experience, or flow.[3]

Following Hal Elrod and *The Miracle Morning*, my morning routine of reading, meditation, gratitude, affirmation, journaling, Yoga, and other like-minded practices has all eight components of flow.[4] A well-designed morning routine is designed to put you in a flow state every morning before you leave home. Csikszentmihalyi describes virtually all the elements of the morning routine in detail in *Flow*, such as "The similarities between Yoga and flow are extremely strong; in fact, it makes sense to think of Yoga as a very thoroughly planned flow activity." Yogis refer to this internal state of flow as *sattva*, a Sanskrit word.[¶]

Csikszentmihalyi says, "Among the many intellectual pursuits available, reading is currently perhaps the most often mentioned flow activity around the world." Finally, he highlights the importance of finding flow in an occupation: "It is true that if one finds flow in work, and in relations with other people, one is well on the way toward improving the quality of life as a whole."[5]

¶   Sattva is one of the gunas, which are described in Appendix 2.

The Twelve Pillars of Mindful Leadership are about Presence and being in flow. Virtually every element of the Twelve Pillars promotes flow—mindfulness, inner purpose, vision, being versus doing, showing up, taking action, being detached from results, fostering relationships, being your word, listening, being grateful, giving generously, being of service, practicing acceptance, dropping resistance and complaint, taking everything impersonally, letting life flow through you, having a beginner's mind, knowing nothing, and being curious. The whole thing is about the flow of optimal experience.**

The second type of flow is how we connect with others. I like to stay in flow with people who make me a bigger person and not with people who make me a smaller person. The people who you are in flow with, or hang around the most, affect who you are. Because of mirror neurons and other factors, we act like those around us. Also, some people are much more helpful and giving generally, and some specifically are helpful to our careers.

For leaders and many high-level businesspeople, the most important group to be in flow with is other leaders. This is the group that makes things happen, and your relationship with other leaders will be one of the most prominent elements of your success. This group makes the buying and selling decisions, knows what makes things work or not, and knows other people who have the same skills.

The most influential leaders to support mindful leadership are possibly those involved in service, who are giving of themselves for the benefit of others. It also important to be in flow with customers, vendors, and other people we work with. Most importantly, we want to be in flow with other mindful professionals who are practicing these concepts.

** For a practical application of flow designed for the workplace, see Larry Kendall's *Ninja Selling*.

Why do you want to have relationships with these people? Because they are willing to give, and abundance comes to givers. Where can you find them? Many hang around nonprofit boardrooms, creating opportunities for others, their companies, and themselves. They are making the best of their affluence. According to the *Tao Te Ching*, "The best businessperson serves the communal good."[6]

Create affluence

> Affluence is the experience in which our needs are easily met and our desires spontaneously fulfilled. We feel joy, health, happiness, and vitality in every moment of our existence.[7]
>
> **—DEEPAK CHOPRA**

Affluence includes money but is more than money. It's the mindset of abundance, flow, and generosity. With abundance, anything within reason is possible. Having a vision is key for its fulfillment, and you've already started creating a life of your dreams. "If you have enough money, you are rich. If you have abundance, you are fulfilled. This is the true aim of Yoga."[8]

All material creation, from a galaxy of stars to a rain forest, human body, or a thought, has the same origin in the universal field of all creation. Thought, ideas, and material creation are simply a pulse of energy and information from and through the unified field of the universe.

Experiences such as joy or sorrow, success or failure, wealth or poverty are seemingly happening to us, but we're making them happen at the primordial level. All things we create begin with a thought, cultivated into an idea, especially those ideas on which we place our focused attention to foster.

The source of all material reality is pure consciousness and awareness through the unified field of all possibilities, or Presence. The quality of our experiences results from the quality of our Presence in whatever we are doing.

As I pointed out earlier, I believe *idea* is a better description than *thought* because we place our attention on a thought and contemplate what we wish to foster into an idea. But the main point remains: A human's ideas are a formless substance and cause the thing you have an idea about to become a conscious creation. The formless substance of abundance has no limit in supply.

We should operate from abundance rather than scarcity if we want to be affluent or wealthy. Abundance is the mindset that will bring us more affluence because abundance doesn't come from the material world; it is part of who we are spiritually. When we start to see the world as abundant, we start to unleash the abundance inside us, and vice versa.

Abundance and scarcity are mindsets that often establish your reality. Even more accurate is that abundance comes to givers. The flow of the universe, the precession effect—or karma, if you will—determines that what you receive is determined by what you give.

AFFLUENCE INCREASES INFLUENCE

Influence is the power to produce effects on and guide others by intangible or indirect means, possibly based on one's financial or social standing. This does not mean to control others, which is a subtle but important difference. With your influence, you have the capacity to affect the character, development, or behavior of someone or something else through your support. Your influence can shape policy to ensure favorable treatment through intellectual capacity, status, relationships, or wealth. Most simply, influence is power, and without influence, you have little power.[††]

Affluence increases influence. If you are looking to be rich so you can help more people, this is an essential concept. When I feel guilty about being affluent, I remember that my affluence increases my influence. As long as I am responsible, wealth, and the affluence it creates, is a positive force. Without affluence I could not have created my nonprofit Living in the Gap, and I could not have written this book. My hope is that these things influence the business community to adapt mindfulness and service in their visions and cultures.

Finally, the real benefits of affluence are opportunities you can offer your family and those close to you. My three kids, Ryan, Kaity, and Kohlton, all graduated college in four years without debt, and my wife and I were able to help them get started owning a home and running their own businesses.[‡‡] Some might say I have done too much for my kids, and to those people I say, look at the results. Each has a meditation practice and works to make people's lives better. They didn't just get financial support; we gave them our attention, tools, and encouragement to practice mindfulness too. They took mindful actions on their own accord with our support.

The path you are on can make a huge difference for your family, friends, business, and community. It starts by you practicing mindfulness. This work has certainly transformed my entire family, business, community, and view of the world.

- Be in the flow of optimal experience, or Presence.

[††] Note that the ability to give and keep your word is a primary source of influence.

[‡‡] If interested, see their business websites: Kohlton's is https://www.credenziostudios.com/, Kaity's is https://www.hertemplehealing.com; and Ryan's is https://www.ryanholsappleguide.com.

- Be in flow with people important to your being a mindful leader and with others important to your business or career.

- Create affluence.

- Affluence increases influence.

Chapter Takeaway

Stay in Flow in both your internal state and with other important people such as other leaders and givers.

Flow Exercise

List all the people in your sphere and note the ones who are a positive influence and those who are not. Work to spend more time with positive influences and less time with those who are a less positive influence. Notice what difference this makes—it's profound.

Pillar 9

BE GRATEFUL, GIVE GENEROUSLY, AND SERVE

The servant leader is servant first. . . . It begins with the natural feeling that one wants to serve first. The conscious choice brings one to aspire to lead. . . . The difference manifests itself in the care taken by servant-first to make sure that other people's highest needs are met first.[1]

—ROBERT GREENLEAF

Many people seem to plan to wait to give or serve until they make it. This is wrong thinking. It's counterintuitive, but due to mindset, karma, and the precession effect, being grateful, giving, and serving are the surest path to success. Additionally, if you haven't given and served along the way, it's unlikely you will automatically have that epiphany later, when you feel you have "made it." You may well donate to worthwhile causes, which is to be commended. I am not judging anyone; I'm just stating that I have personally found service essential to business success and personal happiness.

Gratitude

> To be grateful means to allow oneself to be placed in the position of a recipient—to feel indebted and aware of one's dependence on others.[2]
>
> **—ROBERT EMMONS**

If there's one simple, easy practice that evokes results immediately, it's expressing gratitude. Gratitude changes the brain and creates the mindset to be present and enjoy the moment.

When you begin to live in gratitude, you begin to look for things to be grateful for rather than looking for the source of irritation or for other things that irritate you. It takes only a couple of minutes to express gratitude. After practicing for a while, the effects of gratitude are felt throughout the day.

Gratefulness is Presence and awareness that we are the recipients of goodness. Gratitude itself becomes the gift, creating a cycle of giving and receiving, like an endless waterfall.

Gratitude is a choice that can be selected from many possible responses. Many people have to work at being grateful and consciously cultivating gratitude. Using a gratitude journal is a great place to start. It's an intentional activity that can influence well-being. Being grateful allows you to be placed in the position of receiving and aware of one's dependence on others.

Robert Emmons is possibly the most renowned researcher in the area of gratitude, and his studies show that participants in the gratitude condition felt better about their lives as a whole and were more optimistic about the future. They were more joyful, enthusiastic, interested, attentive, energetic, excited, determined, and robust than those not engaging expressly in gratitude. Those maintaining a gratitude journal as a long-term commitment reported better sleep and feeling more refreshed upon awakening.

Generally, grateful individuals feel alive and vital during the day. People who kept gratitude journals reported feeling closer and more connected to others, were more likely to help others, and were seen as more helpful by those in their social networks. This is why we suggest practicing gratitude daily and keeping a gratitude journal.

Based on Emmons's work and my personal experience, here are my top five methods of practicing gratitude:

- Keep a gratitude journal with a vow to make daily entries.

- Remember the bad (how much worse life might be than it is).

- Use visual reminders (such as positioning the words "give thanks" where you can see them).

- Watch your language (grateful people have a particular linguistic style).

- Go through the motions (attitude change often follows behavioral change).

William Wattles said, "There is a Law of Gratitude . . . thankful praise to the Supreme is a liberation or expenditure of force; it cannot fail to reach that to which it is addressed . . . it is gratitude that keeps you connected with POWER."[3]

Give generously

Giving sets off a chain reaction. It evokes a response to give in return. It's a mirror neuron response. Our natural reaction is to give something when we receive something. Not necessarily a tit for tat, but a karmic reaction to receiving. Give because it's the right thing to do, and simply be aware to notice responses and be open to receiving.

Receiving is a gift in itself. But the main reason to give is because you can, and that's what makes humanity work. Giving takes the focus off ourselves and puts it onto someone who is in need. Our lives improve significantly when we stop focusing on ourselves and start to focus on others.

Bob Burg and John David Mann highlight the Five Laws of Stratospheric Success in their book *The Go-Giver*.[4]

1. The Law of Value: Your true worth is determined by how much more you give in value than you take in payment.

2. The Law of Compensation: Your income is determined by how many people you serve and how well you serve them.

3. The Law of Influence: Your influence is determined by how abundantly you place other people's interests first.

4. The Law of Authenticity: The most valuable gift you have to offer is yourself.

5. The Law of Receptivity: The key to effective giving is to stay open to receiving.

Many people struggle with the counterintuitive nature of giving. They are either stuck in survival mode and don't feel they have anything to spare, or they can't believe anything so benign can be instrumental in success. In my opinion, it's not possible to convince someone to give or to provide service. You can give to them without expectation of anything in return and see what happens. Fortunately, the only one you have to convince is yourself. What's the downside? You give something to someone in need? Giving is an act of gratitude and compassion. Anything returned is a bonus.

Adam Grant, who wrote *Give and Take*, found there are givers, takers, and matchers.[5] The first two are obvious, but matchers are those who try to match their giving and receiving equally. Note that giving to a taker, or even a matcher, isn't going to have the same impact as giving to another giver. One reason I suggest doing service work is because it exposes you to other givers who can significantly impact your success.

Grant found that givers were at the top of the ladder of success. He further found that givers don't believe life or business is a zero-sum game but that the pie can be grown to offer more to everyone. Here are five "Actions for Impact" offered by Grant:

- Run a reciprocity ring, in which people get together to get and provide help in a variety of areas to reward people for giving in ways that leaders and managers rarely see.

- Embrace the five-minute favor, a rule that states you should do anything for someone that takes five minutes or less.

- Practice powerless communication but become an advocate. This requires a change in habit from talking to listening, from self-promoting to advice seeking, and from advocating to inquiring.

- Join a community of givers.

- Try random acts of kindness to see what shows up.[6]

There is one more that is a stumbling block for many but a key to success: seek help more often. If you want others to give, you often have to ask.

When you ask someone to give, you must realize you don't know what is going on in their lives. They may say yes, no, or maybe, depending on their situation. It has nothing to do with you, so don't take it personally. The most significant element to getting to yes is to ask and give space for someone to say no.

After giving and serving being the right things to do, the biggest reason for giving and serving is that they change our mindsets to one of abundance. Remember, from an abundant mindset, anything within reason is possible.

The fullest expression of gratitude and generosity is possibly service. In *Thanks!*, Robert Emmons states, "The self, by itself, is a very poor place to find happiness or meaning in life. Gratitude takes us outside ourselves where we see ourselves as part of a larger, intricate network of sustaining relationships, relationships that are mutually reciprocal."[7]

SERVE

Giving generously of your money is excellent; however, service is giving of your most valuable asset—yourself. Service is gratitude in action and the humblest form of leadership. Serving is a natural expression of the Soul.

Through service you create affluence and influence and get into flow with other giving leaders and make yourself available to receive. With affluence and influence, you increase your impact where it matters most. You'll become all about making a difference.

Service is positive action that sets karma and the precession effect in motion.

Think of your life as a life of service to your family, community, and the world. Of course, your needs must be met, but that doesn't have to be your dominant focus.

Providing service is the right thing to do. It also sets the karmic winds in motion, unleashes the precession effect, and it puts you in flow with other givers. I am not attached to whether you or anyone provides community service; that's a personal decision for each of us to make. Some of the benefits I have personally received from giving and serving follow.

MY STORY

When I was first teaching as an adjunct facility member at CSU, the full-time professor left, and they asked me to run the Real Estate Center to avoid losing a grant. Entrepreneur is a dominant subpersonality or part of me, and it saw the opportunity to make a tremendous difference for the university, the community, and especially the students. Long story short, I ended up endowing a chair in the real estate program with my partner Don Marostica, helping to get the center endowed, and generating memberships to run the center. All told, over $5 million was raised in a fairly short time. At the time, I contributed a good percentage of my net worth, as I wasn't even on the radar screen of the College Development Office.

Probably my favorite activity was creating an internship program that helped place students who had been working in fast food and retail to get real estate experience. We hired a number of them at LC Real Estate, and today four of them are partners in our firm and movers and shakers in the industry. When someone didn't fit, and it was usually their choice to live in Denver versus Fort Collins, I helped place them with a firm in Denver, and as their number grew, I knew people in all the large firms in Denver. Many of the attendees at our workshops have been former students who stayed in touch with me over the years.

I also ran the center at three different periods, including running the academic real estate program full time for two years as the Executive Director of Real Estate when the industry collapsed during the Great Recession. The graduating class in real estate was down to five students, and the college feared losing a program that had one of the largest endowments in the college.

While running the center, I organized large conferences where I was the host, including market area forecasts and events and a student real estate competition, and these gave the college and the students great visibility. I loved teaching and the students, and I might still be there today if my entrepreneurial spirit didn't lead to so much stress in a bureaucratic college system. The people at the college were wonderful. It's just a different world.

After the endowment and all the effort I gave to the center, many in our industry looked at me in dismay. How could you give so much time and money away? I did it out of gratitude, generosity, and service and from my heart. I loved the students and saw their raw potential. I often ran my primary business on the side with the generous help of my partners. I can only tell you that the relationships I made with the community, area, businesses, and students, who are now some of the top professionals in the industry, made me one of the best-connected people in the real estate industry in Colorado.

The precession effect and the related karma meant I could walk in anywhere and be known, liked, and trusted. I have significantly increased my net worth since giving that initial gift to get the center launched and have gained trusted partners from the experience who now run our company while I continue in gratitude, generosity, and service.

I have learned by direct experience that abundance comes to givers.

Giving takes a lot of confidence, and the express feeling that you are enough, and realizing that no amount of material possessions will increase who you are in essence. It also takes trust in yourself and trust in the universe, that good does win out in the end.

My experience is the more you give, the more you get. Not every time, so there are lessons you will learn along the way too, including who not to trust.

But with the mindset of abundance, you'll see more opportunities and options to promote success and be more likely to take appropriate actions. This is simply mirror neurons at work; when someone gives something, the response is to give something in return. As William Wattles said, "You cannot receive what you don't give. Outflow determines inflow."[8]

Having gratitude, giving generously, and serving are acts of self-actualization that indirectly and directly serve and affect others' perceptions of you. That's the precession effect and karma of gratitude, generosity, and service.

- Be grateful.

- Use a gratitude journal and practice gratitude.

- Give generously.

- Serve, and be aware of the precession effects.

- Abundance comes to givers.

Chapter Takeaway

De-Scrooge yourself by being grateful, giving, and serving your communities: realize a new mindset and the precession effect.

Personal Notes Exercise

Write personal notes and send them to people you are most grateful for.

Random Act of Kindness Exercise

Perform a random act of kindness for someone each day for the next week, and don't let them know it was you.

Pillar 10

ACCEPTANCE MEANS TO STOP RESISTING AND COMPLAINING

And acceptance is the answer to all my problems today. When I am disturbed, it is because I find some person, place, thing, or situation—some fact of my life—unacceptable to me, and I can find no serenity until I accept that person, place, thing, or situation as being exactly the way it is supposed to be at this moment.[1]

—ALCOHOLICS ANONYMOUS

One of the biggest lessons I have learned in this work is that acceptance does not mean complacency; in fact, my experience is that acceptance is the primary ingredient in lasting change and transformation. Without acceptance, there is limited potential for awareness and growth.

Acceptance

> I teach one thing, and one thing only, a deep and fearless accep-
> tance of whatever comes your way.[2]
>
> **—JEFF FOSTER**

Acceptance is simply being present and noticing what is—what already is—for what you are is acceptance itself amid your present experience. Acceptance is the path to stop resisting and complaining. Acceptance means to see reality, see things as they actually are, not as we wish them to be. Presence springs from acceptance of what is, and from Presence comes love, compassion, creativity, and mindful action.

Acceptance is an opening; resisting and complaining means to close yourself off to the possibility of real change.

Ask yourself the following:

- Do I accept my body as it is? My weight, my hair, my face?

- Do I accept my mind as it is? My intelligence, my humor, my thoughts?

- Do I accept my emotions and moods as they are?

- Do I accept my family and friends as they are?

- Do I accept my financial situation, living arrangement, and current opportunities as they are?

A big misconception is that if you accept yourself as you are, you'll lose your motivation to change and grow. However, it's from an awareness that acceptance allows that real change is possible. Acceptance means bringing mindful attention to our limitations, capacities, and external realities without allowing them to determine our happiness.

Acceptance doesn't ignore self-indulgence or make us passive. Instead, it gives us the option of mindful action in the face of persistent desires and problems, coupled with surrender and acceptance of what is and what we cannot change. Renowned psychologist Carl Rogers said, "The curious paradox is that when I accept myself just as I am, then I can change."[3]

Nonacceptance also means nonawareness, which shuts us off from the problem or situation, whereas acceptance creates awareness and an opening. Jeff Foster says, "We seek purity, perfection, and completeness outside of this present experience because we see our present experience as broken, as incomplete, as imperfect, as not whole in some way."[4] Presence is often curative. The constant judgments, criticism, and complaints come to an abrupt end with the wand of acceptance. Self-acceptance is amazingly liberating and transformative. My experience is that acceptance opens the mind with awareness and possibility, whereas nonacceptance closes off the mind and limits growth. Let me give you a personal example.

MY DEEPEST ACCEPTANCE

About fifteen years ago, I was in a golf mastery program with Extraordinary Golf. It was a transformational experience with golf as the medium for living a more meaningful life. In one exercise, we were tasked with accepting our golf swing to become more aware of it. When I watched a video of my swing, I viewed it as totally unacceptable, making me cringe. It was even more cringeworthy when compared side by side with the technique of a PGA Tour player. But I accepted the challenge and went to work on simply accepting my golf swing without trying to fix anything.

It took some time, but I slowly began to accept my swing, and awareness around it grew dramatically. I began to just play golf without needing an extensive warm-up on the range or even a practice swing. I could just play with awareness of my swing, the ball, and the target. For me, golf went from stressful to relaxing and restorative. These were great results, but the kicker was that I chose to see where else in my life I was not accepting reality. I meditated regularly and started contemplating acceptance in my life at the end of my daily meditation sessions. Quite soon, I realized that not only were there parts of myself I didn't accept but I also didn't accept myself in totality.

All the little things, like big ears, being short, curly hair, added up. Some work I did around my dad not spending time with me or not making an emotional connection when I was growing up revealed that at the core was a belief that I wasn't accepted. Suddenly, I understood deeply that I was the biggest perpetrator by not accepting myself. It had nothing to do with my dad. By that point, we had a close, loving relationship, and I'd grown to accept who he was and to accept his love the way he offered it.

Initially, acknowledging that I didn't accept myself was pretty upsetting, and I had several meditation sessions that concluded with teary acceptance practices. I went to work on accepting myself. Looking in the mirror and saying, "I love and accept you unconditionally" was tough at first. I would say it with a cringe as the little voice in my head would whisper, "Yeah, right." But eventually I got there, accepting every freckle, every curl, and even my sarcastic wit.

A new awareness opened for me, and I could finally admit that I drank too much. Acceptance led me to quit drinking and discover the enormous life improvements that unfolded in a life of sobriety. Because I accepted myself, I could accept that I was an alcoholic. Before, even with a ton of evidence that my drinking was a problem, I couldn't stop. With self-acceptance, I no longer needed to drink, and I'm sober to this day.

From that point, I started accepting others, like my wife and kids, the way they were, and our relationships bloomed. I had the belief that if I accepted them, it signaled that I didn't want them to improve. The fact is that I couldn't change them; I'd tried and tried. What resulted was that my acceptance gave them space to grow their own awareness and desire to improve. It was unconditional acceptance and space that was effective. Love filled the space.

I also applied acceptance at work and learned that I didn't have to do everything if I was willing to accept how someone else wanted to do it. Additionally, I learned that people grew exponentially when they were accepted and trusted. I accepted imperfect work from attorneys, accountants, and consultants whom I found competent but not perfect. If they weren't competent, I changed firms to ones I could accept and trust. Suddenly, I found people more willing to work with me, and they delivered better work. If something wasn't right, I'd correct it without emotion or arrogance because it was my job to get it right.

With acceptance and space, people shine. And if they don't, move on to someone who will. The stress levels at work will drop significantly. This was the start of a dramatic transformation for me. Who says golf can't transform a person? "What does life look like when you know yourself to be the wide-open space of acceptance, in which all thoughts, all sensations, all feelings, all waves of experience are deeply allowed to come and go?"[5]

Stop resisting "what is." The good news is that you have likely been trying to change for some time, because surrender is effective only after we've tried for a while. It happens only after we've resisted with all our might and noticed nothing is changing because we're fighting what is. Once we become aware of what is, surrender and acceptance become the best and only practical option. We don't have to like it or agree with it. All we have to do is stop resisting and surrender to what is, surrender to reality, and live in acceptance of what is.

Complaints

Don't complain about anything, not even yourself.[6]

—JOSEPH PARENT

When we start to be more aware, we start noticing other people's complaints first. Next, we start noticing our own inner dialogue that constantly complains too. Some of us have a pattern of complaining that is nonproductive and termed a racket.[7] A racket has four key elements:

- The complaint has persisted for some time.

- There is a pattern of behavior that goes with the complaint.

- There is a payoff for the complaint.

- There is a cost associated with the complaint.

A perfect example is that my wife was often late and I complained about it. The pattern was that I would be irritated with her for being late. The payoff was that I got to be right, since we all know we're supposed to be on time. But there was a cost. We were not as close or as intimate as we could have been because I was often angry, and it led to arguments.

The main thing to know about rackets is that they exist to a much greater extent than we realize until we start paying attention. Rackets are not productive or helpful. In essence, the complaint describes something deeper, but we may never get to the source of the underlying issue as long as we keep complaining. To find the source, start taking note of when you complain, and if it happens regularly, consider journaling. Try to stop complaining for a week, and journal when you do complain. Contemplate the underlying cause of the complaint. You will start to notice as a complaint surfaces through Presence and detachment. Keep it to yourself by hearing your internal dialogue: *There it goes again.* If it surfaces as a verbal complaint directed at someone, apologize.

Apologizing is pleasant for the other person and trains you to know that it will take work to apologize and clean up the aftermath if you complain. Also, pay attention to the underlying cause.

In my earlier example of my wife being late, the underlying belief I held from childhood that I wasn't accepted was triggered when my wife was late; I took her being late as rejection. Once I discovered this underlying belief, it didn't bother me as much. Besides, my wife never responded to my irritation by showing up on time the next time. I must say that when I stopped getting upset, she wasn't late as often. It's counterintuitive but true.

Death

I am home now.

—Last words spoken by my mom,
BETTY HOLSAPPLE, may she RIP*

---

* These last words from my mom inspire me, may she rest in peace. I want that feeling when taking my last breath. I credit my mom for my spiritual bent. Although she never meditated, she was one of the most mindful people I have ever met. I miss her, and she is with me as I write this book.

Perhaps the most significant acceptance, and the one with the greatest payoff, is the acceptance of death. We tend to treat death as a disease or sickness in the West. In essence, death is an unavoidable outcome of each of our lives. Early in my mindfulness practice, I learned that contemplating death was a good way to renounce the ego, or our exclusive identity with form. Contemplating death can help secure our inner purpose and identify us with a higher spiritual calling. If we can accept the end of life, it may bring more Presence and meaning to our lives in each moment. It's death that makes life meaningful, and learning to embrace death each day is a powerful spiritual practice. Death isn't a disease or an unnatural occurrence but rather the most natural thing in the world. Andrew Holecek writes in *Preparing to Die*, "Death is one of the most precious experiences in life. It is literally a once-in-a-lifetime opportunity."[8]

When death happens and form dissolves, it's also a rebirth or manifestation into new forms. You don't have to believe in reincarnation. Just think logically. Where does form go after dissolution? Into other forms. Where does my consciousness go after it leaves my form (body)? Back to universal consciousness.

Death doesn't need to be sad or a tragedy, although an untimely death may indeed be sad. By accepting the inescapability of death and residing in our inner purpose, which is eternal, we can come to terms with death. A daily practice of contemplating death for some time can help you accept death and be present in the moment. Additionally, when your time, or the time of someone close to you, does come, it may make it easier to deal with the actual event.

Bronnie Ware wrote about the top five regrets of the dying:

- Living the life expected of them rather than a life true to oneself

- Working too hard rather than having purpose, intention, and simplicity

- Not having the courage to express their feelings

- Not staying in touch with close friends

- Not letting oneself be happy now, waiting to be happy someday[9]

It's best not to wait to address these potential regrets, and living the principles in the Twelve Pillars of Mindful Leadership addresses each of these five regrets in different ways while you still have time, so you will have no regrets when that fateful time comes. Feeling complete with life, and accepting our life as it is, can assist in accepting death too.

Eckhart Tolle offers more advice: "In the last few moments before physical death . . . you then experience yourself as consciousness free of form. Suddenly, there is no more fear, just peace and a knowing that 'all is well' and that death is only a form of dissolving. Death is then recognized as ultimately illusory—as illusory as the form you had identified with as yourself."[10]

- Acceptance is simply being present and accepting what is.

- Acceptance is often the key to change.

- Continual complaining can be a racket.

- Become aware of complaining.

- Complaining is resistance to what is.

- Accept and embrace death.

Chapter Takeaway

Live with Presence and accept what is.

In conclusion, I would like to share a poem with you that I wrote about resistance.

RESISTANCE

So what do I resist?
Only everything!
What I resist persists?
Oh, that's what's going on!

Drop my resistance?
Try Acceptance and Surrender?
It's so counter me.
I would have to, well, just "be."

I can feel myself get tight;
As I was taught to fight,
Surrender was not acceptable you see;
But now I see I am fighting me.

So let it go,
Turn into the resistance
Surrender and accept
Is the necessary next step.

To finding me;
Who I really am.
To just be.
Such simplicity.

Two Obituary Exercise

Write two obituaries: one written as though nothing changes and you continue on the path you have been on, the second as though you make changes to become more mindful. The best way to predict this future is to create it by following the Twelve Pillars of Mindful Leadership.

Savasana Exercise

At the end of each mindful Yoga or stretching session, practitioners recommend lying stretched out on the four corners of your mat or carpet, and just rest, breathe naturally, and be aware of your body with your eyes closed. Do a body scan as described previously, from your toes to the top of your head, and experience being in the body. Next, let it all go. Let everything go. Let your flesh drop from the bones and melt into the mat or floor. Experience death while you are alive, die to this life, and let it all go. Visualize your own death, letting flesh go until all that is left is awareness. Rest for 5–20 minutes depending on your rest state and time availability. This Savasana pose is also called corpse pose or the little death. Practice it as often as you can.

Pillar 11

TAKE EVERYTHING IMPERSONALLY AND LET LIFE FLOW THROUGH YOU

Whatever happens around you, don't take it personally. If I see you on the street and I say, "Hey, you are so stupid," without knowing you, it's not about you; it's about me. If you take it personally, then perhaps you believe you are stupid. Maybe you think to yourself, "How does he know? Is he clairvoyant, or can everybody see how stupid I am?"[1]

—DON MIGUEL RUIZ

I started the development on a housing parcel next to my home where I had lived with my family for the prior twenty years. I will never forget showing up to a neighborhood meeting with the development on the agenda and finding 100 of my neighbors in the room. Unbeknownst to me, they were upset about the development, and many had written letters to the planning department documenting their objections to the development. I had neighbors calling me names under their breath.

And then, the miracle: I did not take the objections personally but let them flow through me. I addressed every concern, one at a time, as if I were the person who had the complaint. A couple of months and two neighborhood meetings later, we won unanimous approval of the development, and the neighborhood was in favor of the development. My wife, who had become uncomfortable with even going to the mail box, was able to resume her neighborhood activities.

We lost some projected profit, but the suggestions reduced our risk and made the development better. It was an amazing feeling to not take the objections personally, and they weren't personal. This is an example of *Profit with Presence*.

Take everything impersonally

It's selfish and arrogant to believe that what another person does is about you because it isn't about you at all; it's about the other person. When people share about themselves with us, our typical response is to apply that to ourselves. But that's just how we're wired: It's all about me. This book is about rewiring ourselves over time.

We're most reactive when someone says something negative about us and, inside, we believe it's true. When we know it's not true, we tend to be more forgiving. If we believe it's true, our fight-or-flight response is triggered and we become defensive.

In truth, we should thank the person for making us aware of a troubling behavior that's true. But that's seldom our typical response. Generally, we respond by taking it personally, reacting, and assuming they're attacking us. Personally, it's much easier to practice this with people who aren't as close to me; for instance, I struggle to practice this when someone in my family makes a comment I take critically. I am aware of it, and am working on it every day, just acknowledging my own issues.

Very seldom is what other people do because of you. It's typically because of themselves. As we discussed earlier, each person projects their own world, which is different from the one you live in. We assume they know and care what it's like to live in our world by taking it personally. In actuality, the comments are about themselves and their own world that you are possibly affecting in a way that motivated the comment or action. Don Migel Ruiz says, "Even when a situation seems so personal . . . it has nothing to do with you. What they say, what they do, and the opinions they give are according to the agreements they have in their own minds."[2]

If we can get over ourselves and start looking outward rather than having everything be about us, we can change this dynamic. We must give up self-importance and the belief that others go out of their way to insult us. Accept that things are either true or false. Someone saying them doesn't make them true or false. If someone calls you an idiot, it doesn't mean you are an idiot. Start noticing your reactions and pause. Being present and having Presence is often curative without any further action.

Let life flow through you

Stress is related to our thoughts and our resistance, and what we resist persists. In particular, we often resist what is rather than accepting or surrendering to it. When we resist, we tighten and block the energy in our bodies and psyche. Apart from being quite stressful and limiting, it drains your essential energy. If you don't take things personally and do learn to accept and surrender to what is, the energy will flow through you and not cause such a disruption. Energy is made to flow; when we are resistant to something, it blocks the energy inside of us rather than letting it pass though us. This blocks our own energy and depletes us rather than increasing our energy.

Byron Katie says, "The only time we suffer is when we believe a thought that argues with what is. When the mind is perfectly clear, what is is what we want."[3] Most of life is dealing with one disaster after another. Birth, accidents, storms, earthquakes, fires, disease, sickness all culminate with certain death for all of us. So learning not to take things personally and to accept and surrender to what is is a powerful spiritual practice. It can lead you to live a life of Presence with more joy, love, and affinity. Resistance to unchangeable life events is what causes the most stress.

If we can learn to accept and surrender, life can start to flow through us rather than manifesting as blocked energy in our bodies and psyche. We learn to change what we can change and to accept what we cannot reasonably change. The Serenity Prayer tells us, "God, grant us the serenity to accept the things we cannot change, Courage to change the things we can, and Wisdom to know the difference."[4]

We are predisposed to give credence to how we think life should be, and we resist everything else. Unfortunately, we don't know how life should be, and we don't acknowledge how life actually is. By growing our awareness and beginning a practice of acceptance, we can gain insight into what is and realize it's not a problem. Our reactions to events are the problem; events are just events regardless of our thinking.

Michael Singer says, "Let your spiritual practice become the willingness to let whatever happens make it through you, rather than carrying it into the next moment."[5] Acceptance and surrender are on the path to nonresistance, and this path allows us to flow with life. We often hear, "I have a life," which is false. You are life, and acceptance, surrender, and nonresistance will allow you to flow as one with life. From this place, Presence becomes the normal state of being, clarity emerges, and you will feel more joy, love, and affinity for life.

Stop taking yourself so seriously. Stop acting as if you could stop life's events from occurring. You can't. Things happen, and resisting them doesn't make them stop. It just creates stress in your body and psyche.

J. Krishnamurti, a great Indian philosopher known and respected around the world, once asked his audience, "Do you want to know my secret?" After a pause, he offered, "I don't mind what happens."[6] I have reworked Krishnamurti's words into an affirmation by stating it in the positive: "I accept what happens." Try it as an affirmation for thirty days and see what opens up for you.

Life does eventually flow through you; however, with a change of mindset and by training the mind, things can begin to flow through you more quickly. You are not as dense or solid as you think, and in fact, you even lack, or are empty of, an independent existence. The Buddhist monk Thich Nhat Hanh's explanation of emptiness may help convince you that you are less dense than you believe:

> If we look into this sheet of paper even more deeply, we can see the sunshine in it. If the sunshine is not there, the forest cannot grow. In fact, nothing can grow. . . . And if we continue to look, we can see the logger who cut the tree and brought it to the mill to be transformed into paper.
>
> Looking even more deeply, we can see we are in it too. This is not difficult to see, because when we look at a sheet of paper, the sheet of paper is part of our perception. . . . You cannot point out one thing that is not here—time, space, the earth, the rain, the minerals in the soil, the sunshine, the cloud, the river, the heat. Everything coexists with this sheet of paper.[7]

The paper is empty of a separate existence. This is the insight of emptiness Thich Nahn Hahn so eloquently explained. This example shows that a simple piece of paper possesses the entire cosmos. We each lack a separate existence and are as wide open as the cosmos. As life's events come and go, keep this in mind, and see if they can begin to flow through you.

It also helps to remember the phrase "this too shall pass" to exemplify the temporary and dynamic nature of our lives.

- Take everything impersonally.

- What others do is usually about themselves, not you.

- Stop resisting "what is."

- You are empty of a separate existence and not as dense as you think you are.

- Let life flow through you.

Chapter Takeaway

Nothing anybody else does is because of you,
it's because of themselves.

Journaling Exercise

When you take something personally, journal about it for the next week and see what you notice.

Affirmation Exercise

Journal "I accept what happens" twenty-five times per day, for the next thirty days.

See what you notice.

Pillar 12

BEGINNER'S MIND MEANS TO KNOW NOTHING ABSOLUTELY AND BE CURIOUS

In the beginner's mind there are many possibilities, but in the expert's mind, there are few.[1]

—SHUNRYU SUZUKI

I thought I was a business expert who had seen everything, having gone through at least four business-cycle recessions in my career and always landing on my feet. Then the coronavirus pandemic hit, and I knew nothing. We had empty buildings everywhere. We hung in there, came out the other side of the pandemic, and learned once again how little we know absolutely.

No matter how smart you are, you don't know everything, and a lot of what you think you know is based on assumptions, judgments, bias, and erroneous information. The mind is wired to say, "I know," culture promotes knowing, and fortunately or unfortunately, the world continues to be a mystery. As the *Tao Te Ching* teaches: "When they think they know the answers, people are hard to guide. When they know that they don't know, people can find their own way."[2]

Knowing closes the mind and limits awareness. Unknowing leaves us open to explore possibilities and expands awareness. Notably, we tend to think we know what's best for someone else, but how could we? We've discussed the new science of consciousness in which we each project our own unique universe, and in that universe, sometimes we create "I know" when we don't. How much do you think you know in all the universe, in all knowledge, in all wisdom? What do you acknowledge you don't know? What don't you know that you don't know? There is literally an entire universe of possibilities.

Saying you know is really a form of resistance—resisting what is, and the fact that you don't know much absolutely. It's also a lack of confidence and humility to say you know something you don't and extreme confidence to acknowledge when you don't. The *Tao Te Ching* states, "Not knowing is true knowledge."[3]

Be patient; it can take a long time to gain the awareness and confidence to acknowledge how little you really know absolutely.

Beginner's mind

I can't tell you how many people have told me, "I can't meditate, it's too difficult." It's not difficult because we have to sit still; it's difficult because our minds run wild without training. Our minds have been like that for most of our adult lives, we just haven't noticed. Taking the time to sit in meditation and observe the mind makes this apparent. Meditation is a very simple exercise, it's just that it exposes the excessive thinking we have done before practicing mindfulness for a while. Frankly, even after twenty-plus years of meditation, my mind can run amok; however, I have tools that allow me to notice it and rest in awareness rather than in thoughts, and other tools to calm thoughts down.

Thoughts create a dualistic situation, whereas Presence is non-dualistic. Shunryu Suzuki says, "The most important thing is not to be dualistic."[4] By keeping a beginner's mind, I am staying in a state of Presence. Once I become an expert who knows, I start labeling and judging, and I lose myself in these concepts and thoughts. A beginner's mind is open, empty, and ready for anything—unlimited options. An expert's mind is often closed to input or awareness, because they already know.

Marc Benioff, Salesforce CEO and avid meditator, said, "Beginner's mind is informing me to step back, so that I can create what wants to be, not what was."[5]

Know nothing and be curious

Know *nothing* is a term from Buddhism that simply means you know very little absolutely. I claim to know two things: who I am, and what I stand for. It might be hard to hear, but you really don't know everything. It takes confidence to say, "I don't know" regularly.

Responding to questions under pressure or out of habit as if we know doesn't typically land very well with others, and a confidently delivered wrong answer is ill advised. You inadvertently undermine your credibility by always having an answer because everyone else knows you don't know everything. Instead of consistently providing an answer, simply say, "I don't know," when you don't know. This is a sign of confidence. You can follow the "I don't know" statement with "and I'm going to find out," or "I'll get back to you," or "what do you think?" Asking questions is how you grow and learn. Acting as if you know when you don't keeps you in the dark and ruins your credibility.

If you're willing to stay curious and ask questions when you don't know, rather than assuming or answering as if you do know, you'll learn faster and be more respected. As Socrates said, "All I know is that I know nothing."

The Work

Byron Katie developed "The Work" to help us uncover what we know for sure:

> The Work helps to reveal that what you think shouldn't have happened should have happened. It should have happened because it did, and no thinking in the world can change it. This doesn't mean you condone it or approve of it. It just means that you can see things without resistance and without the confusion of your inner struggle.[6]

As the backbone of The Work, Katie provides four questions to be applied to any problem or situation:

1. Is it true?

2. Can you absolutely know it's true?

3. How do you react—what happens—when you believe that thought?

4. What would you be without the thought? Turn the thought around and find at least three specific, genuine examples of how each turnaround is true for you in this situation.

The Work helps us answer the question, "What do I really know for sure?" Let me give you an example: I had a business associate who I'll call Sue to protect her identity. Sue misappropriated money from a company we were involved in together and threw the company into a tailspin costing me years, hundreds of thousands of dollars, and my reputation because I was subsequently dragged into several lawsuits attacking my character.

This situation bothered me; I mean, how could she? I'd supported her, believed in her, and didn't deserve to be treated this way. The hurt was profound because I didn't just lose money and a business relationship, I lost one of my closest friends.

I had done the forgiveness exercise and cut the energetic cord explained in Pillar 7 with Sue. I decided to also do The Work because I was still bothered, and this is another exercise that can help facilitate forgiveness and let us move on.

1. Is it true? Yes, it is true, she misappropriated the money and ruined the company, and I had to fix it. It is true relative to these facts.

2. Can I absolutely know it's true? Not for sure in the absolute sense of universal knowledge. I know the money is gone, and I had a mess to deal with. But I wasn't there. I didn't file charges and there was no investigation. Someone else could have forced her into it, or she could have been mentally incompetent at the time. I don't know in absolute terms.

3. How do I react when I believe that thought? I am hurt and upset, and I don't want to trust others again.

4. What would I be without the thought? Less angry and more aware so as to deal with the situation as what is. The money was gone, and I had to repair the damage to the company. I could afford it and will learn something in the process of cleaning up the mess.

Turnaround: Sue didn't betray me; she betrayed herself. It cost her everything she had. She lost all her money, her reputation, and her business community of friends. In fact, looking back on it, I knew she was struggling, and I ignored the signs. I tried to get out of the partnership rather than trying to help Sue. In truth, I betrayed Sue by not paying attention and ignoring the situation. In the end, I got what I deserved.

Now, I'm still not happy, nor do I agree with what Sue most likely did, but it wasn't personal. I relived the gift of her friendship, which included providing a house for my sister-in-law and her family to live in with their two small children for free for a year when they were down on their luck. The next morning, after The Work, I named Sue as who I was grateful for. The hurt was deep, and it honestly still hurts, but I've chosen to forgive Sue. I've also decided not to have anything to do with her going forward, because no one I want to call a friend would have done that to me. Yes, I've forgiven Sue—not for Sue, but for myself. I have drawn a boundary to protect myself and ensure this won't happen again.

Also, Sue was cooperative when I needed her to sign things as I cleaned up the mess, and she may not have been if I had retaliated.

What I didn't do was use this incident to lose trust in other partners who have not betrayed me. In fact, one of my other partners did most of the work cleaning up what Sue did to the company for little or no compensation, as he was involved in the company too.

I gained a new level of appreciation and gratitude for my partners. I also learned there was a cost to my not paying attention. Through this process, I've gained some clarity and wisdom.

The other interesting thing is that we really don't know the total or final impact of events. Sometimes, events seem horrific, but in the end, they triggered subsequent events that were positive. There's a famous Taoist parable that makes this point well.

Who knows what is good and what is bad?

An old Chinese farmer lost his best stallion one day, and his neighbor came around to express his regrets, but the farmer just said, "Who knows what is good and what is bad?" The next day the stallion returned, bringing with him three wild mares. The neighbor rushed back to celebrate with the farmer, but the old farmer just said, "Who knows what is good and what is bad?" The following day, the farmer's son fell from one of the wild mares while trying to break her in and broke his arm and injured his leg. The neighbor came by to check on the son and give his condolences, but the old farmer just said, "Who knows what is good and what is bad?" The next day, the army came to the farm to conscript the farmer's son for the war but found him invalid and left him with his father.

The neighbor thought to himself, "Who knows what is good and what is bad?"

—TAOIST PARABLE[7]

We all experience ups and downs in life, but it's important to remember that we should never get caught up in these moments. To enjoy the whole experience of life, we must learn to see past the individual highs and lows and instead focus our perspective on the big picture, hopefully resting securely in our inner purpose and our vision. In the end, knowing makes us old, and curiosity keeps us young. Curiosity is another antidote for judgment, and what makes life interesting.

Stephen Hawking said, "Remember to look up at the stars and not down at your feet. Try to make sense of what you see and wonder about what makes the universe exist. Be curious."[8] Having a beginner's mind means to know nothing absolutely and to be curious. Beginner's mind helps us get over ourselves and stay present, leading to joy, happiness, and fulfillment.

The mind is a garden

Our brain is constantly manufacturing thoughts from its previous experiences and current situation. The only time it's not producing thoughts is when the mind is in Presence, like when being mindful, or experiencing a transformational shock.

Through meditation and body awareness practices like Yoga or martial arts, the mind can be trained to focus on what you wish to focus on versus following a seemingly random thought. Thoughts are like seeds— some manifest and flourish, and some wane and die. What makes the biggest difference in determining which thoughts flourish and which die? Consciousness, awareness, and the power of attention. I, for one, am glad that everything I think does not manifest, as I have some very unholy and unproductive thoughts.

In an untrained mind, which thoughts, or seeds, manifest and which die is largely random. Making our thoughts conscious and reducing the manifestation of our nonproductive thoughts is key to determining what happens.

Remember the last time you committed to something only to sabotage yourself a few days later? Like deciding this is the year to get your finances in order, only to find yourself purchasing an expensive new toy a few days later? Many of us have done something like this. The mind runs constantly, and without awareness it often leads to counterproductive activities that we are unaware of until it's too late.

Meditation is a practice of watching our thoughts and growing Presence. It's a practice that allows us to take a pitch or let a thought pass through without impact or manifestation. It's a practice that allows us to be aware of our thoughts and to have a choice as to which thoughts are fertilized and fostered and which thoughts simply pass though like bubbles in a glass of champagne or a poor pitch. It's also a practice that allows us to grow a gap between thoughts and simply be Presence, which can help us grow awareness and experience joy. You can think of meditation as gardening, in which we foster the thoughts we choose into ideas and discard the weeds, or thoughts we don't choose to foster.

Practices such as visualization, reading, or affirmation allow us to plant seeds we wish to develop and manifest. For instance, visualizing myself accomplishing a great deed, like finally launching that new business enterprise, causes the seed to be planted and fostered. Reading a book titled *How to Launch a New Business Enterprise* would plant seeds of successful actions. An affirmation like "I am a successful entrepreneur" written perhaps twenty-five times daily reaffirms the thought or seed and helps it grow. The more someone can fill the mind with desirable and productive thoughts, the less room there is for unproductive thoughts. Performing these activities while simultaneously weeding out counterproductive thoughts through meditation has the best effect, in my experience.

Interestingly, thoughts are energy because everything is energy, and thought energy can be manifested into something material or solid. For instance, the thought *I want a new business enterprise,* supported with the visualization of working in the business, putting up a picture of your dream business where you can see it each day, reading a book titled *Profit with Presence,* and all complemented by writing an affirmation such as "I enjoy launching my new business" twenty-five times each day, would be incredibly supportive of actually launching the new business enterprise. Bringing awareness to your current finances and savings, credit rating, and other parts of the process of launching a new business while simultaneously bringing awareness to what is counterproductive to launching a new business, like taking an expensive vacation during the launch and not paying your bills on time (i.e., having a poor credit score), so they can be minimized, is crucial to success. The mind is a garden, and gardens need maintenance.

- Acknowledge you know very little absolutely.

- Be curious, as another antidote to judgment.

- Do The Work when stuck in a situation.

- Who knows what's good and what's bad?

- The mind is a garden, and gardens need maintenance.

Chapter Takeaway

Be curious and ask probing questions rather than knowing.

Conclusion to Part 2

The Twelve Pillars of Mindful Leadership and your personal mindfulness practice have the potential to radically change your life from one full of stress and strains to one of Presence, filled with joy, success, and happiness. There are the potential impediments of skepticism and intellectualism; that is, you either don't legitimately give the practices a try because they seem odd or different, or because "you get it" intellectually and thus don't need to practice. Unfortunately, you must practice mindfulness to reap the benefits. I hope you will give it a go, to whatever level you are comfortable with to get started. My experience is that the more consistently and longer you practice mindfulness, the more inviting it is. So just start where you are, but start.

I hope we have dispelled any myth that you don't have time to practice mindfulness. For those who already have, or do start a mindfulness practice, perhaps the most significant danger to the essential slow boil practices espoused in this work is that you get bored, even when you are doing well and enjoying the benefits, as James Clear wrote in *Atomic Habits*. I have found this to be surprising, but true.

Your commitment and habits will be the first line of defense against boredom. Then it helps to keep learning and deepening your practice to keep it fresh. There may be days when you may need to "go through the motions," but doing that is a million times better than ditching the practice for the day. If you miss a day or two, use your commitment to motivate you to get back on the path the next day. Keep with the intention of being mindful, and the commitment to practice as the path to achieving and maintaining Presence.

I've found that my antidote to boredom is to read inspirational books and attend workshops regularly that deepen my existing practice and give me new tools to add to my practice. For instance, Yoga has numerous layers, and you can go as deep as you wish or have time to explore. Going deeper in a pose or learning a new pose can keep you present and interested. If you have chosen to include Yoga in your practice, the references in Appendix 2 will help you explore available options, and Yoga is exploding across the globe.

Meditation is similar. We introduced a straightforward breath meditation practice, but there are numerous paths to follow in meditation. You can simply increase time as you progress at your own pace. A meditation workshop or silent retreat can be helpful to keep you on the path.

Another useful suggestion is to find others to share the practice with because you can help keep each other going through periods of boredom or life's disruptions and challenges. Just be careful not to depend on others solely to keep yourself going in the practices. I am so blessed to not only have a family committed to mindfulness, but also to have a work environment that supports mindfully creating community.

In the next section, we explore mindfulness in the workplace, where we spend most of our prime time. You may find a rich community of practitioners there to share with eventually. But if you can't find it there, keep looking, because a mindful community, or at least a mindful friend, can be essential to maintaining mindfulness practice. You will find information on our workshops on the resources page at the end of the book, and one benefit of our professionals-based workshops is meeting like-minded professionals.

Boredom is not the enemy; mindlessness is the enemy. Accept periods of boredom and be curious about them while doing what you can to make the practice more interesting. Your commitment and habits are essential. Clear wrote, "Professionals stick to the schedule; amateurs let life get in the way. Professionals know what is important to them and work toward it with purpose; amateurs get pulled off course by the urgencies of life." He went on to state, "When a habit is truly important to you, you have to be willing to stick to it in any mood. Professionals act even when the mood isn't right. They might not enjoy it, but they find a way to put the reps in."[9]

This is especially important when training the mind; it takes repetition and boredom to fully ingrain a new habit. Become thrilled with being Present and fascinated by all the little things you never noticed before, while you train your mind to work on your conscious objectives 24/7.

Next, we'll explore the potential of mindfulness in your professional life and business.

PART 3

PRACTICING MINDFULNESS IN YOUR BUSINESS AND CONCLUSIONS

A truly great leader is appropriately uncertain but well equipped to deal with that uncertainty through open-minded exploration.[1]

—Ray Dalio

Now that you have stepped onto the path of mindfulness and Presence, it's very helpful to have a friend who is also on the path. Even better is to have a mindful community to support you, and where you can support others. Remember, our culture generally is less, rather than more, mindful, and although that is changing, it's the current reality or "what is." Without support, it's more difficult to maintain a mindfulness practice long term.

I had my brother Bruce and the Yoga community to support me as I got started. Later, I had my family and a blossoming community of mindfulness practitioners at work that inspired my practice and inspired me to write this book. It was me who started the mindful community at work, and this part of the book will show how to initiate or support a similar situation in your workplace. So, look for support for your practice and look for where you can support the mindfulness practice of others too.

Another difficulty is time for practice in a busy, distracted world. But I think this is also an opportunity if you are in a position to influence corporate culture. Recently one of the participants in one of our Living in the Gap programs, Nate Melchior, asked me how to get this amazing work into his company, Dunton Commercial. He was the number-two person and a principal in the company. We designed an eight-week corporate mindfulness program, and I told him if he could get the CEO to attend, I would make time to deliver it. The CEO agreed, but he was a skeptical participant for the first several sessions. And then something switched. He became engaged, curious, and more positive in the sessions. In fact, he later enthusiastically signed up for our Mindful Leadership Program. Comments from the staff were phenomenal, not just about what mindfulness added to their lives, which was a reduction of stress and an increase in appreciation, among other benefits, but also about management caring about them as people.

Afterward, Nate said,

> The program taught our company some initial skills and guide-
> lines for living a more mindful, present, intentional life. This
> included practicing Yoga, meditation, book discussions, and
> building a morning routine as a foundation for our mindful
> practice. In just eight weeks, we saw immense benefits in stress
> relief, productivity, focus, and the overall happiness across the
> company. It has brought us all closer personally and improved
> the culture across the organization.

Nate persuaded another firm, Sullivan Hayes Corporation, to join
their eight-week program. Brian Shorter, the company's managing partner, also appreciated the experience, and his company is joining Nate's
company's follow-up program as well. Brian said,

> Eric was generous to introduce our company to an eight-week
> Living in the Gap workshop. We had about half of our team
> take advantage of the wonderful opportunity to learn. Not only
> did this program open our eyes to the benefits of living in a
> more intentional way; it brought our extended team together in
> ways I couldn't have ever imagined. The ripple effect throughout
> our organization was tremendous. I am confident the dividends
> of the program will be lifelong.

Long story short, at the conclusion, they decided to continue on
their own and created their own internal group that meets regularly to
practice meditation, read inspiring books, and get to know each other
personally. The simple fact is, most of us know our coworkers' names and
some niceties, but we don't really know each other, our struggles, our

celebrations, and each other's families. Mindfulness is a huge opportunity to change corporate culture, which you will hear more about in the upcoming chapters.

The point that the CEO or top management have buy-in to mindfulness and corporate culture is critical. To return to why I think too little time outside work is an opportunity, it's because everyone at work struggles to find time to practice mindfulness, so why not promote mindfulness at work, where we spend most of our prime time? My experience is that the gains in focus and efficiency more than offset paid time off to practice mindfulness. I have yet to meet a professional who adopted mindfulness practices that did not experience an increase in business performance and a reduction in stress.

Let's move on to discuss the mindful CEO, and then on to the mindful company discussion. If you are not a CEO, do not want to be a CEO, and you would like to find a mindfulness culture, it may be you need to look for a company and/or CEO with these qualities. If you are not a CEO but would like to be, this may be great information for you, and I will offer the advice I got from my dad, Don Holsapple, continually while growing up: "There is always room at the top. They are turning over every day. If you are having trouble finding a position, you are setting your sights too low."*

---

* My dad, may he rest in peace, taught me how to be a man and how to show up and work. He was not mindful, but he was a solid gentleman. He gave me the drive to write this book. I miss him.

Chapter 5

THE MINDFUL CEO

I began to realize that an intuitive understanding and consciousness was more significant than abstract thinking and intellectual
logical analysis.[1]

—STEVE JOBS

A CEO doesn't have to be enlightened to be mindful, but the
word *enlightenment* is thrown around so much, and by a culture that really has no idea what it means, that I thought it
would be instructive to visit the topic of enlightenment.

First is the enlightenment period, an intellectual and philosophical
movement that dominated Europe in the seventeenth and eighteenth
centuries with global influences and effects. I designate this meaning of
enlightenment with a lowercase *e.*[*]

---

[*] For an interesting synopsis on enlightenment then and now, see Stephen Pinker,
Enlightenment Now (New York: Penguin Random House, 2018).

Second is what Buddhists refer to when they use the term *Enlightenment*. Buddhists believe that human life is a cycle of suffering and rebirth but, by achieving a state of Enlightenment (nirvana), it's possible to escape this cycle forever. Siddhartha Gautama (563–483 BC) was the first person believed to reach this state of Enlightenment and is known as Buddha. Without making a comparison, of course Christ was Enlightened and lived later. I will designate this definition with an uppercase *E* because this is the definition most closely tied to mindfulness and Presence.

One simple way to think of this Eastern concept of Enlightenment is that it means you reside in consciousness, or Presence, as your primary self, and when your body is abandoned at death, your consciousness returns to universal consciousness. This is similar to the theory of analytic idealism, which is gaining steam in the academic community, as we discussed in chapter 1.

Importantly, and why I am bringing up the subject, these two definitions are merging in the current scientific and mindfulness research, and they are helping both fields to explain, understand, and grow mutually, each supporting the other. Especially for CEOs, enlightenment means they will be guided by facts and science, and now that science is starting to better understand and embrace consciousness, CEOs have permission to also embrace mindfulness and the usefulness of Presence. Thus this book's title, *Profit with Presence*.

Now let's get a little less lofty and use this background, and the Twelve Pillars of Mindful Leadership, to define a mindful CEO, mindful leader, and mindful professional more generally. I use *CEO*, but if another word works better for your situation, feel free to substitute. These principles apply to any professional. I use *CEO* or *leader* because of that position's ability to influence culture, which is critical to get organizations on board. These findings apply to professionals generally as well.

The mindful CEO

The benefits of mindfulness are important for everyone in the company, however it's especially important for the CEO and members of the executive team. Using the Twelve Pillars of Mindful Leadership as a guide, mindful CEOs, leaders, or professionals have the following characteristics:

- They are present and mindful, know their purpose, and create clarity, vision, intention, commitment, and habits around things that matter for themselves, their families, and their organization.

- They reside in Presence regardless of what they're doing and show up with Presence, take appropriate actions from looking within for guidance, and detach from results.

- To them, profits are important but not the purpose of their life or organization.

- They take responsibility, practice nonjudgment and compassion, and foster relationships through service, the integrity of their word, and listening to others.

- They stay in Flow both with a regular routine supporting these principles and by staying connected to others.

- They create affluence for their families, organization, shareholders, executives, and employees (as applicable) to improve their lives and to influence others in a meaningful way.

- They are grateful, give generously, and serve others and their communities while accepting what is without resistance or complaint.

- They take everything impersonally, let life flow through them, realize they know very little absolutely, and are genuinely curious.

- They do not require perfection in these things from themselves or others, but they have these principles, or similar ones, as a paramount intention.

- They keep these standards as ideals to work toward as they move through the world and complete their journey.

WHAT THE MINDFUL CEO IS NOT

I've been around many transformational leaders and high-level CEOs who've taught me a lot. I have also witnessed their blind spots to various degrees, despite their high levels of awareness in other areas. Far from taking that to mean they're not extraordinary and present, I take it to mean they're human and not perfect. They are as close to being Enlightened as I have seen for householders with responsibilities in the world (i.e., excluding renunciants). They are searching for the important balance between the spiritual and material worlds, and I applaud them.

They've also taught me what Enlightenment (for most of us) is not:

- Perfect

- In a state of Presence 24/7

- Void of material possessions

This may be a relief for you; I know it was for me. Keep your intention, do your best, and practice compassion for yourself when you fall short—and you will because you're human.

Mindful leadership is a choice

What does mindful leadership look like in this moment? Choose that!

After all, mindfulness is a choice and a series of choices in each moment. First, you choose to get on the path of mindfulness and discover and honor your inner purpose of Presence in all that you do. When presented with a situation, you sense a choice, and when you honor that choice, you've made a selection consistent with your inner purpose. This is the mindful choice in that moment.[2]

To illustrate, let's say you are presented with the possibility of cutting a corner that you know won't be discovered and will save money. Thoroughness was promised, but completing the task as promised will reduce profit. One choice is to take the shortcut. The mindful choice is to do what's promised and learn from it for the next time. The mindful leader makes a series of mindful choices and if they result in errors, fixes them when possible. They are not perfect but endeavor to do the right thing in each moment. When the moments are added up, it makes a meaningful difference for the leader, their family, organization, community, and the world. What you choose in each moment matters. You matter.

If this sounds too lofty, remember that it's a process, and getting on the path with an ideal or vision in mind is what's important. Furthermore, these are my principals, and what matters more is what a mindful CEO (or leader or professional) is to you, and what principles you have or adopt. Feel free to modify this to reflect your situation and see how you can move the needle toward a more mindful world.

It may be comforting to know that there are many joining the ranks of being mindful CEOs, and you are not alone. If you Google "mindful CEOs," you will see an array of high-powered CEOs leading Fortune 500 and smaller companies using mindfulness to guide them and their organizations, and I listed some of them at the end of Pillar 1, for instance Ray Dalio, Marc Benioff, and Andrew Cherng, to pique your interest. Corporate mindfulness coach and consultant Elizabeth Prather thinks the world is ready for mindfulness. "From figures like Bill Gates and Oprah Winfrey and mega-corporations like Google and Nike, more high-level names and renowned companies are raving about the positive impact mindfulness has on business."[3]

- The mindful CEO is guided by mindfulness principles.

- The mindful CEO is not perfect, residing in Presence 24/7, or void of material possessions.

- Mindful leadership is a choice and a series of choices.

Chapter Takeaway

The mindful CEO is the key to building a mindful company culture.

Mindful CEO Exercise

Look at your calendar and track your time for the next month to see where you may be wasting time that could be used to support your mindfulness practices.

Answer the question: Of all your duties, what can only you do?

Make a list of all your work associates and start to consider who may be open to practicing mindfulness and whom you might be willing to share these practices with first when you are ready. Put the list away in a safe place.

Search for other CEOs, leaders, or professionals in your communities who practice mindfulness and reach out to ask them what their experience has been.

Chapter 6

THE MINDFUL CORPORATION

You can't force people to be mindful at all, as it turns out. . . . I think you can make it easier to be mindful. . . . If it's on your calendar, and there's a room over there to sit in, and there's someone there to guide you, you're 10,000 times more likely to do it.[1]

—EVAN WILLIAMS, cofounder of Twitter

You cannot transform your business to become mindful until you transform yourself.

The truth is, companies cannot be mindful; only the people in the company can be mindful. Mindful leaders can establish an environment that fosters and rewards mindfulness. Most organizations are corruptible unless the people within them are virtuous and strong.

Of course, the company needs to make a profit, and more profit is better than less profit, but profit is not a vision, mission, or purpose. To continue the theme of cultural lies, the charge to maximize profit puts all the employees in an expendable situation and all company actions under a single lens. Instead, create a powerful vision statement for the company, and let the vision guide your decisions. Be present to what you're doing in the moment and leave the ultimate profit report to other forces. You will check in on profit and other metrics as regularly as you feel necessary; however, the main focus each day and each moment within the day is Presence.

For the mindful corporation, the most influential person to be mindful is the CEO. But everyone matters, and one mindful person can be a seed for transformation. The CEO or leader implements the tone, the vision, and the mission of the company.

At a retreat for our company, LC Real Estate Group, which I helped facilitate with one of my mentors, Garry Lester, the partners and managers came up with the vision statement Mindfully Creating Community, which was a powerful statement and guides our actions. Who says the statement is always important, and if this had been based on my vision only it would not have been nearly as empowering to the company.

Unfortunately, I cannot tell you *exactly* how to implement mindfulness for your organization because I don't know you or your business. I can tell you what we've done that's worked and what hasn't worked. Admittedly, LC Real Estate is a small organization, but companies as large as Google have done it too.

Don't share before you've achieved

My first piece of advice to you is that you should not even try to share mindfulness with your company until you've personally achieved a stabilized practice and formed habits that support it. Generally, that takes at least a year of regular mindfulness practice.

Several reasons are behind this advice, beginning with how easy it is to be thrown off your practice by the skepticism of others, which is rampant in our society. Also, if you are just learning, sharing too soon may turn your focus away from gaining depth in your own practice toward getting someone else to start.

One of the biggest traps for someone learning mindfulness (or any transformation, for that matter) is to immediately identify others in their lives "who really need this." The only one that needs to practice mindfulness is you, and that's only if you say so. Of course, after reading this book, I hope you decide to get on the path to mindfulness if you haven't already. Although I am the one suggesting ways to introduce mindfulness into your company, I am also cautioning against doing so too soon or implementing it too rapidly.

When you change, others will change because of your perception and because of the Presence and example you have given to them. The single most powerful way to share this work is to have people notice a difference in you and ask you, "What's going on?" Go to work on your own practice, show up with Presence, and trust that you will know when it's time to share with others. There will be a time to share what you've learned. In fact, it's essential for your practice and for the world that you not only practice mindfulness, but that you also share it with others.

Keep in mind that we are trying to create a corporate mindfulness culture, not necessarily to have everyone in the organization meditate regularly. Before mindfulness was infused into LC Real Estate Group, for years I was a closet meditator who still rushed in and out of the office, barely noticing who was in the office unless I needed something from them.

\\|//

Fortunately, meditation opened me up to some other work, such as that in Arbinger's book *The Outward Mindset* and the program of the same name, which is specifically designed to transform corporate culture (without formal meditation).[2] The first thing we did company-wide was to implement the Outward Mindset program, which I classify as leadership training. The "we" in this statement is important, because even though I was the CEO, I knew it was critical to get my partners and management team to be on board with completing the training. Don't miss this step.

The Outward Mindset isn't a meditation program but rather teaches how to view others as people and what roles we each have in various circumstances. It's a powerful approach, and Arbinger trains people in your organization to deliver the training and oversee it on an ongoing basis.*[3]

The Outward Mindset program is beneficial as a start because it's not likely that everyone in your firm will meditate regularly, even with the CEO supporting the effort and even when offering free meditation training. These types of programs, and there are many others, give something for everybody. We had zero employee resistance to company-wide mandatory Arbinger retreats.[3] The Outward Mindset program or a similar program is a good step because it gives many of the virtues of the mindfulness mindset without requiring meditation for everyone.

---

* It's a unique feature in that, rather than having an outside person who doesn't know the people or culture, the CEO (preferably) or an HR representative leads the discussion. I trained to be a facilitator with the Arbinger Institute, as have Rollin Goering and Nick Galluzzo with LC Real Estate.

Of high importance is what partners and employees report finding at home after attending whatever programs you decide upon. We had many employees find an immediate benefit of better relationships at home and in the office with a mindset change alone. At LC Real Estate we say, "When you can learn something at work that makes your home life better, that's a company worth working for." I witnessed all my partners benefit personally, and Rollin Goering and Rico Devlin transformed their personal lives via their commitment to this type of approach.

\\|//

Leadership training of the right type starts a cultural shift toward mindfulness, which is good by itself and helpful, and makes it easier when you're ready to share your meditation training with others.

Another highly effective program for my real estate company was Ninja Selling. This program targets real estate sales professionals, but as much as 80 percent of the principles apply across the board to the marketing of any business. The workshop teaches the value of gratitude and being in flow, along with many other helpful mindfulness tools. It was founded by Larry Kendall, one of my mentors, whom I taught with at CSU for ten years and who has become a good friend.[†] If your industry is not real estate, you may find a suitable program for your industry.

My cousin Steve Wiley founded the Lincoln Leadership Institute (LLI), in Gettysburg, Pennsylvania, and he has been a great resource

---

† You can check out Larry Kendall's book, *Ninja Selling*, and for more information about the program, check out the website, https://ninjaselling.com. An interesting precession effect is that Larry introduced me to the term precession effect when I was searching for how to describe the phenomenon I was living and am now writing about. When it came time to write this book, Larry introduced me to Greenleaf Book Group, which also published Larry's book, *Ninja Selling*.

in how to best deliver CEOs and top-level executives the Living in the Gap Mindful Leadership Training. I have attended his trainings numerous times. They contain many mindfulness principles and are attended by representatives of Fortune 500 companies.[‡] LLI programs are great for both leadership and marketing teams.

I am sure there are many other worthwhile programs that can help to transition your company toward a mindfulness mindset. Research on your own, and check with colleagues and your leadership groups to see who's had a good experience with a program and check it out. A leadership training program may not be an essential step, but we had great results, and it moved the needle on mindfulness and allowed us to take the next step. Realizing everything in mindfulness is a process, it may help if you are patient.

By mentioning leadership programs, I am not downplaying meditation; I find it essential. However, some of the tools available to transform corporate culture do not promote sitting meditation, even if the facilitators use the practice themselves, because of cultural resistance to it, or because they are not trained to lead meditation. Meditation, being a daily practice, keeps on giving, day in and day out. Mindfulness and meditation can make people more open to positive changes in company culture. Programs have limited duration, and even I tire of constant programs (after many years). I have never tired of meditation; in fact, I typically crave the daily experience.

It's time to share

Consider mindfulness as the seed of Presence. Plant these seeds with little acts and accept that certain people you know will be open to mindfulness concepts, but not everyone will be open to mindfulness, and

---

‡   For more information, see the institute's website, https://www.gettysburgleadership.com.

some may be especially resistant to meditation. Others will crave it and thrive when it's introduced. I started by sharing with one person in my organization and then it grew to a few. Rollin Goering and I started a seed group that began a monthly meeting to learn meditation and read and discuss mindfulness books together. This was a safe space to attend or not attend, to share or not share, and to learn mindfulness. My partner Wayne Lewis started getting deep into mindfulness, and he interested the group in the book *The Miracle Morning*, which set out a morning routine that many adopted.[4] It caused me to add gratitude and affirmations to my morning routine, which provided instant results. Be prepared to allow others in the group to contribute to you; it's key to empowering the group and yourself.

Sometimes simply sharing a book is an excellent way to introduce mindfulness. If your colleagues are interested and actually read it, great, and you'll likely hear about it. If you get silence, well, that's communication too. Be patient and gentle. If they don't reply, it's likely they aren't interested or struggle to read. Offering an audible option would likely help. Don't force it, and don't take it personally. I am surprised how few people actually read, but I know it's difficult for some, and I believe the difficulty is tied to our distracted world and inability to focus.[§]

You could offer centering meditations at your partner or management meetings, as we did, and then later at all-company meetings. It's helpful to start with verbiage like "centering" or "breathing exercises" like the 5-3-6 sequence in the practice exercise introduced in Pillar 1. Always introduce things gradually to avoid alienating people who are less open to new things, which is almost everyone.

---

§   One of the gifts from our extended workshops is getting people into the habit of reading. As you can tell from the citations in this book, I am a voracious reader today, but I got the reading habit completing my PhD program. It's a very rewarding flow activity and support for your practice with the right type of books, ones that directly affect your mindfulness practice.

I think the biggest shift for us, and the one that gave us permission to start a larger conversation around mindfulness, was the creation of the vision statement Mindfully Creating Community by the management team. The management team had just enough mindfulness experience to be curious and were willing to be vulnerable and explore.

We let our seed group ripen with a few years of meditation for the attendees, and then we seemed ready for the next step. We brought Mindful-Based Stress Reduction (MBSR), an eight-week program of mindfulness, to the entire company. Now, our company is small, with about twenty-five employees, and so we made the training mandatory. If yours is a large firm, making it voluntary may be the best approach. It depends on your relationship with the employees.

The MBSR organization, founded by Jon Kabat-Zinn, has about forty years of history and is approved by a number of large organizations, including the University of Massachusetts. This exposed everyone to mindfulness—some reluctantly, admittedly. We also instituted a thirty-minute mindfulness period before lunch each day and started offering a thirty-minute Yoga class once a week.¶

Know that the corporate world is taking mindfulness seriously. A recent study from Wharton confirms companies can instill mindfulness through leadership training, meditation training, and mindfulness micro-practices, which are repetitive practices of basic skills essential to promote mastery. Christian Greiser says companies that undergo a transformation through mindfulness are seeing positive returns both on an individual level and on an organizational level.[5]

Many companies and even more studies consistently find that the key benefits of mindfulness include the following:[6]

¶   David Gelles's *Mindful Work* (Boston, MA: Houghton Mifflin, 2015) lists other options for corporate mindfulness training to research on your own. Google's Search Inside Yourself is open to outside participation, although I have no direct experience with the program.

- Better decision-making and problem-solving through better listening, more mental clarity, creativity, and less reactivity

- Calmer, less stressed employees with better attention spans, more focused efforts, and improved task performance

- Better relationships among employees and clients, leading to better engagement, increased collaboration, and higher resiliency

- Improved job satisfaction and less turnover, resulting in better engagement, increased productivity, less burnout, and happier employees

- Positively impacted company culture when mindfulness was practiced company wide

Mindfulness works for companies as large as Google or as small as LC Real Estate. Or even for professional associates.

The coronavirus pandemic hit and disrupted our corporate journey into mindfulness and sent everyone into the world of remote work. We continued our seed group over Zoom, which did help, but I think we could have done more. Frankly, I was busy solving issues with empty buildings and my personal mindfulness practice was essential. But looking back, I wish we had done more to promote mindfulness in such a stressful time for everyone.

The seeds of mindfulness are planted at LC Real Estate Group. I admit often wondering what others are actually doing (or not doing), but generally, I've chosen to pay more attention to what people are doing. I find it more effective to notice mindful behavior than to make comments when my expectations aren't met. Drop your expectations and accept what happens. What you focus on expands.

Remember, some will start on the mindfulness path because you, or the CEO, are on the path, and they want to please the CEO. That's okay, and a benefit to having a person in your position promoting mindfulness. Be careful, however, not to reward people disproportionately for following the mindfulness lead, so as not to promote the deception of mindfulness. Once you're on the path, see what the management team comes up with on their own, because it matters whose idea it is. We always like our own ideas more than someone else's.

It's totally appropriate and empowering to set the corporate vision to include mindfulness if you can get that done with shareholders, the board, and the management team. To do that, they will need to be introduced to mindfulness, if they aren't already practicing themselves. William George, board member of Goldman Sachs, says,

> The main business case for meditation is that if you're fully present on the job, you will be more effective as a leader, you will make better decisions, and you will work better with other people . . . I tend to live a very busy life. This keeps me focused on what's important.[7]

Implementation of mindfulness will only work companywide if it is supported by top executives, and if it is collaborative rather than authoritative.

Some sound advice in this area comes from the Three Laws of Performance Leadership Corollaries:[8]

- Leaders have a say and give others a say in how situations occur.

- Leaders master the conversational environment.

- Leaders listen for the future of their organization.

Go slow, be mindful, and remember that the most important person in the organization to practice mindfulness is you, regardless of your position. Also remember that, as necessary as it is, profit is not a purpose. Create an empowering purpose and company vision for the organization and its people to live into.

Consider these guiding principles:

- Start with yourself, then a few select individuals with whom to share the work.

- Let others know the company values mindfulness, and possibly revisit the company vision to ensure it's consistent with your own.

- Create mindfulness offerings, like a seed group, or mindfulness training with a trained mindfulness teacher.

- Create policies that allow time off and support employees attending mindfulness training.

- Allocate a space and time during the day for employees to be mindful.

- Be mindful in all you do, because you matter individually, and others are watching.

Mindfulness is an amazing corporate culture and benefit, and well worth whatever effort it takes to implement. Additionally, here are three pertinent questions applicable to most companies today, and I apply relevant pillars from the Twelve Pillars of Mindful Leadership to answer them:

- How can mindfulness improve the bottom line?

- How can business maintain connection and culture in a world of remote work?

- How can business lead us out of divisiveness through mindfulness?

Mindfulness improves the bottom line

This one is easy, so I will tackle it first.

- Being mindful creates purpose, clarity, vision, intention, and commitment. The state of "being" vs. "doing" creates awareness, connection, and Presence.

- Showing up and taking action is the premise to results, including precessional effects.

- Being detached from results means to be fully engaged in the process of business in intimate detail, without forgetting we are in business to produce results. Additionally, detachment allows letting go of substandard activities more easily.

- Being responsible gives employees power and trust; and being nonjudgmental allows a fuller awareness of the intimacies of business and promotes inclusion.

- Fostering relationships through service, being your word, and listening means you have deep, lasting, trusting contacts through good times and bad.

- Being in Flow makes employees feel better, be more productive, and be connected with other important contacts.

- Generating profits increases affluence, which allows us to influence our environment, communities, and politics.

- Being grateful changes employees' mindsets to be more open and productive; giving generously and being in service are the right things to do and produce precessional effects that are enormously beneficial to business.

- Having employees who accept their roles, are not resistant to what they have to do, and who do not constantly complain is an obvious production gain and stress reduction.

- Taking everything impersonally and letting business events flow through us means we are not making emotional decisions and not emotionally drained by every dip in stock price. If there is something to do about it, do it. If there is nothing we can do about it, accept it.

- Having beginners' minds and staying curious allows us to be open to possibilities and to see the enormous potential for business growth.

Google's Search Inside Yourself Program's website reports to have reached tens of thousands of executives and professionals, from companies like Procter and Gamble, 3M, and Ford. One company, SAP, reported:

- 200 percent ROI for their mindfulness training,

- 6.5 percent greater employee engagement,

- 13.8 percent improved focus,

- 6.9 percent better communication, and

- 5.2 percent better collaboration.[9]

In addition, SAP also reported in 2018 that it more subjectively found mindfulness gave it a completive edge.

Additionally, you can improve the health of your employees and the bottom line at the same time. Mark Bertolini, former CEO of Aetna, a Fortune 100 company with more than $30 billion in revenues and more than 20 million members, had over 13,000 employees participate in mindfulness training. The results were astounding:

- Employees' stress levels improved and Aetna's overall health-care costs were reduced by approximately $2,000 per year; and

- Productivity gains alone amounted to $3,000 per employee, an eleven-to-one return on its investment.[10]

There is no doubt that following these principles will increase the bottom line, while at the same time improving peace of mind, focus, joy, and important relationships.

Additionally, one of the key issues facing companies' bottom lines today is navigating the dramatic evolution of remote work.

How can business maintain connection and culture in a world of remote work?

The COVID-19 pandemic has spawned the "Great Resignation," during which millions of employees are leaving their positions. That means remote work accelerated by the pandemic is a fact of business today.

An article by Larry Kendall in *Real Trends* reports most employers, in fact 74 percent, plan to keep at least some of their workers remote permanently.[11] Interestingly, over 70 percent of managers have reported being just as satisfied or more satisfied by remote work performance as they were when everyone was in the office.[12]

When you combine this result with the Great Resignation experienced during the pandemic, one thing is clear: Remote work is here to stay because workers are demanding it, and because employers are in dire need of workers.

How do we employ remote work strategies that make the most out of the situation?

Kendall's article reports that researchers have found three major themes that are important to employees: relationships, security, and acknowledgment.[13]

Think about something: Employers save money when employees "successfully" work from home because of a reduction in overhead, so why don't all employers embrace remote work?

The main reason I have found is a lack of trust and a reluctance to lose control over their employees' day. That attitude certainly doesn't promote relationship, security, or acknowledgment.

"Command and control" can be used in an office setting but is impossible to utilize in a remote work setting. Command and control leaders are the ones destined to do the worst in a world of remote work.

Who will do the best in a world of remote work?

Some companies, like Jumpstart, have reported improved company culture since the gravitation to remote work. David Patcher of Jumpstart wrote *Remote Leadership* in 2021 and identified three pillars of great remote organizations: reflective leadership, coaching mindset and culture, and peer learning.

- Reflective leaders are self-aware and focused on acting mindfully.

- A coaching mindset flips command and control to a training and trust culture.

- Lastly, peer learning is about creating deeper conversations between people across the organization who may never meet. Co-workers can share personal experiences and create trust (like during the leadership or eight-week mindfulness trainings we have discussed).[14]

The simple truth is that remote work exposes underlying motivations of either command and control leaders who seek to achieve their agenda, or reflective leaders who coach and lead by honoring the employees' agendas while still retaining necessary corporate outcomes.

Importantly, trust is a two-way street, and if employers want to be able to trust their employees, then employees need to be able to trust their employers.

You cannot fake caring about someone, and remote work may force us to be mindful and happy for it to succeed. And that is a good thing.

Pachter says:

You can build a high-performing organization based on deeper relationships, a sense of community, self-acceptance, courageous questioning, and mutual accountability. A place where you won't need to have all the answers so you can ask better questions. You won't teach; you'll share. You won't give orders; you'll bring out the best in others while trusting them to guide themselves, each other, and sometimes you.[15]

Mindful leadership is more important in a world of remote work. In fact, mindful leadership may be the only way it works for many organizations that depend on culture, creativity, and trust. Transactional companies may survive in the old-world style; however, companies that depend and thrive on culture and creativity will need to transform to survive. There is no substitute for truly caring about employees as people, and no intuition about remote employees without regular and effective communication with them.

There are several key elements for remote work to be successful:

- Top managers and the CEO must participate in peer learning for it to be a genuine offering.

- CEOs and managers need to be more mindful.

- CEOs and managers should have a system to stay in flow, not only with outside stakeholders, but also to stay in flow on a regular basis with employees working remotely.

Culture describes how a company does business and what's important to a company, in addition to making money. In fact, mindfulness is a "sticky" culture, meaning it doesn't just exist when employees walk through the office door or log in on their home computer; mindfulness is a way of being that permeates the entire life of an employee. Once the match is made between mindful employers and mindful employees, it becomes very solid or "sticky."

When employees know they are valued at work, and work in turn promotes mindfulness, this makes their home lives better too. Employers know it's not that easy to find mindful employees that fit a specific job description and are careful to hang on to them.

Importantly for remote work, mindfulness is virtual. You don't need to be in physical proximity to be mindful of each other, although it is helpful. A leader who is more aware knows to reach out and connect regularly with employees, giving acknowledgment where due.

A deep relationship can be formed between employers and employees through mindfulness. Mindfulness creates a relational, versus transactional, connection, especially once mindfulness is adopted in the company vision statement. We had zero employees resign during the Great Resignation at LC Real Estate, although this is admittedly a small sample size.

Mindfulness is a culture, and a "sticky" culture. And it can be of great assistance to maintaining connections and culture in the world of remote work.

Next, let's return to possibly the most important topic of our time, which I discussed briefly in the preface. It's not meant to be "political," but rather mindful and practical. If it seems political, my apologies, and I hope you will bear with me for a brief divergence, as I am not a politician or a podcaster; business is my platform to make change. However, I can't sit by and watch this phenomenon without doing something to try to move the needle toward a more mindful world that works for everyone, including you and me.

Can business lead us out of divisiveness through mindfulness?

A major reason for writing this book is to help mobilize businesses to mindfully engage in influencing often-divisive behavior and politics. The entire US political system is dependent on donations from political activists, most of whom are funded by someone who has initially generated their wealth through business ventures either directly or indirectly. In an era of super PACs, it's difficult to track, but my economics training allows me to have confidence that most all money originates from business of some type or another. The most recent presidential election showed this, as reported by *The Conversation*: "Election 2020 sees record $11 billion in campaign spending, mostly from a handful of super-rich donors. . . . corporations are the predominant contributors to the huge growth in so-called 527 organizations since 2010."[16]

And the problem (or opportunity) is growing: "In total, the [2020] election cost an unprecedented $14 billion, making it twice as expensive as the previous presidential election cycle."[17]

The $3 billion difference in reporting is not lost on me, and neither is what else could be done with the $11 or $14 billion. But that's not my main point. Politicians know they are beholden to business interests, and while businesses historically preferred to stay apolitical, as not to alienate the other side of the aisle, the fact is that this has changed for many businesses in the current environment, and businesses have tremendous influence if and when they choose to use it. And if the Fortune 500 companies decided to band together in an apolitical manner to make unified progress toward meaningful political transformation, this issue actually *would* be solved by next Tuesday.

The current political narrative is so stalled and divisive that it is detrimental to businesses, both because too little gets done and because the state of politics is too unpredictable. The current threats to the US democratic system make investments in the US risky and impair business and consumer confidence in the system.

As I mentioned in the preface, as told by Barbara Walter, the business community in South Africa was instrumental in solving the political divisiveness from apartheid:

> But then something happened to bring South Africa back from the brink. . . . If the economy collapsed so would white

wealth. . . . South Africa was closer to civil war than the United States is today . . . . No one thought that white South Africans would reform a system designed specifically to cement their dominance. But when the costs of maintaining that dominance became too high, and business leaders who were hurt by sanctions by the international community insisted on reform, they dismantled it [apartheid]. If South Africa could reform, so can the United States.[18]

And we could indeed do the same here. Maybe it has to get worse before people are willing to set aside their political ideals and goals to "defeat the other side" in order to pull together as one business community and insist politicians do the same thing to move us forward.

Businesses could do this anytime they choose and back this up by withholding funds to politicians who are divisive and being generous to politicians who are acting in the common good to move us forward as a country, and by bringing national attention to the issue. The more businesses can come together to implement this strategy, the more effective it will be. It doesn't matter if you are a Democrat or Republican, you are a professional, and political divisiveness is bad for business.

I believe it's better and less risky to promote your ideologies personally and at the ballot box , not in your business that represents such diverse stakeholder interests. Alternatively, we will experience a trend that has already started, where customers and shareholders target where they buy or invest based on the political leanings of the companies. This seems to be a very slippery slope to hang business success on to me. For instance, recently *Newsweek* reported a number of retailers will no longer sell MyPillow Products due to founder Mike Lindell's involvement in the 2020 election.[19]

The hope, dream, or vision of this book is to accelerate this conversation, and hope the conversation reaches the Fortune 500 CEOs. That group has the visibility and influence to move the needle from zero to sixty any time they choose to band together as one voice.

On another level, it would be even better if politicians would be more mindful on their own, and this may happen eventually, especially with modeling from successful business executives.

Some politicians, like Tim Ryan of Ohio, author of *A Mindful Nation*, have already started. Tim noted, "It seems to me that it would do us all good to act from our heart more often. We'll be surprised how small acts of attention and kindness can release the energy, enthusiasm, and imagination bottled up in our overstressed minds and bodies."[20]

And it's not just Democrats who are practicing meditation. Ryan hosts a weekly "quiet time" in Congress attended by both parties.[21] The number of Democrats who meditate at least once a week hovers slightly over 40 percent, and the number of Republicans who meditate at least once a week hovers slightly below 40 percent, which is encouraging. In my experience, we may notice a significant difference in behavior when these numbers tip into the majority and each exceeds 50 percent.

A recent study published by the journal *Group Processes & Intergroup Relations* found that meditation did reduce partisanship: "The results suggest that befriending meditation can reduce affective polarization between Democrats and Republicans by increasing positive feelings relatively more for the political outgroup than the political ingroup."[22]

There is hope, but the sooner the business community can act with one voice and demonstrate to the politicians that it can be done, the better. Business can lead us out of divisiveness through mindful action. Businesspeople just need to unify and use their influence mindfully. Blue Beyond recently surveyed and found:[23]

- Eight in ten employees want company values to align with

their own, however, only 57 percent said that was currently the case.

- One in four knowledge workers would accept a job that did not align with their values.

- Three in four expect employers and businesses in general to be a force for good in society.

Thus, employees are expecting their employers to step up and be a force for good, as well as to make a profit. In other words, pursue *Profit with Presence*.

Summary

Those are the tools of mindfulness available to business as laid out in the Twelve Pillars of Mindful Leadership. I hope they have also planted the seed of conversation for business once again to be the catalyst for creative destruction of the old system and generation of the new system that includes mindfulness and works better for everyone—including you and me.

If everyone was willing to "move the needle" according to their individual positions, skills sets, and abilities, I have no doubt we have a bright and mindful future.

Follow these mindfulness best practices:

- Don't share mindfulness in your business until you have achieved some stability in your personal practice.

- Consider starting with mindfulness trainings that don't include formal meditation.

- You'll know when it's time to share.

- Ponder planting seeds of mindfulness.

- Consider offering training and time in the workday to practice meditation.

- Mindfulness can increase the bottom line.

- Mindfulness can help navigate the trend toward remote work.

- Business can lead us out of divisiveness through mindfulness.

Chapter Takeaway

The goal of the mindful corporation is not to have everyone meditate, it's to transform the employees and company culture.

Preparing to Share Exercise

- Do your own mindfulness practice and to be ready when it's time to share.

- Do your research on what companies are already practicing mindfulness and contact your industry peers to see how they did it.

- Start reading up on corporate mindfulness.

- Make a list of all the people in your company who you feel may be the most open to mindfulness. Keep the list in a safe place so you can find it when you are ready to share.

Chapter 7

CONCLUSION: TOWARD A NEW CULTURAL WORLDVIEW

The most beautiful thing we can experience is the mysterious. It is the source of all true art and science. He to whom the emotion is a stranger, who can no longer pause to wonder and stand wrapped in awe, is as good as dead; his eyes are closed.

—ALBERT EINSTEIN

This concluding chapter uses the framework outlined in the book and my personal experience as the basis of an exploration of the possibility of a new cultural worldview. As an eternal optimist, I see a world that works for everyone with Presence.

I am not presenting this view as a fact or truth, just my perspective on the possibility for the future of human existence and business's potential role in creating it.

The day the world woke up

Close your eyes. Notice the dark, black, nothing, and everything at the same time. By removing visual distractions this points to reality, the universe, and universal consciousness. This points to your mind and universal mind. This points to Presence.

Open your eyes. Notice what you see. Notice your world is smaller and more defined. Notice the shapes, contours, and colors of life. That's your visual perception of the world and the human story of existence. This is not reality, it's your perception and a creation of the brain to make life actionable and for survival. The universe we see is of our own creation, as is the separate world we have created within it. We share this separate world through universal mind, and typically choose to live in only a small corner of it.

The truth is the world, the universe, consciousness, and our existence are a mystery. However, we were given human form to take action with Presence; our human form and the distinction of a separate world is what makes life actionable, and how we have survived as a species up until now. The way we take action is to know things in a relative sense, and we do that by our perceptions and by creating stories or myths we have mistaken for truth: The world is flat, the Sun revolves around the Earth, consciousness is created at conception, and the body is the limit of human existence, etc.

Humans believe they know things about how the world works and call it science and fact. Science tells us a lot about how things work in a relative sense, in relation to other material things, but has made scant inroads to explaining fundamental reality or why things work the way they do in any absolute sense. This would not be a problem if we acknowledged the mystery, but mostly we don't. We don't even really understand ourselves, what makes us act the way we do, what makes us happy, or how to get along with each other in a world that's a mystery.

Rather, we make up stories and call them knowledge of reality to make ourselves feel better, and as we each create our own universe and our own stories to explain it, we exaggerate our separateness, create large divisions between ourselves that we call counties, religions, culture, truth, or politics, and dig in trying to defeat the other side whose stories we find ludicrous and dangerous.

This works for a while despite infighting, political arguments, division, wars, and gradual planet degradation, until it becomes so toxic and divisive that it doesn't work anymore and planet Earth and its inhabitants face extinction. I don't know if we are there yet, it's a mystery, but the writing is on the wall. How bad does it need to get before the world wakes up?

What does waking up mean?

Waking up means residing in Presence and acknowledging what we know absolutely and what is a mystery. I know that I exist because I experience my existence through Presence. Presence is what I experience when I close my eyes, and I practice mindfulness to experience Presence with my eyes open as I go out and about, taking action in the material world. In Presence I know and experience love and compassion, which are there with my eyes closed, and I practice mindfulness to experience love and compassion with my eyes open as I go out and about in the material world taking action with Presence. So, I know I am Presence in reality and that I stand for a world that is present, mindful, loving, and compassionate. Everything else is a story.

The day the world wakes up is the day the people in the world realize it's okay to live in mystery, that it's healthy to have different stories and to disagree, that not knowing much absolutely is a strength that could hold us together, and that it's our fixed mindsets and inability to acknowledge the mystery that separate us. Disagreements are healthy as long as we are resolved to compromise on the path to inner and outer peace and prosperity. If we are going to live in a story—and we must, to some extent, have stories or myths to make life actionable and survive—why not make it an empowering story or myth in which the world works for ourselves and all of the world's inhabitants?

The Self-Soul-Spirit model

According to analytic idealism, each individual's consciousness may have many "sub-persons" within it. Historically, these have been referred to as archetypes, complexes, or sometimes alters. According to the Self-Soul-Spirit model, this phenomenon is posited as subpersonalities. Following that proposition, I use the term subpersonalities to refer to the multiple parts of an individual personality. Subpersonalities are not necessarily universal like archetypes were thought to be; rather, everyone has unique subpersonalities, which contribute to their overall self. Through awareness, Presence, and intention, you can intentionally direct the expression of subpersonalities from the energy of your soul, which stands for the deep essence and whole of yourself.

One of the beauties of the Self-Soul-Sprit model we first introduced in Pillar 2 is that a person, and their subpersonalities, is not good or bad, or right or wrong, they just are what exists. It's what each of us do with each subpersonality and our lives that matters. The key is to do something about it, which means to accept the possibility that subpersonalities exist within your overriding personality, become aware of the subpersonalities within yourself, and to embrace and accept them as part of you. I believe if each of us becomes aware and responsible for the parts or subpersonalities that drive our behavior, our problem and issues, and the world's problems and issues, may not be insurmountable mountains, but rather signposts pointing the way toward prosperity and peace. This is a possible path of a new cultural worldview in which mental health becomes personal empowerment. The potential is enormous.

In the Self-Soul-Spirit model, Self is determined by an interaction between genetic predispositions a person receives at birth and environmental conditions they are exposed to during their life. One's life further develops their subpersonalities in life experience through attraction and connection to elements of environmental and cultural experience, which correspond to their innate temperament. The multifaceted genetic contributions to particular psychological predisposition are then fostered through further attractiveness of life's experiences (e.g., athletic subpersonalities may find their love for sports, artists may find their love for art, or depressed subpersonalities may get reinforced by distressing circumstances at school or home, etc.).

Therefore, what you bring in genetically develops and grabs on to available experiences in the immediate environment, thereby expressing definite preferences or tendencies. Subsequently, the brain is further wired by neuroplasticity to reinforce the initial predisposition through continued use. This is a nature and nurture approach, rather than relying on conceptions that are limited to either nature or nurture. As such, while one's soul may change a subpersonality's expression through focus and intention, Self-Soul-Spirit holds that you are not in fact changing your subpersonalities or getting rid of them, you are directing, redirecting, or repurposing them with focus and consistent effort.

You are now possibly wondering how one becomes aware of these subpersonalities. A person can have many life situations during which one or another subpersonality may voice a thought or take action. For instance, when you have the thought or feeling, "A part of me wants [this] . . . yet another part of me doesn't," this is the dynamic of subpersonalities playing out within you. Like right now, a part of you (or a subpersonality) may want to embrace this approach, and likely another part does not.

A subpersonality may be helpful to the outcome in one situation and harmful to another situation. With awareness and practice, a person can direct which subpersonalities are dominant at a given time, and which ones are more dormant. This helps us excel and/or avoid self-sabotaging behaviors.

Ultimately, the self comprises a complex set of subparts that form a gestalt, or an organized whole that's greater than the sum of its parts. The totality of the parts is referred to as a "Mandala"—a symmetric circle representing the whole, or gestalt. The soul also stands to represent the essence of wholeness. As mentioned, the soul is the deep essence of who you are and has the capacity to direct life with intentional designs and meaningful expressions. Awakening the soul is a deep feeling where one becomes very connected to their felt sense of inner energy. This can take a lot of practice, but in my experience is well worth the effort.

Spirit is the great mystery, the universal consciousness, and that from which each individual's soul is ultimately derived. Individual's souls, as life forces created by the universe, also provide the opportunity for opening and connecting with universal Spirit. Seeking spiritual meaning and connection is crucial to many people's lives, and Self-Soul-Spirit supports spiritual-seeking as a unique, individualized process open to many interpretations. I have a subpersonality called "wise elder yogi" who loves seeking spirit through meditation, yoga, mindfulness, and transformational shocks of all types.

The epitome of success in this realm is discovery and development of your concept of an organizing Soul, and the intention of leading a Soul-directed life, versus a subpersonality-directed life, a.k.a., a life run amok.

Self Soul Spirit Gestalt

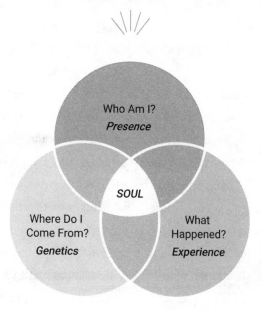

Your unique subpersonalities

While having a facilitator may help you discover this process more deeply, you can become aware of the competing subpersonalities within yourself right now; just begin to look inside yourself and examine your ways of being and self-expression. Do you have a part of you who is reading this book and another part of you operating at work, or possibly at home with family? If you begin to look at all your various moods, behaviors, and desires, you may find you have a community of distinct subpersonalities living inside of you. You and I, and all of us, may have been unaware of the existence of the various subpersonalities within ourselves. These subpersonalities can run our lives, for good or bad, until we become aware of their existence and reconcile them through our personal concept of Soul. If you try to focus, you will easily be able to start to identify major subpersonalities on your own to get started with the discovery of your innermost self.*

Looking inside yourself is not easy, but nothing rewarding is easy, and it does become easier with acceptance of yourself, and all the parts of yourself. By choosing Presence and discovering your personal Soul concept, you can accept responsibility for your own life and begin understanding how awareness of these subpersonalities can transform your life. Self-Soul-Spirit is a model, and therefore not espousing to be the truth or a doctrine of absolutism, but rather a process without a fixed destination.

Great thinkers and scientists note that while we cannot know truth, we can generate closer and closer approximations to what may be true. Therefore, the empowering process presented in this model may assist us in being more functional and intentional with our lives. Although many individuals may get along fine without such methods or interventions, often, parts of people run their lives without deeper intention and meaning, as was true for me for many years. This can sometimes lead to havoc, shame, division, and self-sabotage. Furthermore, without deep self-awareness, some lives will be continuously lived in a dull state of discontent. If we do create awareness and take personal responsibility for our complete body of selves and development of our Soul, then we can lead lives filled with joy and meaning, rather than in some state of dissatisfaction or discontent.

The same havoc, shame, division, and sabotage we are witnessing in our own countries and across the globe has possibly originated within each of us and been exaggerated due to our lack of awareness

---

* For additional information, you can read Dr. Roger Strachan's original paper, with Mado Reid, "Self • Soul • Spirit: A Current Working Model for Understanding Human Development," Center for Creative Choice, February 2011, https://drive.google. com/file/d/0B4056K8o_aRebWRtN2k5b0ktZkwwZ2E2ZEx0WDh3REpxMVQ0/ view?usp=drivesdk&resourcekey=0-PR_qMRlVBmEEqyBY725vjQ. You can also contact us at https://livinginthegap.org and get information on our Mindful Leadership Program where we support participants in this approach, and we have videos posted online, or we can point you in the right direction. You can also contact The Director of the Center for

and acknowledgment of what we know and what we don't know about ourselves and our world. It's likely that the people who are creating most of the havoc are largely not aware and accountable of the underlying causes and implications of their divisive behavior.

I do know that the place to begin to resolve divisiveness in the world is to search inside of ourselves with Presence to resolve our own inner conflicts and to understand ourselves better. Here you will find the love and compassion to yield a more empowering view the world.

If there is individual mind and universal mind, the concepts of Soul and universal Soul are not too abstract to consider. Universal mind and universal Soul may be signposts of where we look to for the future, and they all may be one phenomenon, like the universe and consciousness. If they exist, and we each search to tap into universal mind and/or universal Soul, the irreconcilable differences and problems in the world will fade as distant memories. It's certainly a mystery that I am not claiming to have solved, but find as an empowering possibility. I am certain that it's worth searching inside ourselves for the possibility of universal existence, as there could not be a more uniting concept.

The role of consciousness and the Self-Soul-Spirit model in my life

As I was raised, my mind evolved by drawing distinctions between things and defining and labeling them as separate, despite everything

Creative Choice, Ryan Holsapple, at RyanHolsappleGuide.com and watch for the website www.centerforcreativechoice.com to come back online. A good published source to learn more about subpersonalities is Fadiman and Gruber, *Your Symphony of Selves* (Rochester, VT: Park Street Press, 2020). Two books that introduce this topic, albeit not to the depth or completeness of the Self-Soul-Spirit model, but good introductions to the topic, are Shirzad Chamine, *Positive Intelligence* (Austin, TX: Greenleaf Book Group, 2016) and Todd Herman, *Alter Ego Effect* (New York: Harper Collins, 2019).

being composed of consciousness and ultimately connected. The result was that I came to understand myself as separate from the world, other things, and other people. This caused a lot of suffering in my life despite material success early in my life and career.

While I was born into this world with innate consciousness, I lived predominantly a life without Presence until I began practicing mindfulness. I was not living in the now with intention and mindfulness, and I was not aware of my Soul. I was unaware of the importance of Presence, and often parts of me would get away with behaviors without accountability and direction from my Soul. Whereas certain subpersonalities used to drive focus and energies toward problematic behaviors, I am now aware and responsible for their expressions.

I learned, through the discovery of the work you have in your hand, that the idea of separation from all else is false in any absolute sense, and of course, true in a relative sense. I am Eric, with my own body and life in relative terms, but my Soul is connected to *all, including you, the reader,* though universal spirit, and "I" am not here in an absolute sense. My physical body is of course here within your purview, but it's merely an icon, or dashboard representation of the immense Presence behind the icon.

By embracing Presence, I found even more awareness was possible through the discovery of my subpersonalities, and that they were seemingly disassociated with each other until I reconciled them through awareness and connection with my Soul.

The following is my personal experience of the phenomenon and reconciliation of my subpersonalities. In 2010 my wife, Tracy, and I entered marriage counseling to address a few longstanding marital and family issues, and after several sessions, Tracy announced, "I'm done with counseling; it's not for me."

Fortunately, a good friend suggested we meet with Dr. Roger Strachan, who worked with families in a different way. Tracy and I agreed to give it a try, and off to Prescott, Arizona, we went to meet with Roger and his partner at the time.

Tracy and I learned that we each exhibited default responses when certain subpersonalities of the other become evident. For example, I have a genetic part labeled "Teacher," and when this part would surface, Tracy seethed, as she did not want to be taught by her husband. Initially, this was surprising to me, although it shouldn't have been, but I learned how to set the "Teacher" subpersonality aside and focus on my "Husband" and "Lover" subpersonalities when I was interacting with Tracy, and things got much better. Of course, there were other subpersonality issues for us to address, too, but you get the point. For Tracy and me, this Self-Soul-Spirit subpersonality work was instrumental to resume a harmonious marriage and family life.

Additionally, I have a subpersonality labeled "Adventurer" and another labeled "Father." When my kids were younger, my Adventurer part was dormant, and my Father part was dominant.[†] This happened naturally and before my knowledge of subpersonalities, because my Father part was strong (and we had a lot of family adventures). It just was the situation at hand, and the subpersonalities organized to meet the moment.

I also have a subpersonality labeled "Driver" that accomplishes complex tasks like completing my doctorate, building a company, developing a shopping center, or writing this book. My Driver possesses an intensity that moves the world when it's called upon. Before gaining awareness of my subpersonalities and development of my Soul, I would allow my Driver subpersonality to surface on vacations,

---

[†] I must point out that physically having children does not automatically mean that one has a father subpersonality that embraces fatherhood; it just means a person has offspring, who may or may not be nurtured, mentored, and led in a positive direction in life.

often texting and emailing to keep things rolling at work and bringing an intensity to the trip that my family didn't find relaxing or appreciate. More recently on family vacations, my Soul set my Driver aside to focus on my other subpersonalities labeled "Adventurer," "Lover," "Father," and "Husband." As a result, everybody had a better time and came home feeling more rested and connected from the experience.

Through this work, my son Ryan and I have also transformed our relationship. Ryan and I have learned that he has a subpersonality labelled "Challenger," and I have a subpersonality labeled "Righteous," and when these two came out together, it was almost always a non-productive argument. We learned how to work to resolve our differences in a peaceful and productive way, by watching those subpersonalities with awareness, especially around the other. We brought other subpersonalities to the conversation that were productive and facilitated bonding for our relationship. Ryan brought out his lover of life, 6-year-old boy, his friend, his shaman, and his Soul; and I brought out my father, my 5-year-old boy, my friend, my wise elder yogi, and my Soul. Before, we argued a lot unproductively. Now we spend personal time together peacefully, and we run workshops together smoothly. Ryan is now completing his doctorate in this field of Depth Psychology and writing his dissertation involving subpersonalities and the Self-Soul-Spirit model.

Kaity and Kohlton each have their own subpersonalities and mandalas, and all of us have learned to get along and be in relationship with one another through thick and thin. It's not that we don't have the normal family issues, but we resolve them fairly quickly with conscious effort and the intention of having a harmonious family relationship, and greatly aided by the development of our Souls and knowledge of our individual subpersonalities.

Through this reconciliation process, I recalled the different lived experiences of several of my most dominant subpersonalities and will share their experience and stories with you now. When I was in high school, my "Athlete" subpersonality, who was rewarded by MVP and All Conference accolades, seemingly had a different lived experience than my "Addict" subpersonality, who was constantly in trouble, had the police over to my home repeatedly, crashed three vehicles during high school, and caused me to spend more time in the principal's office than I care to admit. My "Philosopher" and "Teacher" subpersonalities were largely dormant while my Addict sabotaged my successes, although later they were largely responsible for achieving my PhD in Economics and writing this book. My Addict subpersonality has now been repositioned to support my spiritual journey and my morning routine, rather than wreaking havoc in less useful places.

To summarize, the Athlete was rewarded, the Addict was reprimanded and shamed until sobered, and the Philosopher and Teacher, once kept in the dark by the shadow and shame of the Addict, were able to thrive once the Addict was tamed.

This conundrum of disconnected and sabotaging subpersonalities was daunting until I found the tools to be aware and reconcile them. It led me to search for answers to my own inconsistent behaviors, and then realize I could only fully pursue those answers once my Addict was embraced, accepted as part of me, and the other parts of me kept me sober. Discovery of the Self-Soul-Spirit approach and organization of my subpersonalities through my Soul was a relief and empowering realization personally, and it positively impacted my entire life.

For instance, the following is an example of my mandala with subpersonalities that were organized by my Soul to complete this book project. At the bottom are the parts that were not relevant to this endeavor. On the left are subpersonalities that were waiting to sabotage the collaborative effort.

Subpersonalities

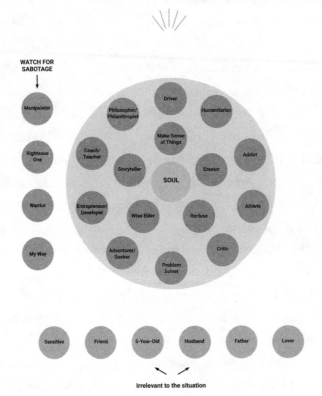

Now for my view of how my unique subpersonalities were possibly formed. My consciousness was first circumscribed or bounded within a human form when I was born in a body with genetic predispositions. Next, as I went out into the world and faced its challenges and traumas, its rewards and self-satisfying activities, my consciousness was further circumscribed when my subpersonalities formed during my development. One subpersonality was seemingly unable to immediately notice, recall, or recollect the experiences of another even within myself; thus, that subpersonality seemingly experienced a different, or separate, life. I often knew and acknowledged what I did, but the other parts of me did not understand and were frustrated by the behavior. They did not know why, or really "who" (or what subpersonality) did it. From the perspective of the Self-Soul-Spirit model, all the parts of us do exactly what they want to do at any given moment and then we try to figure out why and come up with a story after the fact to rationalize the behavior. What I learned is that some part of me was doing what it wanted to do, and the rest of me, including my Soul, was flabbergasted and angry while trying to pick up the pieces.

Now I know who did it, what they were up to, have reconciled the behaviors, and directed my subpersonalities through my Soul. I don't have those sabotaging events like I used to; the tendencies still exist, but with awareness of the subpersonalities and their tendencies, I am typically able to pause and reset, and do not allow them to derail me.

APPLYING THIS MODEL TO WORK

In the work context, I have become aware of the subpersonalities of "Entrepreneur/Developer," "Make Sense of Things," "Problem Solver," and "Coach/Teacher." Others in my company have identified their own mandala of subpersonalities.

I don't have a Manager subpersonality and do not do well with managerial or routine tasks. Fortunately, my partner, Blaine, has subpersonalities of "Manager" and "Organizer," so typically I create the business and he runs it. My professional subpersonalities have allowed me to rise to the top of most professional engagements; however, my sabotaging parts often left others resentful, causing many of my negotiated successes to collapse after I left the room.

I have worked hard at becoming more of a collaborator, but it's not one of my genetically spawned subpersonalities, so it does not come without focused intention. Negotiation comes naturally to me and is a subpersonality expressed as "My Way." This is helpful in transactional relationships, but can be disastrous in collaborative environments, so

I have learned to set that subpersonality aside in most instances. My awareness of this dynamic has made a tremendous difference in my professional relationships and related successes.

The entire LC Real Estate Group is on this path to different degrees, which, along with its vision statement, Mindfully Creating Community, has helped to simultaneously create *Profit with Presence*.

New cultural worldview

What got us here is not going to get us "*here*."

I have created an empowering vision of the world for myself in which world transformation with Presence starts with me. So, as you read these words, I hope that transformation has started with your adoption of mindfulness and Presence as being of paramount importance; and after you have secured your personal mindfulness practice, I hope it will further spread as you begin to share these principles with your work and professional associates, family, friends, school boards, churches, sports teams, communities, and literally the world.

I see a world in which business wakes up as a unified voice for transformation and is the melting pot for all ideologies, religions, races, cultures, politics, and beliefs. A world in which the next stage of creative destruction is to adopt and promote mindfulness and Presence through the powerful tools that science and business have already created, and many more that we haven't even dreamed of yet. Not long ago, we couldn't dream of traveling to the moon or communicating around the world instantly via the internet. This is a world where capitalism thrives, and we make *Profit with Presence* and use our abundance to make a difference for ourselves and for everyone else in the world too.

I see a world in which most people wake up and realize that most things in life are a mystery. This is a world where the existence of Presence, love, and compassion are not mysteries, but rather exist as reality for those of us who are willing to look inside of ourselves with Presence and practice mindfulness like our lives depend on it (and our lives, and the lives of our loved ones, may indeed depend on it).

I see a world in which psychology is transformed with more meditation and less medication, and a focus on awareness of ourselves and responsibility for our choices, including our subpersonalities, awareness of others, and our ultimate impact on the world.

I see a world in which most people wake up and accept themselves and each other just as they are, and differences, while debated, are also understood and celebrated, while divisiveness and aggression are rare and frowned upon.

I see a world in which people each create their own empowering story or myth to navigate the mystery of the world, and in which people acknowledge the mystery and the stories they create to exist in prosperity and harmony with each other, and with the entire planet and universe.

I see a world in which we all still have different opinions, but in which wars, poverty, starvation, drug addiction, homelessness, political divisiveness, and climate degradation exist, but are rare and short-lived occurrences.

I see a world in which we were born to take action with Presence, and all who do live with peace, joy, success, and happiness.

I see a world of *Profit with Presence.*

Where do we go when we die?

My view of the process of death has changed dramatically with Presence. In a relative sense, my body will die and dissolve back into the earth, and some people in my life will be sad. But I take comfort in the belief that my essence of consciousness will leave my body and be freed from the boundaries occurring at birth—and my skin bag—to once again swim in the great ocean of universal consciousness.

I look at death as an inevitable part of life and a pending adventure. We cannot do anything to avoid physical death, other than be as healthy as we can be, so why not accept death rather that dread it? The acceptance of death can be quite liberating, and potentially a homecoming, as my mom said in her last words spoken on earth: "I am home now."

I don't know where we go when we die; like consciousness, the universe, birth, and life, death is a mystery. My Adventurer subpersonality is standing by and dying to find out when the time comes.

This new cultural worldview is my story. I am not asking you or anyone else to take this as their story or their truth. I will assert that this new cultural worldview—which is not truly new but literally thousands of years old within the history of Yoga and meditation, once championed by the likes of Albert Einstein and Carl Jung, and more recently by scientists including Robert Lanza, Bernardo Kastrup, and others—is gaining acceptance and momentum in the world, and that is exciting.

That's my story of a new cultural worldview, and I am sticking to it until a more empowering cultural worldview comes along. You've generously read my book and my story. Now the pertinent question is:

What's your story?

Life is a series of choices. The main choice is whether or not to wake up, adopt Presence and accept life for the mystery it is, and realize we have a choice of what story or myth to live out in our lives. As you have read, you don't have to forgo material success; you can create *Profit with Presence* and make even a bigger difference in the world if you choose to do so. You, too, are possibly a bundle of subpersonalities awaiting Presence and your personal concept of Soul to take responsibility and direct your own subpersonalities, take charge of your life, and make the difference you were born to make.

For instance, right now part of you may be urging you to jump on the path of mindfulness and search for Presence, and to be optimistic and hopeful, while another part may be more skeptical about the state of the world and your current list of daunting responsibilities and see this approach to be impractical. Look to your concept of Soul to resolve the conflict and listen. Fortunately, it doesn't start with you abandoning your life and immediately setting out to save the world. It starts by simply searching inside yourself mindfully to examine yourself and your own experience of existence. It starts with the simple mindfulness practices you have been reading about in this book.

My suggestion and hope are that, whatever you choose, you acknowledge the mystery and make your story empowering and uniting rather than small and divisive. You have the tools to create an empowering life that moves the needle on your own personal vision for the world. Have beginner's mind, know nothing absolutely, and be curious. The world is waiting for you to take action with Presence. It's your turn and you matter. Start with small things and be consistent. Start with the practice of mindfulness in your own life. Possibly volunteer at a nonprofit if you have the time and inclination. That's enough for now. Pleasant, constant, persistent action with Presence will change the world.

Conclusion

Humans have the capability to evolve and manifest with Presence. Humans can maintain physical form and create *Profit with Presence*. Presence must be discovered, cultivated, maintained, and nurtured, much like a garden, if it's going to grow and be accessible in everyday life. To establish and maintain Presence as the default state takes intention and the practice of mindfulness.

If you want peace, joy, happiness, and satisfaction, establish Presence as your inner purpose in life, practice mindfulness, and simply be open to the possibility of life playing out as the most empowering story you create for it to be. Then see what shows up with Presence. You are the best laboratory of your own self, so begin to search inside yourself for the answers to life's biggest questions and let your concept of Soul captain your ship. *Profit with Presence* can point you to the way.

You are the seed of Presence, and the hope for a more mindful world. You matter. I wish you success traveling on the path with Presence, wherever it leads you. I appreciate your Presence. Thank you for reading *Profit with Presence*.

Remember that:

- The world is largely a mystery.

- We know we exist, and that Presence, love, and compassion exist.

- Business and creative destruction can be the melting pot for our perceived differences, and impetus for spreading mindfulness and Presence around the globe.

- We largely live in a story, either one that culture creates for us or that we create for ourselves.

- Make the story yours and make it empowering.

- You matter.

- Create *Profit with Presence*.

Final Takeaway

The world is a mystery; "waking up" is adopting Presence as your purpose, accepting the mystery, and creating an empowering life story, starting now.

AFTERWORD

It's amazing to me how creating a mindfulness program and writing a book made it so difficult to practice mindfulness. Being required to post and be on social media, create and promote a website, and log in three-week editing stretches of twelve-plus hours a day have made mindfulness more difficult in one way.

On the other hand, the precession effect of starting out to share what I have learned with the business community ended up with me learning way more about myself and the topic. Has it been worth it? Yes. In fact, the process has been worth it even if not one copy sells.

As for social media, it has some problems today, but those can be resolved, and like consciousness, it's virtual, so can be a powerful tool to promote mindfulness and do good in the long run.

This book is one of my first major writing assignments since my dissertation in 1996, and I have certainly appreciated the efficiency of Google's search engine. Social media and the internet are not going away, so we must resolve the issues, eventually.

Yes, I am an optimist. That's my story, and I hope I am right.

ACKNOWLEDGMENTS

While writing and editing this book, it became obvious that it was a "we" rather than a "me" endeavor. So, for my acknowledgments, let's play baseball:

At home plate, I would like to acknowledge Presence in my own life, which keeps pulling me forward and motivating me to learn and share more, so that others may experience the amazing effects of Presence in their lives, and especially at work. A world full of people with Presence is what pulls me forward when my ego screams, "What about me?"

At first base are my family and friends. Thank you to my wife, Tracy, who always has my back and has more intuition in her little finger than I have in my entire body. She has helped compensate for my lack of technical skills, and her help and intuition were invaluable. She also had to put up with my high level of intensity while writing and editing this book, which admittedly was not always completely mindful. Thank you, Tracy.

I also acknowledge my three grown children who are all on their own metaphysical journeys and have been my greatest teachers in life— you all inspire me. I was told not to be friends with my young children, and I am glad I didn't listen because I now have three best friends with whom to enjoy the journey of life:

Ryan, who co-facilitates our Living in the Gap workshops, is the director of the Center for Creative Choice and is finalizing his PhD in Depth Psychology at Pacifica;

Kaity, who runs her own Yoga and Somatic Yoga therapy workshops at Her Temple and assists with Yoga in our workshops; and Kohlton, who was the first one to apply to my Mindful Leadership Program when it launched and runs Credenzio Studios Game Development Company.

You are all equal to me in essence and ahead of me in most other areas of life. I love and appreciate you more than can be expressed in words here. Thank you.

Three others in my extended family have been an enormous influence on the direction of my life and ultimately the work in your hand:

My brother Bruce, who is a poet and one of my earliest and most consistent mentors. Bruce taught me how to be an intellectual, how to meditate, and how to live a scholarly life on my own terms. Please don't blame him for the poetry—it's my own. Thank you, Bruce.

Frank Spizuoco, or "Spook," has been my mentor, coach, teacher, and one of my best friends since birth. He means so much, he is family. He has taught me not to ever underestimate the impact you may have on someone by listening to them and treating them as an equal. He taught me never to give up on someone; people do change. He also taught me the value of community and of giving of yourself generously. Thank you, Spook.

Thank you to my cousin Steve Wiley, founder and president of the Lincoln Leadership Institute, who wrote the foreword, gave me constant encouragement, and convinced me that it's possible for a kid from rural Maine with a public education to be great. He also taught me the value of family and friends, and how to extend yourself for family and friends without hesitation. His encouragement and advice have been invaluable. Thank you, Steve.

I dedicate first base to my family. Thank you.

At second base is my work environment, where everyone who works with me is mindfully creating community. This book would not be possible without Erica Ellis and Chris Johnston. They are the prime movers on my Living in the Gap team and were always there to help when I most need it. Erica is our graphic designer and event coordinator, and is amazing. She never misses a deadline and has creative genius. She created the graphic images for this book. Chris, whom I met as a student at CSU, worked with me at the CSU Real Estate Center and later followed me to LC Real Estate and Living in the Gap. Chris has been instrumental once again in this endeavor. There seems to be no bottom to his reservoir of energy. These two compensate for my deficiencies. Thank you both so much—you are appreciated more than you know.

As highlighted in my dedication, I want to acknowledge the LC Real Estate Group, and all the fantastic participants of the Living in the Gap program. The lives they have created and changed by using the material contained on these pages gave me the inspiration to offer this work in a book format and share it with the broader business world. Thank you.

I dedicate second base, my work environment, to the people who work with the LC Real Estate Group and Living in the Gap. Thank you.

At third base are those providing community service to the world of mindful Presence through their astounding work in meaningful areas. There are three individuals who have directly contributed to the material and book's production. They have not only directly helped me in understanding and completing the process of creating the content and writing the book, they inspired me to write the book.

I appreciate the support of Larry Kendall, founder of Ninja Selling

Installations, and author of the highly successful book *Ninja Selling*. He has been a fantastic resource, describing the process and introducing me to Greenleaf Book Group, who allowed me to write the book I wanted to write. But more importantly, I watched Larry re-create himself in his sixties; he created Ninja Selling to change lives through business, taught with me at CSU, and wrote a successful business book. I don't think I would have known it was possible to make such a transformation late in life without his example, encouragement, and coaching. He also recommended invaluable books that expanded my perceptual map and opened my mind to a new approach to business. Many of those books are referenced within this one.

Thank you to Andrew Holecek, whom I met at his Dream Yoga retreat in Sedona several years back. Andrew similarly left a career in dentistry to create a life of sharing transformation though successful books, workshops, and more recently, his podcast, *Edge of Mind*. Andrew has led me down a path of inner discovery that has been transformative and introduced me to cutting-edge authors who have rocked my inner landscape, many of whose books are also referenced within this one. He is truly an intellectual and spiritual inspiration. We also enjoy golfing and snow skiing together, which is so much fun.

Thank you to Dr. Roger Strachan, who developed the Self-Soul-Spirit model, helped my family during a rough patch, trained Ryan and me in how to use and facilitate the model, and was a mentor and inspiration to create Living in the Gap and write this book. As I uncovered new research for this book, it became evident that he was way ahead of his time, and his work could eventually transform the way we perform therapy, from medication to meditation. Additionally, he has taken on mentoring my two sons and is turning his Center for Creative Choice over to my son Ryan.

To all three of these individuals, I offer my sincere appreciation and gratitude—thank you for helping me along the way in producing this book, and most of all, thank you for being an inspiration. Any misuse or misinterpretation of their teachings and guidance is my own.

Also at third base, I never would have gotten to the point of being able to write this book without the support and guidance of numerous mentors and teachers along the way. Many have been cited already, and there are simply too many to mention here, but all of their contributions are significant. Thank you to all my mentors and teachers along the way.

I dedicate third base, community service, to all my mentors and teachers who have taught me by example that community service is not just a calling that pulls you forward; it defines a life of "we" that is **worth living.** Thank you, all.

Finally, Greenleaf Book Group has a unique approach of allowing the author to have a say in the production and marketing cycle, which was particularly attractive to me as a successful entrepreneur who loves to be part of the process. Thanks to my project manager Brian Welch, fantastic editor Erin Brown, and the entire Greenleaf team for producing a great product on schedule, even with my finger in the middle of the process. Thank you for allowing me to bring this incredible life story to the business world and helping me "move the needle" on my vision for the world, that world transformation starts with me. That's a home run in my book.

I dedicate home plate to Greenleaf Book Group. Thank you.

I could go on, but please know there are too many who have been part of my journey to name here. Thank you to all who have been on my path and contributed in any small or significant way. It's sincerely appreciated.

Finally, I would like to express my appreciation and gratitude to the reader for your personal interest in mindfulness and Presence, not just in this book, but in becoming more mindful and considering sharing it with others when you are ready. You are the seed of Presence, and the hope for a more mindful world.

I will leave you with a final reminder to control your environment and load your bases with family and friends, work, and community service that are supportive of obtaining lasting Presence. If your bases are loaded and you hit one out of the park, it's not just an individual home run, it's a grand slam. **Loading your bases happens one hit at a time, and all the hits are sourced from home plate by residing in Presence and doing your personal mindfulness work.**

You matter. Thank you.

LIVING IN THE GAP
ADDITIONAL RESOURCES

L iving in the Gap is a nonprofit 501c3 corporation, and its website, www.livinginthegap.org, has the latest information on our workshops, events, and other material. We publish a monthly newsletter that is free to subscribe to on the website, highlighting key mindfulness concepts applicable to business and professionals.

There are also free resources available on the website that will allow you to get started with guided meditations, body scans, visualizations, mindful stretching, and more.

We regularly offer briefer introductions to our longer programs, and these offerings, when available, are posted on the website.

We currently have a popular annual offering of a nine-month Mindful Leadership Program in the fall of each year, and space is limited, so apply early.

We have an online three-week introduction to mindfulness program, and an online eight-week corporate mindfulness program and an online guide to complement this book are in the works, expected to be available in 2023.

Please follow us:

facebook.com/livinginthegap

linkedin.com/company/living-in-the-gap-501c3

youtube.com/channel/UCUQAoUMGzsoCYOrSaCyT6Hw

instagram.com/livinginthegap501c3/

Instagram handle: @livinginthegap501c3

We greatly appreciate your feedback and reviews. Thank you.

Appendix 1

SUMMARY OF CHAPTERS AND PILLARS, EXERCISES, AND MINDFULNESS PRACTICES

Chapter 1: Presence

- *Presence* is used as a universal term to denote a class of nondual state in which you can recall or reflect on experiences.

- *Presence* is the primary purpose of life and business.

- Duality and nonduality are both critical concepts to live a meaningful life, in which you accomplish things in the material world and make a *Profit with Presence*.

- Analytic idealism proposes that we each create our own universe, and together create the universe.

- Training and practice are what allow us to reside in Presence and still accomplish our personal, professional, and business goals.

CHAPTER TAKEAWAY

Presence is the primary purpose of life and business.

Chapter 2: Transformation

- Slow boils are small daily practices.

- Transformational shocks shift you directly into Presence.

- Slow boils allow transformational shocks to make a permanent, lasting difference.

CHAPTER TAKEAWAY

Transformation means the only thing that's permanent is your state of mind. Until you say otherwise.

Chapter 3: The Precession Effect

- Bodies in motion operate at ninety-degree angles.

- Service work can create opportunities, as well as an enhanced mindset.

- Be aware of the total impact of your actions, both positive and negative.

CHAPTER TAKEAWAY

The precession effect means the side effects of
an intentional action are often the main event.

Chapter 4: Spiritual Cross-Training

- A secular and multidiscipline approach allows broader access to mindfulness.

- The teachings are rafts to be discarded when no longer useful.

- Take what works to achieve Presence and discard the rest.

CHAPTER TAKEAWAY

These teachings are simply rafts to help you to achieve Presence
and should be released when no longer necessary.

Pillar 1: Be Present and Practice Mindfulness

- Practice mindfulness.

- Be present.

- If possible, meditate regularly.

- Use less formal practices of mindfulness while performing mundane tasks.

- Make physical activity mindful by noticing the inner energy body.

- Adopt the body scan and other tools to gain awareness of the inner energy body.

CHAPTER TAKEAWAY

Practice mindfulness as if your life depended on it.

Breathing Exercise[1]:

Sit in a quiet place with few distractions, with your spine erect so the breath can flow without restriction, and you can notice the breath. Keep your eyes open with a softened gaze focused downward in front of you several feet. Relax your body and find a comfortable position, in which the body does not distract you. Take 3 deep breaths through your nostrils. Next, count to 5 on the inhale, hold your breath for a count of 3, and count to 6 as you exhale slowly through the nose. Do this several times and notice the movement of the belly and ribs as you breathe. Don't manipulate the movement, just observe the movements as you breathe. Do this for several minutes to positively activate the vagus nerve. The longer you can do the exercise, the more it will impact the vagus nerve, but I always suggest starting with short durations consistently, and increasing the time gradually as you become familiar and comfortable with the practice. This is a great preparation for the meditation practice that follows in the next section.

How to Meditate

If you are not already experienced in meditation, here is a simple breath meditation practice.* Find a quiet spot to sit where you won't be interrupted. Start in a chair or on a cushion. Rock back and forth a few times on your sit bones and find a comfortable position with your spine erect.

Next, set a timer or alarm for two minutes.

I suggest having your eyes closed to begin with, but if that makes you anxious or uncomfortable, keeping your eyes open with a soft downward gaze two to three feet out in front of you is fine.† Place your hands in a comfortable position in your lap or on top of your thighs.

Breathe through your nostrils. Start focusing on your breath, just noticing and listening to the in breath and out breath. Follow your breath in and out of your body. Notice your stomach rise on

continued

---

* If you have meditation experience, have beginner's mind, as discussed in Pillar 12. Also, this may be an ideal time to lengthen your sessions or add some of the other practices coming up in later pillars.

† Meditation instruction is split on whether to have eyes open or closed. I have found that when becoming inner focused, especially when first learning meditation or when first sitting down, eyes closed generates the best experience of the inner world. When becoming outer focused, or bringing my meditation out to the world, I find eyes open generates the best result. I recommend eyes closed when beginning to establish a meditation practice or when starting a session, even for advanced meditators. And when concluding the session, keeping eyes open while continuing to meditate for several minutes aids in bringing the meditative state into daily life. Nothing says you can't do both. It's also fine to meditate exclusively with closed eyes or open eyes if that's your preference. Feel free to experiment.

the inhale and contract on the exhale. Be aware of your breath as it enters and exits the body.

Notice when you are distracted by a thought, noise, emotion, or anything else. As soon as you notice, let the distraction go and return your attention to your breath. You are teaching yourself the skill of detachment, as well as how to be present in the moment by being one with the breath.

If your mind is particularly busy, that's normal; you are meditating, so don't change anything. Notice the distraction, then let it go and return your attention to your breath. Keep returning your attention to your breath until the alarm goes off. It's like training a puppy; be persistent and gentle.

When time is up, open your eyes and continue to focus on your breathing for a few breaths before getting up. This is how you bring your meditation to the outside world.

That's it. You have just completed your first meditation session.

Commit to two minutes a day until it's a habit.

It's also okay to take a certain day of the week off if that's important to you.

Try to meditate at the same time and place each day.

If you miss your scheduled time, make it up later in the day. If you miss a day, don't miss the next day. Your goal is to do two minutes for twenty-one days straight. Then consider going to three to five minutes.

The most essential ingredient is consistency, so be as consistent as you can.

If focusing on your breath alone isn't working for you, counting can be helpful too. Instead of focusing on the breath, focus on the numbers while counting to 10 on the out breaths. Once you've reached 10, let the counting go and return to the breath. If you lose count, which is to be expected when beginning the practice, start over at 1. Once you can get to 10 easily, count backward from 10 to 1.

Even if you are very distracted, keep practicing. Noticing you are distracted, and returning to your breath, is meditation. As soon as you are aware you are distracted, you are present, which is something you can use all day long.

Body Scan Exercise

A body scan is a way to place your consciousness in your body while sitting still. It takes only a few minutes.

Find a comfortable chair or cushion and sit with your back straight and eyes closed.

Place your awareness in your feet. Notice that you can direct your conscious attention where you choose in the body. Start with the soles of your feet, slowly move on to your toes, and then to the tops of your feet. Spend several moments at each body part before moving to the next.

Now, carefully place your awareness in your ankles, shins, and then calves. Slowly continue up to your knees, thighs, and hamstrings. Gradually, move the focus of your awareness to your buttocks, genitals, and midsection.

Slowly become aware of your solar plexus, ribs, and lower spine. Move up to the heart area and upper spine. Become aware of your shoulders, biceps, forearms, wrists, and hands. Reverse the sequence and move awareness from your hands to wrists, elbows, biceps, and back to shoulders. Gently and slowly move

continued

your awareness to your neck, cheeks, ears, nose, eyes, brow, fore-head, and the top of your head.

At this point, flood your entire body, from the top of your head to your toes, with awareness. Notice any tension in your body and place your attention in those areas. Notice your ability to place awareness in your body and the lack of extraneous thoughts when you do so.

This is being in your inner energy body as a refuge from the mind, an exploration of consciousness and an accessing of your intuition, or gut.

Exercises

Try a body scan, mindful massage, or acupuncture and be open to feeling the inner energy body.

Pick your exercise of choice and go as slow and gently as you can to feel and notice the inner energy body. If you haven't yet, consider trying gentle Yoga for thirty days to get the feeling of the inner energy body. Then continue if you like it, or take that experience to your exercise of choice.

A note on practices: Perform practices regularly, daily if possible. Record the practices in the Practice Journal that follows or your own journal. This will heighten your awareness of what you are doing and track how regularly you do them. Try to do these practices while you continue to read this book for the maximum benefit of both.

- Read ten pages per day from an inspirational book, starting with *Profit with Presence*.

- Journal your dreams and whatever is coming up or bothering you.

- Gratitude: Journal three things you are grateful for and why.

- Breathwork sequence (5-3-6): 1 minute

- Body scan: 3 minutes

- Mindful movement: 5 minutes (activity of your choice)

- Meditation: 2 minutes

- Estimated duration: less than 30 minutes

Practice Journal

Date: ___ / ___ / ___   Woke: ___ : ___   Bed: ___ : ___

Any dreams?

_____

_____

_____

_____

_____

What are you grateful for?

1. _____

_____

Why?

_____

_____

_____

2. _____

_____

Why?

_____

_____

_____

3. _____

_____

Why?

_____

_____

_____

Breathwork sequence? Yes___ No___

Body scan? Yes___ No___

Meditation: _____ minutes

Yoga or mindful movement of choice: _____

Minutes: _____

Pillar 2: Identify Your Purpose in Life

- Your inner purpose is Presence.

- Soul connects our inner and outer purposes.

- Outer purpose is your various roles.

- Find your Element.

- The Self-Soul-Spirit model.

- The journey into your innermost self is a continuous process.

CHAPTER TAKEAWAY

Your inner purpose is Presence.

Exercise 1. How to explore the inquiry "Who am I?"

Once you have established your meditation practice, you can find your way with a meditation that changes the focus from breath to the question "Who am I?" Repeat the question silently and expect no answer during the session.

I typically do it for a few minutes and just let the question hang. Keep asking yourself, "Who am I?" silently on the out breath. It could be done for hours if you have the time and patience. As you sit with the question, you are in meditation or Presence itself. Allow Presence to fill the space of the inquiry. Keep practicing this until you identify yourself as Presence.

continued

Exercise 2

Point Finger.[2] Sit in a chair at least ten feet from the wall. Point your index finger at the ceiling and look at your finger and the ceiling. Next, point your finger to the wall and just look.

Now, point your finger to the floor and look. Notice how the ceiling, wall, and floor are "out there."

Continue by pointing your finger at your foot, then at your knee, then at your stomach.

Then move to point your finger at your eyes. Does anything shift?

You see your finger, but who is seeing the finger? Is it "little you" (i.e., your material body) within the eyes, or is there a "BIG YOU" (i.e., Presence) behind the eyes? Notice what's looking at your finger. Could it possibly be bigger than your eyes? Possibly even bigger than your face or body?

Ask yourself, "Who or what is looking?" Consider that it is your true essence or who you really are: Awareness, Consciousness, or Presence.

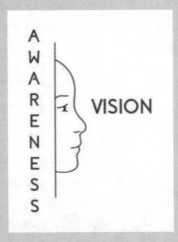

Exercise 3

Inner World. Find a quiet spot and sit with your spine erect and your eyes closed. Focus on listening to your breath for several rounds, then let the focus on your breath go. Dive deep within your inner self and sit in the darkness. Notice the space of the inner self. Let your body disappear in the vastness and notice the enormity of the space; in reality, the space is as large as the universe. Once you notice the enormity of the space, open your eyes, and notice the space shrink to fit within your visual landscape. Close your eyes again and regain the enormity of the inner space. Open your eyes and see if you can gain the awareness and spaciousness your noticed with your eyes closed, with your eyes open.‡ This enormous black hole of your inner world is the universe and Presence.

Exercise 4

Constricted Space. Stand in the middle of a quiet room with an open doorway in sight. Try to expand your vision as wide as possible and see as much of the room as you can with your peripheral vision. This is known as *wide angle vision*, and it slows down your brain waves. Close your eyes and notice the vastness and enormity of the space within the darkness. Open your eyes and try to gain as much of the feeling and sense of vastness

continued

‡ It's much harder to experience the feeling of vastness and the enormity of Presence with your eyes open, so don't be discouraged if you can't. Just close your eyes and regain the spaciousness. We do some more advanced practices to experience Presence in our workshops. Presence is a process, so be patient with yourself.

and enormity as you can and keep your vision within as wide an angle as possible. Next, slowly walk toward the doorway and notice the space shrink as you approach the doorway. Stand in the doorway and notice the space contract. Close your eyes and notice the vastness and enormity return.

Open your eyes. What difference do you notice? Your vision constricts your felt awareness or Presence; that's its job and allow you to focus.

Pillar 3: Create Clarity, Vision, Intention, Commitment, and Habits

Create:

- Clarity

- Vision

- Intention

- Commitment

- Habits

CHAPTER TAKEAWAY

Your habits are who you are—make Presence a habit.

Steps to Creating Your Vision

Creating our future is communicated through language. Future-based language transforms how situations occur to us and others.[3] The default future is a projection based on the past and told through descriptive language. What we resist persists. Future-based language transforms or literally replaces the default future, like Martin Luther King Jr.'s "I Have a Dream" speech, which put listeners in the future world without discrimination. State your vision using positive phrases, similar to affirmations.

1. Create clarity through mindfulness and discover your inner purpose and your Soul.

2. Go big and bold. Set your "vision for the world." This vision is overarching and personal. It could be for world peace, opportunities for all, equality, or a world where art is fully appreciated. It's your distinct vision for the world.

    Mine is "world transformation starts with me." I found mindfulness to be missing in much of the business world. From this vision, I created Living in the Gap Workshops and this book.

    What's important to you? Hunger? Education? Peace? Don't be shy. What matters to you? Notice any resignation or skepticism, and LET IT GO! Come back to your breath to create your personal vision for the world. To be honest, when I first attempted this, I couldn't sleep because I saw the world in such disarray, as I described in the preface.

3. Make a "life list" by setting out what you want to accomplish in important areas of your life. I suggest focusing on four main categories.

   - To Learn

   - To Be

   - To Do

   - To Have[§]

4. Create a vision board.

   - What is your vision for your life? Ask yourself, "How can I 'move the needle' on my vision for the world through the vision for my life?" (For instance, you don't have to solve world hunger, but you might join your local food bank.)

   - Make a 2' x 3' (poster size) color vision board that represents your life vision. Use magazine and online images or draw your own in color. Use as few words as possible.

The emphasis is on your life list and demonstrating Presence. Keep materialistic images to a minimum. But if you need a house, a house should be on your vision board. Being secure in a home may foster Presence. Also display what ways of being the house will provide, whether that is a close-knit family space, your sanctuary, or a haven for relatives. It is important that you

---

[§] For more detailed guidance, check out famous explorer and adventurer John Goddard's life list: https://johngoddard.info/index.htm.

place the vision board where you will see it daily. This will help you continually download your vision to your brain and the RAS (reticular activating system).

In our workshops, attendees also complete the extensive personal vision and plan exercise to include family, professional, financial, health, spiritual, relationships, service, hobbies, and more. You can write about these areas on your own; we set aside an entire day to draft it.

Once you complete your vision, you will have two points: 1) where you are, or "what is"; and 2) where you want to go, or "the vision." Having these points established, you can then chart your "path of development"—how to get from point 1) "what is" to point 2) "the vision."

Vision is critically important to create a future to live into and to be present. The clearer your vision is, the greater your ability to detach from it and be present. Training and practicing your morning or daily routine are key to achieving your vision and goals with Presence.

A promising future allows us to be present in the *now*, although it takes mindfulness practice, and specifically detachment, to accomplish it.

Visualization

Now that we have a vision, we need to visualize. Visualization is a practice of internally creating the vision to be as authentic and real as possible. Look at your vision board.

continued

Close your eyes, and picture yourself achieving one aspect of your vision in minute detail.

Consider the steps and process necessary to fulfill this vision in minute detail. Highlight the journey, celebrating 10 percent, 25 percent, 50 percent, 75 percent, 90 percent, and the most difficult, final 10 percent of the journey. Then celebrate achieving 100 percent of the goal!

Pick one word that best describes your feeling of accomplishment. Embody this felt emotion as it lifts you toward achieving the goal.

Consider how you will feel once you accomplish 100 percent of your vision and feel that emotion. Are you safe, secure, fulfilled, loved? Who are you with? Who will you call to share your accomplishment? Pick one word that best describes your feeling of accomplishment. Embody this felt emotion as it lifts you towards achieving the goal.

Embody that feeling in Presence as you prepare for the day ahead.

Take a few minutes each morning to look at your vision board and visualize, with emotions, making it as real as possible. When complete, review the steps you visualized and write them in your journal. Your intention will lead you to what the appropriate actions are to achieve your vision and goals. What actions can you take today?

Pillar 4: Success Is a Mindset of Be-Do-Have

- You can have it all.

- Success and happiness are states of being, not destinations.

- Success is a mindset of be-do-have.

- Train the mind so that you can live in Presence and still accomplish you vision and goals.

- Foster the mindset of being rich and of abundance.

CHAPTER TAKEAWAY

Be happy and successful now and achieve
your vision and goals with Presence.

Visualization Exercise

Select a professional or personal goal that is important to you, that you feel is reasonably achievable, but you haven't achieved yet. Keep it simple; there will be time to stretch later on.

Now let's turn the goal into a vision. For vision, we need to visualize. Visualization is a practice of internally creating the vision as authentically as possible. When you have some time and space to complete this exercise, find a quiet place and, while seated, do the following:

1. Close your eyes and focus internally, possibly after meditating or practicing breathwork, at least briefly.

continued

2. Call forth your goal with the intention to make it a reality, to complete it now.

3. Picture yourself achieving each aspect of your goal and envision it in minute detail. Picture yourself achieving each step in the process as you slowly progress through 10, 20, 30, 40, 50, 60, 70, 80, 90, and finally 100 percent of goal achievement, and notice how you feel, and what emotions are felt, at each step.

4. Take several minutes to mentally create each step you know has to be completed to achieve this goal and vision.

5. See yourself after completing 100 percent of the goal: Who are you with? Who do you tell? What emotions do you feel? Are you safe, secure, fulfilled, loved?

6. Consider all these feelings or emotions and pick one word that best describes the feeling of having accomplished your goal and vision.

7. Open your eyes and write down your word.

What was the one word? I have done this in all kinds of workshops and events and the participants have listed amazing things they have felt: unstoppable, invincible, free, successful, happy, joy, content, satisfied—the list goes on and on.

Next question: Is this feeling you wrote down real? I mean, come on, all you did was sit there. Did you really feel happy? How could you? You didn't achieve the goal! That's the point.

You have possibly been withholding happiness from yourself until some future event, rather than deciding, choosing, and allowing yourself to be happy (or unstoppable, invincible, etc.) now. Presence and happiness are choices you can make now.

Yes, it's that simple. And the good news is that having this improved mindset will make it even more likely you will accomplish this goal and the bigger ones coming up after you have been in this work for a while.

Journal this experience. Repeat the exercise after meditation for the next week. See what you notice. Do it when you feel down or are trying to accomplish something that's not going well. The more you practice visualization, the harder the tasks you can take on through this technique. Success begets success.

Pillar 5: Show Up, Take Action, and Detach from Results

Balancing Priorities
Don't Miss a Base

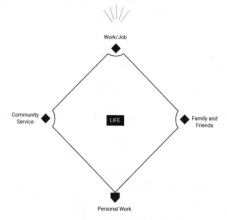

- Align your inner and outer purpose to assure motivation.

- Showing up starts by having a morning routine.

- Prioritize your duties, using the baseball analogy.

- Mindful leaders ask, "What can only I do?"

- Detach from results so you can be present.

- Train and trust the mind to deliver your vision, so you can be present.

CHAPTER TAKEAWAY

Detach from results and be present in the process.

Exercise

Notice when you show up and take action and when you don't, and then journal about what you notice about the experience and how you felt.

Pillar 6: Be Responsible, Practice Nonjudgment and Compassion

- Be responsible; you got this.

- Practice nonjudgment and start seeing people as people.

- Practice compassion; be connected rather than disconnected.

CHAPTER TAKEAWAY

An antidote for judging others is compassion.

Meditation on Compassion Exercise

Meditation on compassion.[4] For the next month, at the end of your meditation session, repeat the following phrases to yourself:

First verse
May you be held in compassion.
May your pain and sorrow be eased.
May you be at peace.

Second verse
May I be held in compassion.
May my pain and sorrow be eased.
May I be at peace.

Work on detaching from results and being present in all activities. Notice when you are attached to outcomes and journal about it for the next month as you meditate on compassion.

Pillar 7: Foster Relationships with Your Word and Listening

- Giving and keeping your word is the key to being trusted and having influence.

- Listening is the key to relationships.

- Forgiveness is important to clearing away negative energy.

CHAPTER TAKEAWAY

Mastering relationships with Presence
is the key to life and business.

Forgiveness Exercise

The Forgiveness Process. Visualize a setting that's familiar and empowering to you, like a nature setting; somewhere neutral for you and the person you wish to forgive.

Meditate for several minutes, following the breath. Visualize yourself as a person of great wisdom and compassion. Call forth an intention to resolve all conflicts in the world. Given your wisdom, you know that the process must start with you and the person who you feel needs to be forgiven. Call forth the intention to forgive this person genuinely, so you can both move on in peace.

You are not agreeing to bring the person back into your life unless you want to. You are free to set any boundary around forgiveness you wish, including never seeing or speaking to the person again. It also works with people you are in regular communication with.

You are forgiving the person to clear the air, to remove the negative energy in your system, and to be the first step in moving the needle toward world peace. It's that important.

Then picture the person you wish to forgive in the scene with you. Quietly, confidently, and nonemotionally, state what the person did to you that has caused negative feelings, attitudes, emotions, and possible resentment toward the person. This can be done silently or out loud; however you feel most comfortable. Take your time and re-create the feelings and resentment as if the person is there and continuing the behavior. Stay in that state until it feels as real as possible.

Next, close your eyes and look within. Search for any and every positive experience you had with this person, no matter how small. Try to remember anything the person ever did for you, perhaps doing good things for you or being a close friend. Maybe you still love the person even though the relationship is toxic. Everybody has redeeming qualities; find them. Maybe the acts committed made you see something about yourself that is fuel for personal growth. Look deeply until you find any positives you received from this person and what they did.

Ask what positives have or could come from it. Were any blind spots uncovered? Did it make you more self-reliant?

Next, return to meditation with your eyes open so you can read. Take a few breaths to reestablish the meditative state. Then recite these lines, either to yourself or out loud, whichever you prefer:

May you be held in compassion.
May your pain and sorrow be healed.
May you be at peace.[5]

continued

Keep your eyes open so you can read the next piece:

\\|//

There are many ways that I have been harmed by you.
I have carried this pain in my heart for too long.
I offer you forgiveness.
I forgive you.[6]

\\|//

Now, through compassion and love, forgive the person for what they did. Actually say the words out loud again with emphasis: "I forgive you."

This part can be challenging, but it's worthwhile. We start to expel the negative emotions by filling ourselves with love. When we're full of love, we have no room for negative emotions. Feel love and be released from negativity. Feel the positive energy flow into you as negative energy flows out.

When you feel a new energy in yourself, check in with your highest self and ask if you are complete.

Depending on what the person did, this can take some time and several attempts. Even if you feel complete, later resentments may creep back into your psyche. Your highest self will know if you're complete or need to repeat the practice to thoroughly forgive and receive the energy shift. Listen to your highest self until it gives you an indication that you are complete. If you try twice and are still not complete, then you may need other methods to achieve forgiveness or more time to pass. The statements "Time heals all wounds eventually" and "This too shall pass" may be helpful.

If you do feel complete, you can decide after this session whether you want to let the person know of your forgiveness or not. That's totally up to you. One effective way is to send a short, friendly letter. My suggestion is not to go into detail or tell a story, just say something like the following:

"I don't appreciate how you treated me, but I have decided to move on through forgiveness. I am still not wanting to see or hear from you; it just hurts too much. But I do forgive you. Love or Sincerely, _____." Sign it with your name.

You can write it and never mail it, or you can mail it. It's your process. Just don't feel as if you have to let the person back into your life unless you want to. If you are not positive you want to send the letter, or you don't want to give the person an opening to return to your life, don't send it. Put it away in a safe place, burn it, or throw it away. Time to move on to bigger and better things.

If this is a business relationship, know that I have found it never pays to burn a bridge. You don't need to burn the bridge; just don't do business with the person again. Businesspeople can resurface when you least expect it, or you need something you never expected to need. Just shut your mouth, close your email, and move on. That's my advice after many years in (mindful) business. As always, of course, it's totally up to you (and your highest self).

continued

Deep Listening Exercise

For this exercise, you will need a partner.

Center yourselves with several 5-3-6 breaths as described in Pillar 1's exercises. Select a partner A and a partner B. Share with your selected partner the following:

Consider that listening is best done from a state of silence and stillness. Listen for this silence and stillness and listen until it hurts. If thoughts come up, or you start thinking about what you want to say, try to set that aside and listen. While the other person is talking, don't say anything, even internally to yourself. Set aside whatever you are in the middle of and just listen for the next several minutes.

Once you both feel present, look into each other's eyes. When you each have this felt sense of connection, proceed with the following:

Partner A: Share when you haven't listened to someone else and when you haven't been listened to. Explain how it felt and how you think it made the other person feel.

Partner B: Listen and ask yourself, "How does the experience of listening impact me? How does the person occur to me? What images come up for me?"

Next, partner B, reflect back what you heard, without personalizing (e.g., I always do that!) or modifying the content. Partner B, then ask partner A, "Did I get it?" or "Do you feel like I heard you?" If your partner hasn't felt heard, ask which part, re-create it, and reflect it back until your partner feels the experience of being heard by another human. When this point is attained, switch. Partner B talks and partner A listens until partner B feels heard.

You will find ways to do this less formally in your conversations. I find this process invaluable in important business meetings when it may take quite an effort to get people back together again. My wife also appreciates when I am present enough to listen.

Practice listening less formally until you can fully hear others, as you were doing in the exercise. Then try this less formally, just by deep listening, and re-creating by simple statements like "Is that what you mean?" for the next month, and hopefully adopt it as a permanent practice.

Your Word Exercise

If you have any trouble with giving and keeping your word, keep a journal of when you give your word for *anything*, big or small, to yourself or to anyone else, for the next thirty days.

Note when you kept your word and when you didn't. When you don't keep your word exactly as you promised to someone else, clean up the situation by going back and correcting it with the person. This trains yourself that it's less effort and less embarrassing to keep your word than to have to clean it up. For promises to yourself, just be aware of them and recommit to yourself; awareness is curative, and you are listening.

Pillar 8: Be in Flow, Create Affluence and Influence

- Be in the flow of optimal experience, or Presence.

- Be in flow with people important to your being a mindful leader and with others important to your business or career.

- Create affluence.

- Affluence increases influence.

CHAPTER TAKEAWAY

Stay in Flow in both your internal state and with other important people such as other leaders and givers.

Flow Exercise

List all the people in your sphere and note the ones who are a positive influence and those who are not. Work to spend more time with positive influences and less time with those who are a less positive influence. Notice what difference this makes— it's profound.

Pillar 9: Be Grateful, Give Generously, and Serve

- Be grateful.

- Use a gratitude journal and practice gratitude.

- Give generously.

- Serve, and be aware of the precession effects.

- Abundance comes to givers.

CHAPTER TAKEAWAY

De-Scrooge yourself by being grateful, giving, and serving your communities: realize a new mindset and the precession effect.

Personal Notes Exercise

Write personal notes and send them to people you are most grateful for.

Random Act of Kindness Exercise

Perform a random act of kindness for someone each day for the next week, and don't let them know it was you.

Pillar 10: Acceptance Means to Stop Resisting and Complaining

- Acceptance is simply being present and accepting what is.

- Acceptance is often the key to change.

- Continual complaining can be a racket.

- Become aware of complaining.

- Complaining is resistance to what is.

- Accept and embrace death.

CHAPTER TAKEAWAY

Live with Presence and accept what is.

Two Obituary Exercise

Write two obituaries: one written as though nothing changes and you continue on the path you have been on, the second as though you make changes to become more mindful. The best way to predict this future is to create it by following the Twelve Pillars of Mindful Leadership.

Savasana Exercise

At the end of each mindful Yoga or stretching session, practitioners recommend lying stretched out on the four corners of your mat or carpet, and just rest, breathe naturally, and be aware of your body with your eyes closed. Do a body scan as described previously, from your toes to the top of your head, and experience being in the body. Next, let it all go. Let everything go. Let your flesh drop from the bones and melt into the mat or floor. Experience death while you are alive, die to this life, and let it all go. Visualize your own death, letting flesh go until all that is left is awareness. Rest for 5–20 minutes depending on your rest state and time availability. This Savasana pose is also called corpse pose or the little death. Practice it as often as you can.

Pillar 11: Take Everything Impersonally and Let Life Flow through You

- Take everything impersonally.

- What others do is usually about themselves, not you.

- Stop resisting "what is."

- You are empty of a separate existence and not as dense as you think you are.

- Let life flow through you.

CHAPTER TAKEAWAY

Nothing anybody else does is because
of you, it's because of themselves.

Journaling Exercise

When you take something personally, journal about it for the next week and see what you notice.

Affirmation Exercise

Journal "I accept what happens" twenty-five times per day, for the next thirty days.
See what you notice.

Pillar 12: Beginner's Mind Means to Know Nothing Absolutely and Be Curious

- Acknowledge you know very little absolutely.

- Be curious, as another antidote to judgment.

- Do The Work when stuck in a situation.

- Who knows what's good and what's bad?

- The mind is a garden, and gardens need maintenance.

CHAPTER TAKEAWAY

Be curious and ask probing questions rather than knowing.

Chapter 5: The Mindful CEO

- The mindful CEO is guided by mindfulness principles.

- The mindful CEO is not perfect, residing in Presence 24/7, or void of material possessions.

- Mindful leadership is a choice and a series of choices.

CHAPTER TAKEAWAY

The mindful CEO is the key to building a mindful company culture.

Mindful CEO Exercise

Look at your calendar and track your time for the next month to see where you may be wasting time that could be used to support your mindfulness practices.

Answer the question: Of all your duties, what can only you do?

Make a list of all your work associates and start to consider who may be open to practicing mindfulness and whom you might be willing to share these practices with first when you are ready. Put the list away in a safe place.

Search for other CEOs, leaders, or professionals in your communities who practice mindfulness and reach out to ask them what their experience has been.

Chapter 6: The Mindful Corporation

- Don't share mindfulness in your business until you have achieved some stability in your personal practice.

- Consider starting with mindfulness trainings that don't include formal meditation.

- You'll know when it's time to share.

- Ponder planting seeds of mindfulness.

- Consider offering training and time in the workday to practice meditation.

- Mindfulness can increase the bottom line.

- Mindfulness can help navigate the trend toward remote work.

- Business can lead us out of divisiveness through mindfulness.

CHAPTER TAKEAWAY

The goal of the mindful corporation is not to have everyone meditate, it's to transform the employees and company culture.

Preparing to Share Exercise

- Do your own mindfulness practice and to be ready when it's time to share.

- Do your research on what companies are already practicing mindfulness and contact your industry peers to see how they did it.

- Start reading up on corporate mindfulness.

- Make a list of all the people in your company who you feel may be the most open to mindfulness. Keep the list in a safe place so you can find it when you are ready to share.

Chapter 7: Conclusion: Toward a New Cultural Worldview

- The world is largely a mystery.

- We know we exist, and that Presence, love, and compassion exist.

- Business and creative destruction can be the melting pot for our perceived differences, and impetus for spreading mindfulness and Presence around the globe.

- We largely live in a story, either one that culture creates for us or that we create for ourselves.

- Make the story yours and make it empowering.

- You matter.

- Create *Profit with Presence.*

FINAL TAKEAWAY

The world is a mystery; "waking up" is adopting
Presence as your purpose, accepting the mystery, and
creating an empowering life story, starting now.

Appendix 2

YOGA IS THE SCIENCE OF CONSCIOUSNESS

An introduction to Yoga

The Sanskrit word *Yoga*—when distinguished with a capital *Y*—means to unite the body with consciousness. Thus, when humans practice Yoga in the ancient traditions laid out in this appendix, they are experimenting with consciousness. Modern yoga—when distinguished with a lowercase *y*—can exist more in the world of exercise and not necessarily embody this experimentation with consciousness, although that potential lies within your intention while practicing anywhere.

Yoga is thousands of years old, and it's only been in the last one hundred years or so that its "asanas," or postures, have become the dominant part of the practice. Historically, Yoga was used in preparation for meditation, and if done with consciousness exploration as a primary impetus, Yoga is meditation with the body. This is the Yoga we are discussing in this appendix. There is nothing wrong with modern yoga that doesn't involve consciousness exploration, but it's not as germane to this discussion.

Yoga involves stretching, particularly stretching that is utilized to bring attention into a specific part of the body. By placing your conscious attention into the stretched, or stressed, part of the body, we detach from thought and allow that part of the body to change simultaneously.

We cannot place our focus in our body while thinking of other things at the same time. This practice proves that multitasking with focus is a myth. When we practice Yoga, we are being mindful and aware of our bodies, especially our inner energy bodies as described in Pillar 1.

As bears repeating, the observer principle tells us that when we observe something with focus, it changes the object. Focusing your attention on a part of your body allows it to change. This makes consciousness, awareness, or Presence "curative."

What follows is a taste of the features of this ancient practice. Yoga was my entry into mindfulness, and I have learned that a person can go as deep into the exploration of consciousness through Yoga as with any other method. (Note: I have not included pranayama—breath work— that accompanies the deeper Yoga practices.) I learned the following practices while obtaining my advanced teacher training at Kripalu Center for Yoga and Health, in Lenox, Massachusetts.*

---

* More information can be found on their website: www.kripalu.org. There are other places and a plethora of information online if you are interested.

Let's begin by learning the Eight Limbs of Yoga. The Sanskrit words are used, and I do my best to give the English equivalent; however, there is not always an equivalent word in English.

The Eight Limbs of Yoga:[1]

1. *Yama*: abstinences

2. *Niyama*: observances

3. *Asana*: Yoga postures

4. *Pranayama:* breath control

5. *Pratyahara:* withdrawal of the senses

6. *Dharana:* concentration

7. *Dhyana:* meditation

8. *Samadhi:* absorption

I am not going to go into the detail of each limb, but you can easily research the Eight Limbs of Yoga by Patanjali, who was the founder of these principles along with the Yoga Sutras.

Let's continue by introducing the knower and the known, the *Gunas*, and the chakras.

PURUSHA AND PRAKRITI

In ancient Indian philosophy, *Samkhya* (reality) is divided into two categories: *Purusha* (the knower) and *Prakriti* (the known). Purusha is never an object of experience; it is the subject, the one who is aware, the one who knows. We have been describing this as consciousness, or as the "watcher," or Presence. Prakriti, on the other hand, is all that is known. It is everything that comes before us in the objective universe. It can be psychological or material.

THE GUNAS[2]

The Gunas are the three fundamental forces that make up the limitless potential of Prakriti. These forces are *Sattva, Rajas,* and *Tamas.* Prakriti manifests as the universe through the interplay of the Gunas. Everything that can be known in the universe, both tangible and intangible, is the manifestation of the Gunas in their various forms.

Guna means "strand" or "fiber" and is similar to the strands of a rope. The universe is formed from the various Gunas as they're woven together. This theory explains what our universe is made up of and how it came to manifest itself as mind and matter.

Awareness of the Gunas tells us whether we are indeed progressing in life (sattva), static (rajas), or regressing (tamas). They are very valuable as you move forward on the spiritual path. By understanding the "feel" of each Guna and utilizing the knowledge, you can move closer to recognition of the knower, Purusha, or Presence.

CHARACTERISTICS OF THE GUNAS

Sattva: Allows light of conscious awareness to reveal itself in the mind and in nature; not enlightenment but unveils what is real. Beauty, balance, inspiration. Promotes life, energy, health, and contentment. This has been described previously as "flow," or simply Presence in English.

Rajas: Energy of change distinguished by passion, desire, effort, and pain. May cause movement to sattva or tamas. It can be positive or negative. Unsteady, agitated, unhappy. Binds us to attachment, the fruits of action, and to sensory pleasures.

Tamas: Conceals the presence of consciousness. Causes dullness and ignorance through the power to obscure, and is heavy and dense. This leads to inaction when action is necessary, and results in lethargy, procrastination, and sleep.

THE GUNAS IN LIFE

Bhagavad Gita

The Bhagavad Gita ("The Song of God") is one of the most revered texts of the Yoga tradition. It encompasses the nature of divinity, humankind's ultimate destiny, and the purpose of mortal life. This ancient Indian scripture is presented as a conversation between Arjuna, a prince, and Krishna, a man and a god, a seeker, and a knower.

THE GUNAS AS GUIDES

The Gunas form an essential piece of *The Bhagavad Gita*. As Krishna so proclaimed, There is nothing on the earth, in heaven, or even among the gods, that is not impacted by the Gunas. The Gunas can be signposts that reveal where you are and where you are inspired to be. Krishna's advice is to hone your powers of discernment and self-observation. The theme of his message is that we can learn to be observers of the Gunas and utilize them with a sense of purpose and balance. In order to do this, it's crucial to discern the look and feel of each Guna. Here's a more in-depth guide to the Gunas:[3]

	Sattva	Rajas	Tamas
The food you eat may:	Taste good and promote health and a pleasant mind	Be over-salted, highly spiced, and cause illness and depression	Be stale, unwanted by others, and not fit as an offering
The gifts you offer to others may be:	Given at the right time with nothing expected in return	Given reluctantly or with the aim of gaining a returned favor	Given at an inappropriate time or place, with disrespect or contempt
The steadfastness with which you approach your spiritual path may:	Help you bring your mind, breath, and senses into harmony	Depend on your acquiring something you want	Preoccupy you with fears, grief, and excessive sleep
Your happiness may:	Arise from inner discrimination and increase over time	Be overly sensual: sweet in the beginning, poisonous in the end	Arise from sleep, lethargy, and negligence

Next, let's explore the chakras, or energy wheels in the body. For a good reference for the chakras consistent with this emphasis on business, see Deepak Chopra's new book, *Abundance*. I will lay out the chakra system and leave it to the interested reader to find additional sources, which are plentiful.

The Chakras

7th Chakra - Crown
Violet
Sahasrara

6th Chakra - Third Eye
Indigo
Ajna

5th Chakra - Throat
Blue
Vissudha

4th Chakra - Heart
Green
Anahata

3rd Chakra - Solar Plexus
Yellow
Manipura

2nd Chakra - Sacral/Naval
Orange
Manipura

1st Chakra - Base/Root
Red
Mulahera

Chakra Attributes

Chakra #	Element	Body	Gland	Purpose	Instinct	Seed Sound	Gems
7th	Prana	Brain, Hormone, Skin Balance	Pineal	Higher Self/ God	Universal Identity	Silence	Diamond Amethyst
6th	Light	Eyes, Nervous System	Pituitary	Intuition	Enlightenment Self-Realization	OM	Lapis Quartz
5th	Ether, Sound	Throat, Vocal Chords	Thyroid, Parathyroid	Logos- Speech	Truth	HAM	Turquoise
4th	Air	Lungs, Heart, Rib Cage	Heart	Home of the Soul	Love and Compassion	YAM	Emerald Tourmaline Jade
3rd	Fire	Abdomen, Liver, Spleen	Adrenals	Fight or Flight	Power	RAM	Amber Topaz Apatite
2nd	Water	Urinary Tract	Pancreas	Will to Live	Sexuality	VAM	Coral Carnelian Yellow Zircon
1st	Earth	Feet, Legs, Pelvis	Testicle/ Ovaries	Reproduction	Survival	LAM	Ruby Garnet Hematite

Next, let's briefly explore the main *nadis* in our system. Nadis are energy channels, pathways for our life force energy, or Prana, to travel.

There are sometimes suggested to be over 72,000 nadis or channels in our system. There are three main channels. It's beyond the scope of this work to go into these, other than to note them and their importance.

Breath runs though the *Ida* (right nostril) and *Pingala* (left nostril).

The largest nadi is the *Sushumna Nadi* that runs along the spine and is the gateway for "Kundalini energy." In Hinduism, this (divine feminine) energy is believed to originate at the base of the spine and bring power and energy to our entire system.

These nadis are one reason why posture is so important. A crimped spine reduces energy flow, and an erect spine promotes energy flow. This is why I am introducing such an advanced concept here.

The diagram below will give you the idea, and those interested can do further research.

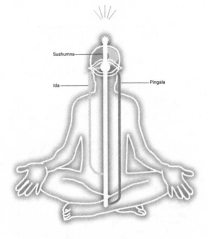

Kundalini
Energy Body
The Three Nadis

What are samskaras?⁴

Samskaras are the subtle impressions of past actions or karma. We continuously perform actions, and many of them contribute to the formation of samskaras. Actions that we perform with full awareness are the ones that make the greatest impression on our minds. It's the intention behind the action that gives power to that action. The literal meaning of the word *samskara* is made up of two parts: "sam" means well-planned, well thought out; and "kara" means "the action undertaken." Thus, samskara means "the impression or impact of the action we perform with full awareness of its goals." When we perform such an action, a subtle impression is deposited in our mind field. Each time the action is repeated, the impression becomes stronger. This is how a habit is formed. The stronger the habit, the less mastery we have over our minds when we try to execute an action contrary to our habit patterns. These habit patterns subtly yet powerfully motivate our thoughts, speech, and actions.

Habit patterns become so ingrained that they alter our body chemistry and are called "addiction." When they become strong enough to alter our thinking process, it is called samskara. We no longer remember when or how this process started. It takes introspection or retentive power to discover the realm of the mind where these samskaras are stored. When our mental world is under the influence of these powerful impressions, they become the determining factors of our personality. Due to these samskaras, our perceptual world is dominated by our habitual ways.

HOW THEY AFFECT US

In life, we have performed all kinds of actions, right and wrong, good and bad. Good deeds create positive samskaras; bad deeds create negative ones. Our mind is a warehouse of positive and negative samskaras. It's up to us whether we exercise our willpower and determination to strengthen or eliminate a particular group of them. Negative samskaras can be eradicated, provided you learn to capture those bright and delightful moments when positive samskaras are in full bloom.

In deep depression, we may lose hope, but we should never lose faith in life itself. The will to live and the desire to find some meaning in life should never die. And if we follow our undying will, we'll be able to overcome the influence of our negative samskaras. We need patience.

Shamanic cord cutting

Sometimes our neural pathways and inner energy body, pain body,[5] or as termed in the Sanskrit language, samskaras have such a significant impression that forgiveness practices aren't enough to release the negative impact of a poor relationship with another.

A powerful and often effective option is trying to reset your electromagnetic field. This is a shamanic practice that can release deep impressions.[†]

Electromagnetism is responsible for practically all the phenomena encountered in daily life. It governs the orbiting electrons in an atom. The electromagnetic field comprising the heart chakra is 5,000 times bigger than the field around the brain.

---

†   I learned this work through a Yoga and Shamanism Program with the Jaguar Path. We perform cord cutting on request in our Living in the Gap workshops.

Energy lines known as "cords" attach from one person to another. When a relationship is alive and healthy, the cords help us communicate with and feel one another. We feel each other deeply as the exchange of energy is visceral. When a relationship is over or perhaps changed, the push and pull sensations being transmitted via cords can become stressful and unhealthy.

Ceremonial shamanic cord cutting is an effective technique to reset the electromagnetic field, establish new boundaries, and end or reestablish relationships on acceptable, healthy terms. If you decide to try this method, you'll need to find someone trained in shamanic work who can effectively help you cut the cord.

Next, a brief Yoga, or mindful stretching, routine is provided to get you started; remember, the actual poses are secondary. Your conscious attention to the body parts being stressed and stretched is the primary objective of Yoga. You can also find free beginning resources on our website, www.livinginthegap.org.

Beginning Yoga & Mindful Stretching Routine

1. Ankle/Toe Rotation
Eight in each direction.

5. Spinal Twist
Legs stationary, arms wrap waist lightly, one in front and one in back, alternating. Head and neck follow.
Eight in each direction.

2. Knee/Ankle Circles
Feet together, knees bent, hands to thighs.
Eight in each direction.

6. Spinal Wave
Eight waves up the spine from tailbone through neck. Knees slightly bent, arms relaxed at sides, just working the spine.

3. Hip Circles
Legs straight, spine loose.
Eight in each direction.

7. Neck Circles
Eight in each direction.
Slow and gentle!

4. Shoulder Rolls
Eight in each direction.

8. Wrist Circles
Eight in each direction.

Adapted from Ron Collins, 'Dasha Chalana (8 Churnings)', www.finishingwellyoga.com/uploads/6/0/5/0/60509535/dasha_chalana.pdf

Beginning Yoga & Mindful Stretching Routine

9. Standing Pigeon
Hold foot in hand with shoulders back, balancing with other foot, balance with hand to wall until you can balance without assistance. Stretch the entire front side of the body. Once each side.

10. Standing Full Extension
Tuck tail bone, stretch to right side, then to left side, then toward rear of room.

11. Standing Forward Fold
Keep knees bent, hands to shins with flat back, then extend hands to floor or block. Roll up slowly, one vertebrae at a time with knees bent.

12. Mountain Pose
Feel feet firmly on the earth, shoulders back, palms forward, looking straight ahead.

Beginning Yoga & Mindful Stretching Routine

13. Tree Pose
From Mountain Pose, shift weight to left foot. Bend right knee, place right foot alongside inner left calf; above or below knee. Adjust position so the center of pelvis is directly over left foot. Press your palms together in prayer position at heart center, with thumbs resting on your sternum. Hold hands in prayer position. Hold for 20 seconds up to 1 minute. Step back into Mountain Pose. Repeat for the same amount of time on the opposite side.

14. Malasana Pose
Squat with your feet as close together as possible. (Keep your heels on the floor if you can, otherwise, support them on a folded mat.)
Separate your thighs slightly wider than your torso. Exhaling, lean your torso forward and fit it snugly between your thighs. Start with your back against a wall and gradually sink until you can sit on a block. Once you have gained flexibility, press your elbows against your inner knees, bringing your palms to together, and resist the knees into the elbows. Hold the position for 30 seconds to 1 minute, then inhale, and straighten the knees.

Beginning Yoga & Mindful Stretching Routine

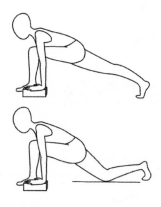

15. Low Lunge Pose: Bring left foot directly under left shoulder. Gently shift weight on left leg and bend downwards. Left knee is bent with hands supporting weight on sides. Use blocks if that is more comfortable. Front foot should be flat on floor, making an angle of 90 degrees. Try to keep right leg stretched out behind you. Stretch head up feeling tension at the back of thighs and shoulders.

Hold the position for 15 to 30 seconds as a beginner. Later you may hold it even longer; a minute or more. Breathe in once.
Gently exhale and revert to the starting position. Repeat on the other side.

16. Crescent Pose: Step right foot forward between hands, aligning knee over the heel. Keep left leg strong and firm. Inhale and raise torso to upright. At the same time, sweep arms wide to the sides and raise overhead, palms facing eachother. Be careful not to overarch the lower back. Lengthen tailbone toward the floor and reach back through your left heel. This will bring the shoulder blades deeper into the back and help support your chest. Draw the front ribs into the torso. Lift the arms from the lower back ribs, reaching through your little fingers. Hold for 20 seconds to a minute and repeat with the left foot forward for the same length of time.

Finally, here are a couple of good books if you are interested in learning more when starting out your practice:

Yoga and The Discipline of Freedom by Barbara Stoler Miller
The Genius of Yoga by Alan Finger and Peter Ferko
Yoga for Pain Relief by Lee Alpert (Kripalu Staff)
The Subtle Body by Christiane Northrup, MD

Appendix 3

MINDFULNESS RESEARCH

To supplement the material you found in the introduction and Pillar 1, the following is a summary of some additional research on the benefits of mindfulness you may find useful.

The book *Altered Traits: Science Reveals How Meditation Changes Your Mind, Brain, and Body* by Daniel Goleman and Richard J. Davidson is a great reference. Goleman and Davidson found long-time meditators' brains were younger by seven and a half years compared with nonmeditators at the age of fifty and that meditation slowed brain atrophy generally.[1] They write, "You may have heard the good news that meditation thickens key parts of the brain."[2]

This landmark scientific research, involving long-time meditators, found that enduring traits such as selflessness, equanimity, and Presence can be altered through epigenetics embodied in our genes. This is one step beyond habits, and if this piques your interest, put *Altered Traits* on your reading list. The most important component is to practice mindfulness, but often we need motivation to practice. Some further research is provided to support your mindfulness journey:

Mindfulness reduces overthinking

In one study, researchers asked twenty novice meditators to participate in a ten-day intensive mindfulness meditation retreat. After the retreat, the meditation group reported increased mindfulness and decreased negative effects compared with a control group. They also experienced fewer depressive symptoms and less overthinking.[3]

As you read in Pillar 1, it's believed we have around 6,000 thoughts per day, most of them repetitive and many negative. If you decreased your negative thoughts and slowed your mind down, you could also lower your stress level.

Mindfulness reduces stress in the workplace

For many of us, we feel the most stress at work. Decisions need to be made quickly, sometimes we are the only ones who can make them, deadlines need to be met, there are meetings with shareholders, employees, investors, banks, etc. All these lead to increased stress.

You employees feel the stress as well. At LC Real Estate Group, employees have experienced less stress as a result of mindfulness practice.

Have you ever walked into a room where an intense meeting has been held or an argument has occurred, and you can *feel* the difference in the air even though no one is in the room? You can feel the stress they left behind.

Your employees feel the stress as well. It has been shown that mindfulness reduces employee stress, mitigates the risk of burnout, and builds one of the most valuable capacities today: resilience.

A few minutes of meditation each day allows your nervous system to return to a state that is deeply rejuvenating and healing.

Mindfulness boosts creativity and innovation

Creativity and innovation are essential assets that enable you and your businesses to stay ahead of the curve.

Researchers at Erasmus University in Rotterdam, Netherlands, set out to understand the impact of mindfulness on creativity and its capacity to increase a clear, solution-oriented state of mind. They found that a mindfulness practice, even in those who had no prior meditation experience, led to significant increases in innovative thinking and the subjects were able to generate an increased range of ideas.[4]

Mindfulness improves focus

Researchers compared a group of mindfulness meditators with a control group that had never meditated before. They found that the meditation group had significantly better performance on all measures of attention and higher self-reported mindfulness, correlating directly with cognitive flexibility and attentional functioning—the ability to achieve and maintain an alert state.[5] I have noticed a dramatic improvement in performance and decrease in stress related to our employees' improved focus achieved through mindfulness practice.

Mindfulness improves memory and test scores

Goleman and Davidson also found that mindfulness improved working memory and students' GRE scores by more than 30 percent.[6] These researchers found that as little as two weeks of practicing produced less mind wondering, and better focus and working memory.[7]

In just weeks, practicing mindfulness can increase your memory. Improved memory has an abundance of benefits, such as being more efficient and reducing stress.

Mindfulness lowers emotional reactivity

Practicing mindfulness will help you reduce anger and anxiety, and stay calm or recover faster.

People who had only one month of meditation practice were able to disengage quicker from emotionally upsetting thoughts while enhancing focus on cognitive tasks.[8]

Disengaging from anger creates calmness for you, your family, and coworkers.

Mindfulness improves relationships and communication skills

A leader's ability to be mindful can improve the quality of their relationships by improving their ability to be compassionate and empathic and to communicate better, even during stressful or challenging times.[9]

Mindfulness helps achieve better health

Evidence suggests mindfulness meditation has numerous health benefits, including increased immune functioning, better sleep, and improvement in overall well-being.

As noted when discussing bottom line impacts, Mark Bertolini, former CEO of Aetna, a Fortune 100 company with more than $30 billion in revenues and more than 20 million members, says that with mindfulness, employees' stress levels dipped and Aetna's overall health-care cost dropped about $2,000 per year. Aetna has had over 13,000 employees participate in mindfulness training. Additionally, Aetna estimated the productivity gains alone amounted to $3,000 per employee, an eleven-to-one return on its investment.[10]

Your company would likely observe decreased call-ins from coworkers and employees, and the decreased strain on health insurance costs for them and your company.

The mindfulness field is becoming widely accepted, even by some ardent skeptics, due the evolution of scientific research. But remember, you are a researcher too, so rely on your own practice and experience to believe the benefits of mindfulness. That's all I needed. Some impacts are immediate, and others take time. Get on the path and trust yourself and the process.

NOTES

Preface

1. Barbara Walter, *How Civil Wars Start* (New York: Crown, 2022).

Introduction

1. Joseph A. Schumpeter, *Can Capitalism Survive? Creative Destruction and the Future of the Global Economy* (New York: Harper Perennial, 2009).

2. David Gelles, *Mindful Work* (Boston, MA: Houghton Mifflin, 2015) 173–177.

3. Rich @ SportofMoney.com, "How Rich Are Americans on a Global Scale? Very Rich!" SportofMoney, September 27, 2019, https://www.sportofmoney.com/how-rich-are-americans-on-a-global-scale-very-rich/.

4. Joni Sweet, "Happiness Doesn't Top Out at $75,000," Verywell Mind, January 26, 2021, https://www.verywellmind.com/happiness-doesn-t-top-out-at-usd75-000-study-says-5097098.

5. Tristan Bove, "Bill and Melinda Gates are giving their foundation a record $20 billion in response to ' the great crises of our time'," *Fortune*, July 13, 2022, https://fortune.com/2022/07/13/bill-melinda-gates-foundation-20-billion-record-donation-warren-buffett/.

6. Robert Frost. "The Road Not Taken." *Atlantic Monthly*, August 1915, https://www.poetryfoundation.org/poems/44272/the-road-not-taken.

Part 1

1. Robert Lanza and Matej Pavsic with Bob Berman, *The Grand Biocentric Design* (Dallas, TX: BenBella Books, 2009) 1.

Chapter 1

1. Peter Senge, C. Otto Scharmer, Joseph Jaworski, Betty Sue Flowers, *Presence* (New York: Doubleday, 2004) 13.

2. Thich Nhat Hanh, *Old Path White Clouds* (Berkeley, CA: Parallax Press, 1991).

3. Bruce Holsapple, *Air Rose* (Portland, ME: Contraband Press, 1975).

4. Donald Hoffman, *The Case Against Reality* (New York: W. W. Norton, 2019) 142.

5. Lynne McTaggart, *The Field* (New York: HarperCollins, 2008) XXIII.

6. Bernardo Kastrup, *Decoding Jung's Metaphysics: The Archetypal Semantics of an Experiential Universe* (United Kingdom: Iff Books, 2019) 110–111.

7. Rupert Spira, *The Nature of Consciousness* (Oxford, England: Sahaja, 2017) 14.

8. Zemeckis, Robert. *A Christmas Carol.* (Walt Disney Studios Motion Pictures, 2009).

9. https://quotefancy.com/jim-carrey-quotes; quote 2.

10. Ideas and Opinions (1954) as reprinted in *Beyond Biocentrism*, 29. Robert Lanza, MD, with Bob Berman, *Beyond Biocentrism: Rethinking Time, Space, Consciousness, and the Illusion of Death* (Dallas, TX: BenBella Books, 2016).

11. Lanza, MD, *Beyond Biocentrism.*

12. Lanza, MD, Beyond *Biocentrism*, 120.

13. Edward F. Kelly and Paul Marshall, eds, *Consciousness Unbound:*

Liberating Mind from the Tyranny of Materialism (Lanham, MD: Rowman and Littlefield, 2021) 267, 275.

14. Bernardo Kastrup, *The Idea of the World* (United Kingdom: Iff Books, 2019) 54.

15. Kastrup, *The Idea of the World*, 2019, 60.

16. Kastrup, The Idea of the World, 2019, 66.

17. Kastrup, The Idea of the World, 2019, 69.

18. David J. Chalmers, *The Conscious Mind: In Search of a Fundamental Theory* (Oxford: Oxford University Press, 1997).

Chapter 2

1. Bruce Hyde and Drew Kopp, *Speaking Being: Werner Erhard, Martin Heidegger, and a New Possibility of Being Human* (Hoboken, NJ: John Wiley and Sons, 2019) 252.

2. Jeff Olson, *The Slight Edge* (Austin, TX: Greenleaf Book Group Press, 2013).

3. Olson, *The Slight Edge*, 2013, 40.

4. Michael Pollan, *How to Change Your Mind* (New York: Penguin Books, 2018).

5. Walter Isaacson, *Steve Jobs* (New York: Simon and Schuster, 2011) 34.

6. Lao Tzu, *Tao Te Ching*, ed. and trans. Stephen Mitchell (New York: Harper and Row, 1988).

Chapter 3

1. R. Buckminster Fuller, *Critical Path* (New York: St. Martin's Griffin, 1982).

2. "Precession," *Britannica*, https://www.britannica.com/science/precession, accessed June 11, 2022.

3. Vin Bhalerao, "How Buckminster Fuller's Principle of Precession Can Change Your Life," Medium, February 2022, https://medium.com/@

vinbhalerao/how-buckminster-fullers-principle-of-precession-can-change-your-life-f4cb39da2c2d?.

4. Christine McDougall, "Precession and Integral Leadership," *Integral Leadership Review*, August 2011, http://integralleadershipreview.com/3285-precession-and-integral-leadership-2/.

5. McDougall, "Precession and Integral Leadership," 2011.

6. Bhalerao, "How Buckminster Fuller's Principle of Precession Can Change Your Life," 2022.

Chapter 4

1. Walter Isaacson, *Steve Jobs* (New York: Simon and Schuster, 2011) 15.

2. The second precept of the Order of Interbeing, from Thich Nhat Hanh, *Living Buddha, Living Christ* (New York: Riverhead, 2007) 2.

Part 2

1. Walter Isaacson, *Steve Jobs* (New York: Simon and Schuster, 2011) 34.

2. Dan Harris, *10% Happier* (New York: HarperCollins, 2014).

Pillar 1

1. Eckhart Tolle, *Stillness Speaks* (Novato, CA: New World Library, 2003) 7.

2. Oprah Winfrey, "What Oprah Knows About the Power of Meditation," O, the Oprah Magazine Online, August 2016, https://www.oprah.com/inspiration/what-oprah-knows-about-the-power-of-meditation#ixzz5AUMcHMHf.

3. Crystal Raypole, "How Many Thoughts Do You Have Each Day? And Other Things to Think About," Healthline, February 28, 2022, https://www.healthline.com/health/how-many-thoughts-per-day.

4. Jon Kabat-Zinn, *Mindfulness for Beginners* (Boulder, CO: Sounds True, 2016) 1.

5. Emma Seppälä, "20 Reasons to Start Meditating Today," *Psychology*

Today, September 11, 2013, https://www.psychologytoday.com/us/blog/feeling-it/201309/20-scientific-reasons-start-meditating-today.

6. Daniel Goleman and Richard Davidson, *Altered Traits: How Science Reveals How Meditation Changes Your Mind, Brain, and Body* (New York: Avery, 2017) 6.

7. Quote Fancy, https://quotefancy.com/quote/856052/Mahatma-Gandhi-I-have-so-much-to-accomplish-today-that-I-must-meditate-for-two-hours, Accessed on August 3, 2022.

8. Jack Dorsey (@Jack), "Just finished a 10 day silent meditation. Wow, what a reset! Fortunate & grateful I was able to take the time. Happy New Year! #Vipassana," Twitter, January 1, 2018, 11:40 a.m., https://twitter.com/jack/status/947885229464805382.

9. Elizabeth Williams, *Daily Vagus Nerve Exercise* (Coppell, TX: Liberty Books, 2020) 17.

10. Adapted from Williams, *Daily Vagus Nerve Exercise*, 2020, 103–104.

11. Thich Nhat Hanh, *The Miracle of Mindfulness* (Boston, MA: Beacon Press, 1999).

12. Cyndi Dale, *The Subtle Body* (Boulder, CO: Sounds True, 2009) 9.

13. "Quantum Theory Demonstrated: Observation Affects Reality," Science Daily, February 27, 1998, https://www.sciencedaily.com/releases/1998/02/980227055013.htm.

14. Deepak Chopra, *Abundance* (New York: Harmony Books, 2022) 1.

15. Moshe Feldenkrais, *Awareness through Movement* (New York: HarperOne, 1977) 38.

16. Chopra, *Abundance*, 2022, 1.

17. Barbara Stoler Miller, *Yoga as the Discipline of Freedom* (New York: Bantam, 1998) 29.

18. Feldenkrais, *Awareness through Movement*, 1977, 48.

19. Feldenkrais, Awareness through Movement, 1977, 59.

20. Feldenkrais, Awareness through Movement, 1977, 58.

21. Feldenkrais, Awareness through Movement, 1977, 59.

22. Feldenkrais, *Awareness through Movement*, 1977, 59.

23. Joseph Parent, *Zen Golf: Mastering the Mental Game* (New York: Doubleday, 2002).

24. Fred Shoemaker, *Extraordinary Golf* (New York: Tarcher Perigee, 1997).

25. George Mumford, *The Mindful Athlete* (Berkeley, CA: Parallax Press, 2015).

26. Phil Jackson, *Sacred Hoops* (New York: Hyperion, 2006).

27. Kayla Kazan, "Huge List of CEOs That Meditate at Work," *Peak Wellness*, March 9, 2020.

Pillar 2

1. Stephen Mitchell, trans., *The Bhagavad Gita* (New York: Harmony, 2002) 191.

2. Eckhart Tolle, *A New Earth* (New York: Plume, 2006) 258.

3. David Deida, *The Way of the Superior Man* (Boulder, CO: Sounds True, 2004) 44–46.

4. Napoleon Hill, *Think and Grow Rich* (Shippensburg, PA: Sound Wisdom, 2017).

5. Laurie Mintz, "Mindful Sex Is Mind-Blowing Sex," *Psychology Today*, November 12, 2017, https://www.psychologytoday.com/us/blog/stress-and-sex/201711/mindful-sex-is-mind-blowing-sex.

6. Mintz, "Mindful Sex Is Mind-Blowing Sex," 2017.

7. Emily Nagoski, *Come as You Are* (New York: Simon and Schuster, 2015) 2.

8. Nagoski, *Come as You Are*, 2015, 3.

9. Tolle, *A New Earth*, 2006, 115.

10. Tolle, A New Earth, 2006, 56.

11. Ramana Maharshi, *Who Am I? The Teachings of Bhagavan Sri Ramana Maharshi* (Tiruvannamalai, India: Sri Ramanasramam, 2008).

12. Doug Harding, *Face to No-Face* (Carlsbad, CA: Inner Directions, 2000).

13. Viktor Frankl, *Man's Search for Meaning* (Boston, MA: Beacon Press, 2006) 69.

14. Ken Robinson, with Lou Aronica, *The Element* (London, UK: Penguin Books, 2009) 42–44.

15. Robinson and Aronica, *The Element*, 2009, 20-25.

16. Carla Tardi, "80–20 Rule," *Investopedia*, March 11, 2022, https://www.investopedia.com/terms/1/80-20-rule.asp.

17. Daniel Goleman and Richard Davidson, *Altered Traits: How Science Reveals How Meditation Changes Your Mind, Brain, and Body* (New York: Avery, 2017).

18. Bernardo Kastrup, *The Idea of the World* (United Kingdom: Iff Books, 2019) 54, 67-71.

19. Adapted from Joseph Campbell, *Pathways to Bliss* (Navato, CA: The New World Library, 2004) xxiii, xxiv.

20. Joseph Campbell, *The Hero with a Thousand Faces*, 3rd ed. (Novato, CA: New World Library, 2008). Adapted and paraphrased, various pages, especially 57: "Supernatural Aid"; 74: "The Belly of the Whale"; and 196: "Master of the Two Worlds."

Pillar 3

1. Herbert Spencer, from *Alcoholics Anonymous*, 4th Edition (Alcoholics Anonymous World Services, 2001) 568.

2. Shakespeare, *Hamlet* (New York: Simon & Schuster, 1992) act 2, scene 2.

3. Emma Young, "Lifting the Lid on the Unconscious," *New Scientist*, July 25, 2018, https://www.newscientist.com/article/mg23931880-400-lifting-the-lid-on-the-unconscious/.

4. Marissa Levin, "The Top 10 Leadership Blind Spots, and 5 Ways to Turn Them into Strengths," *Inc.*, July 13, 2017, https://www.inc.com/marissa-levin/the-top-10-leadership-blind-spots-and-5-ways-to-tu.html.

5. Joan Shafer, Adam Bryant, and David Reimer, "Revealing Leaders' Blind Spots," *Strategy+Business*, April 29, 2020, https://www.strategy-business.com/article/Revealing-leaders-blind-spots.

6. Wallace Wattles, *The Science of Getting Rich* (Langhorne, PA: Jon Rose, 2015) 19.

7. John Assaraf and Murray Smith, *The Answer* (New York: Atria Books, 2008).

8. Lynne McTaggart, *The Intention Experiment* (New York: Free Press, 2007) 143.

9. Joe Haefner, "Mental Rehearsal and Visualization: The Secret to Improving Your Game Without Touching a Basketball!" Breakthrough Basketball, https://www.breakthroughbasketball.com/mental/visualization.html?filterreviews=upvotes; Alan Richardson, "Mental Practice: A Review and Discussion, Part 1," *Research Quarterly* 38 (1967): 95–107.

10. Karin E. Hinshaw, "The Effects of Mental Practice on Motor Skill Performance: Critical Evaluation and Meta-Analysis." *Imagination, Cognition, and Personality* 11, no. 1 (1991): 3-35, 7, 27.

11. James Clear, *Atomic Habits* (New York: Avery 2018).

12. Steve Hagen, *Meditation: Now or Never* (New York: HarperCollins, 2007) 83.

13. Clear, *Atomic Habits*, 2018.

14. Clear, Atomic Habits, 2018, 236.

Pillar 4

1. Shawn Archor, *The Happiness Advantage* (New York: Crown Publishing, 2010) 15.

2. Archor, *The Happiness Advantage*, 2010, 15.

3. *Merriam-Webster*, s.v. "rich (adjective)," accessed May 19, 2022, https://www.merriam-webster.com/dictionary/rich.

Pillar 5

1. Stephen Mitchell, trans., *The Bhagavad Gita* (New York: Harmony, 2002).

2. Andrew Holecek, *Dream Yoga* (Boulder, CO: Sounds True, 2016) 67.

3. Sadhguru, *Karma: The Yogi's Guide to Crafting Your Destiny* (New York: Harmony, 2021) 39.

4. Mitchell, *The Bhagavad Gita*, 2002, 54–55.

5. Mitchell, The Bhagavad Gita, 2002, 55.

6. Thomas M. Sterner, *The Practicing Mind* (Novato, CA: New World Library, 2005) 23.

Pillar 6

1. Bruce Hyde and Drew Kopp, *Speaking Being: Werner Erhard, Martin Heidegger, and a New Possibility of Being Human* (Hoboken, NJ: John Wiley and Sons, 2019) 507.

2. Steve Hagen, *Meditation: Now or Never* (New York: HarperCollins, 2007) .

3. Jack Kornfield, *The Wise Heart* (New York: Bantam Books, 2008) 34.

Pillar 7

1. Eckhart Tolle, *Stillness Speaks* (Novato, CA: New World Library, 2003) 97.

2. Arbinger Institute, *The Outward Mindset* (Oakland, CA: Berrett-Koehler, 2016).

3. Eckhart Tolle, *A New Earth* (New York: Plume, 2006) 109.

4. Melinda Fouts, "Being Mindful in Your Relationships," *Forbes*, July 19, 2018, https://www.forbes.com/sites/forbescoachescouncil/2018/07/19/being-mindful-in-your-relationships/?sh=5b9bfe20ceaa.

5. Jack Kornfield, *The Wise Heart* (New York: Bantam Books, 2008) 33–34.

6. Adapted from Kornfield, *The Wise Heart*, 2008, 351.

7. Jessica Morales, "The Heart's Electromagnetic Field Is Your Superpower," *Psychology Today*, November 29, 2020, https://www.psychologytoday.com/us/blog/building-the-habit-hero/202011/the-hearts-electromagnetic-field-is-your-superpower.

8. Bob Burg and John David Mann, *The Go-Giver* (New York: Penguin, 2007) 27.

9. Burg and Mann, *The Go-Giver*, 2007, 27.

Pillar 8

1. Larry Kendall, *Ninja Selling* (Austin, TX: Greenleaf, 2017) 58.

2. Mihaly Csikszentmihalyi, *Flow: The Psychology of Optimal Experience* (New York: HarperCollins, 1990) 2.

3. Csikszentmihalyi, *Flow*, 1990, 49.

4. Hal Elrod, *The Miracle Morning* (Temecula, CA: Hal Elrod International, 2014).

5. Csikszentmihalyi, *Flow,* 1990, 105, 117, 144.

6. Lao-tzu, *Tao Te Ching*, ed. and trans. Stephen Mitchell (New York: Harper and Row, 1988) 68.

7. Deepak Chopra, *Creating Affluence* (San Rafael, CA: Amber-Allen and New World Publishing, 1998) 21.

8. Deepak Chopra, *Abundance* (New York: Harmony Books, 2022) 59.

Pillar 9

1. Robert Greenleaf, *Servant Leadership* (Mahwah, NJ: Paulist Press, 1977) 27.

2. Robert Emmons, *Thanks! How Practicing Gratitude Can Make You Happier* (New York: Houghton Mifflin, 2008) 29.

3. Wallace Wattles, *The Science of Getting Rich* (Langhorne, PA: Jon Rose, 2015) 43.

4. Bob Burg and John David Mann, *The Go-Giver* (New York: Penguin, 2007) 19, 37, 59, 77, 97.

5. Adam Grant, *Give and Take* (New York: Penguin, 2013), 9.

6. Grant, *Give and Take*, 2013, 261.

7. Emmons, *Thanks!*, 2008, 54.

8. Wattles, *The Science of Getting Rich*, 2015, 91.

Pillar 10

1. *Alcoholics Anonymous*, 4th ed. (Alcoholics Anonymous World Services, 2001) 417.

2. Jeff Foster, *The Deepest Acceptance* (Boulder, CO: Sounds True, 2012) xiii.

3. Carl Rogers, *On Becoming a Person* (New York: Mariner Books, 1961, 1989) 17.

4. Foster, *The Deepest Acceptance*, 2012, 42.

5. Foster, The Deepest Acceptance, 2012, 65.

6. Joseph Parent, *Zen Golf: Mastering the Mental Game* (New York: Doubleday, 2002) 14.

7. Steve Zaffron and Dave Logan, *The Three Laws of Performance* (San Francisco, CA: Jossey-Bass, 2009) 45.

8. Andrew Holecek, *Preparing to Die* (Boston: Snow Lion, 2013) 3.

9. Bronnie Ware, *The Top Five Regrets of the Dying* (Carlsbad, CA: Hay House, 2019) summary.

10. Eckhart Tolle, *Stillness Speaks* (Novato, CA: New World Library, 2003).

Pillar 11

1. Don Miguel Ruiz, *The Four Agreements* (San Rafael, CA: Amber-Allen, 1997) 47–49.

2. Ruiz, *The Four Agreements*, 1997, 49.

3. Byron Katie with Stephen Mitchell, *Loving What Is* (New York: Harmony, 2002) 1.

4. *Twelve Steps and Traditions* (Alcoholics Anonymous World Services, 2009) 125.

5. Michael Singer, *The Untethered Soul* (Oakland, CA: New Harbinger, 2007) 153.

6. J. Krishnamurti quote from Eckhart Tolle, *A New Earth* (New York: Plume, 2006) 198.

7. Thich Nahn Hahn, "The Heart Sutra: the Fullness of Emptiness," *Lion's Roar*, February 10, 2022, https://www.lionsroar.com/the-fullness-of-emptiness/.

Pillar 12

1. Shunryu Suzuki, *Zen Mind, Beginner's Mind* (New York: Weatherhill, 1997) 90.

2. Lao-tzu, *Tao Te Ching*, ed. and trans. Stephen Mitchell (New York: Harper and Row, 1988) 65.

3. Lao-tzu, *Tao Te Ching*, 1998, 71.

4. Suzuki, *Zen Mind, Beginner's Mind*, 1997, 21.

5. Matthias Birk, "Why Leaders Need Meditation Now More Than Ever," *Harvard Business Review*, March 22, 2020, https://hbr.org/2020/03/why-leaders-need-meditation-now-more-than-ever.

6. Byron Katie with Stephen Mitchell, *Loving What Is* (New York: Harmony, 2002) 2–3.

7. Noah Rasheta, "Who Knows What Is Good and What Is Bad?," *Secular Buddhism*, August 2015, https://secularbuddhism.com/who-knows-what-is-good-and-what-is-bad/.

8. Michael McGown, "'Remember to Look Up at the Stars': The Best Stephen Hawking Quotes," *Guardian*, March 14, 2018, https://www.theguardian.com/science/2018/mar/14/best-stephen-hawking-quotes-quotations.

9. James Clear, *Atomic Habits* (New York: Avery 2018) 236.

Part 3

1. Ray Dalio, *Principles* (New York: Simon & Schuster, 2017) 465.

Chapter 5

1. Walter Isaacson, *Steve Jobs* (New York: Simon and Schuster, 2011) 35.

2. Adapted from Arbinger Institute, *The Anatomy of Peace* (San Francisco, CA: Berrett-Koehler, 2008) 131.

3. Rob Dube, "Why More Companies Are Cultivating a Culture of Mindfulness," *Forbes*, March 25, 2019, https://www.forbes.com/sites/robdube/2019/03/25/why-more-companies-are-cultivating-a-culture-of-mindfulness/.

Chapter 6

1. Evan Williams, Wisdom 2.0 Conference, San Francisco, CA, 2013.

2. Arbinger Institute, *The Outward Mindset* (Oakland, CA: Berrett-Koehler, 2016).

3. Arbinger Institute, *Leadership and Self-Deception*, 3rd ed. (Oakland, CA: Berrett-Koehler, 2018); *The Anatomy of Peace*, 4th Edition, (Oakland, CA: Berrett-Koehler, 2022).

4. Hal Elrod, *The Miracle Morning* (Temecula, CA: Hal Elrod International, 2014).

5. Christian Greiser, "How Companies Can Instill Mindfulness," *Knowledge at Wharton*, April 19, 2018, http://knowledge.wharton.upenn.edu/article/how-companies-can-instill-mindfulness/.

6. Shelley Abrams, "Mindfulness in the Workplace: Is It Worth the Hype?" Transcend Strategic Consulting, September 1, 2020, https://www.transcendstrategic.com/blog/2020/9/1/mindfulness-in-the-workplace-is-it-worth-the-hype.

7. David Gelles, "The Mind Business," *Financial Times*, August 24, 2012, https://www.ft.com/content/d9cb7940-ebea-11e1-985a-00144feab49a.

8.   Steve Zaffron and Dave Logan, *The Three Laws of Performance* (San Francisco, CA: Jossey-Bass, 2009) 207.

9.   Abrams, "Mindfulness in the Workplace," 2020.

10. David Gelles, *Mindful Work* (Boston, MA: Houghton Mifflin, 2015) 173–177.

11. Larry Kendall, "Real estate culture-building template for virtual teams, agents," *Real Trends*, November 11, 2021, https://www.realtrends.com/articles/real-estate-culture-building-template-for-virtual-teams-agents/.

12. David Pachter, *Remote Leadership* (Herndon, VA: Amplify Publishing, 2021).

13. Kendall, "Real estate culture-building template for virtual teams, agents," 2021.

14. Pachter, *Remote Leadership*, 2021.

15. Pachter, Remote Leadership, 2021, 15.

16. Richard Briffault, "Election 2020 sees record $11 billion in campaign spending mostly from a handful of super rich donors," *The Conversation*, October 13, 2020, https://www.theconversation.com/election-2020-sees-record-11-billion-in-campaign-spending-mostly-from-a-handful-of-super-rich-donors-145381.

17. Marc Davis, "Where Presidential Campaigns Get Campaign Funding," *Investopedia*, August 31, 2021, https://www.investopedia.com/financial-edge/1012/where-presidential-candidates-get-campaign-funding.aspx.

18. Barbara Walter, *How Civil Wars Start and How to Stop Them* (New York: Crown, 2022) 195–197.

19. Khaleda Rahman, "MyPillow Products Will No Longer Be Sold by These Companies," *Newsweek*, January 19, 2021, https://www.newsweek.com/mypillow-products-no-longer-stocked-these-companies-1562510.

20. Tim Ryan, "Lead with Your Heart," *You Can Heal Your Life*, March 23, 2013, https://www.healyourlife.com/lead-with-your-heart.

21. Alex Seitz-Wald, "Meet the 'mindfulness' caucus: Politicians who meditate!" *Salon*, July 10, 2013, https://www.salon.com/2013/07/10/meet_the_buddhist_caucus/.

22. Otto Simonsson, Jayanth Narayanan, and Joseph Marks, "Love thy (partisan) neighbor: Brief befriending meditation reduces affective polarization," *Group Processes & Intergroup Relations*, July 13, 2021, https://journals.sagepub.com/doi/full/10.1177/13684302211020108.

23. Blue Beyond Consulting, *Closing the Employee Expectations Gap*, 2022, https://www.bluebeyondconsulting.com/closing-the-employee-expectations-gap-the-undeniable-and-promising-new-mandate-for-business/.

Appendix 1

1. Adapted from Elizabeth Williams, *Daily Vagus Nerve Exercise* (Coppell, TX: Liberty Books, 2020) 103–104.

2. Doug Harding, *Face to No-Face* (Carlsbad, CA: Inner Directions, 2000) 9.

3. Steve Zaffron and Dave Logan, *The Three Laws of Performance* (San Francisco, CA: Jossey-Bass, 2009) 20.

4. Jack Kornfield, *The Wise Heart* (New York: Bantam Books, 2008) 34.

5. Kornfield, *The Wise Heart*, 2008, 33–34.

6. Adapted from Kornfield, *The Wise Heart*, 2008, 351.

Appendix 2

1. Swami Satchidananda, *The Yoga Sutras of Patanjali* (Buckingham, VA: Integral Yoga Publications, 1990).

2. Rolf Sovik, "The Gunas: Nature's Three Fundamental Forces," Yoga International, https://yogainternational.com/article/view/the-gunas-natures-three-fundamental-forces.

3. Sovik, "The Gunas: Nature's Three Fundamental Forces."

4. Pandit Rajmani Tigunait, "What Are Samskaras and How Do They Affect Us?" Yoga International, https://yogainternational.com/article/view/what-are-samskaras-and-how-do-they-affect-us.

5. Eckhart Tolle, *A New Earth* (New York: Plume, 2006).

Appendix 3

1. Daniel Goleman and Richard Davidson, *Altered Traits: How Science Reveals How Meditation Changes Your Mind, Brain, and Body* (New York: Avery, 2017) 180.

2. Goleman and Davidson, *Altered Traits*, 2017, 179.

3. R. Chambers, B. C. Y. Lo, and N. B. Allen, "The Impact of Intensive Mindfulness Training on Attentional Control, Cognitive Style, and Affect," *Cogn Ther Res* 32, 303–322 (2008), https://doi.org/10.1007/s10608-007-9119-0.

4. Marianne Littel and Birgit Mayer, "Workplace Mindfulness," Erasmus University Rotterdam, Netherlands, November 10, 2022, https://www.eur.nl/en/working/training-eur/academic-staff/personal-development/mindfulness.

5. Adam Moore and Peter Malinowski, "Meditation, mindfulness and cognitive flexibility," *Consciousness and Cognition* 18, 176–186 (2009), https://web.colby.edu/cogblog/files/2014/05/Moore-Malinowski-2009-.pdf.

6. Goleman and Davidson, *Altered Traits*, 2017, 139.

7. Goleman and Davidson, Altered Traits, 2017, 251.

8. C. N. M. Ortner, S. J. Kilner, and P. D. Zelazo, "Mindfulness meditation and reduced emotional interference on a cognitive task," *Motiv Emot* 31, 271–283 (2007), https://doi.org/10.1007/s11031-007-9076-7.

9. M. Dekeyser, F. Raes, M. Leijssen, S. Leysen, and D. Dewulf, "Mindfulness skills and interpersonal behaviour," *Personality and Individual Differences*, 44(5), 1235–1245 (2008), https://doi.org/10.1016/j.paid.2007.11.018.

10. David Gelles, *Mindful Work* (Boston, MA: Houghton Mifflin, 2015) 173–177.

BIBLIOGRAPHY

Abrams, Shelley. "Mindfulness in the Workplace: Is It Worth the Hype?" Transcend Strategic Consulting, September 1, 2020, https://www.transcendstrategic.com/blog/2020/9/1/mindfulness-in-the-workplace-is-it-worth-the-hype.

Adler, David. "Schumpeter's Theory of Creative Destruction." *IRLE blog*, September 30, 2019, https://www.cmu.edu/epp/irle/irle-blog-pages/schumpeters-theory-of-creative-destruction.html.

Aikens, Kimberly A., John Astin, Kenneth R. Pelletier, Kristin Levanovich, Catherine M. Baase, Yeo Yung Park, and Catherine M. Bodnar. "Mindfulness Goes to Work: Impact of an Online Workplace Intervention." *Journal of Occupational and Environmental Medicine* 56, no 7 (2014): 721-731. https://experts.arizona.edu/en/publications/mindfulness-goes-to-work-impact-of-an-online-workplace-interventi.

Akram, Waseem, and Rekesh Kuar. "The Positive and Negative Effects of Social Media on Society." *International Journal of Computer Sciences and Engineering* 5, no. 10 (2017): 351–354.

Alcoholics Anonymous. 4th ed. Alcoholics Anonymous World Services (2001).

Allen, James. *As A Man Thinketh*. New York: Tarcher/Penguin (1902/2008).

Arbinger Institute. *The Anatomy of Peace*. San Francisco, CA: Berrett-Koehler (2008).

Arbinger Institute. *Leadership and Self-Deception.* 3rd ed. Oakland, CA: Berrett-Koehler (2018).

Arbinger Institute. *The Outward Mindset.* Oakland, CA: Berrett-Koehler (2016).

Archor, Shawn. *The Happiness Advantage.* New York: Crown Business (2010).

Asprey, Dave. *Fast This Way.* New York: HarperCollins (2021).

Asprey, Dave. *Game Changers.* New York: HarperCollins (2018).

Assaraf, John, and Murray Smith. *The Answer.* New York: Atria Books (2008).

Birk, Matthias. "Why Leaders Need Meditation Now More Than Ever." *Harvard Business Review,* March 22, 2020. https://hbr.org/2020/03/why-leaders-need-meditation-now-more-than-ever.

Brown, Tom, Jr. *The Vision.* New York: Berkley (1988).

Burg, Bob, and John David Mann. *The Go-Giver.* New York: Penguin (2007).

Byrne, Rhonda. *The Secret.* Hillsboro, OR: Beyond Words Publishing (2006/2018).

Campbell, Joseph. *The Hero with a Thousand Faces.* 3rd ed. Novato, CA: New World Library (2008).

Chopra, Deepak. *Abundance.* New York: Harmony Books (2022).

Chopra, Deepak. *Creating Affluence.* San Rafael, CA: Amber-Allen (1993).

Clear, James. *Atomic Habits.* New York: Avery (2018).

Colzato, Lorenza, Ayca Szapora, Dominique Lippelt, and Bernhard Hommel. "Prior Meditation Practice Modulates Performance and Strategy Use in Convergent- and Divergent-Thinking Problems." *Mindfulness* 8, nos 10–16 (2017). https://link.springer.com/article/10.1007/s12671-014-0352-9.

Cziksentmihalyi, Mihaly. *Flow: The Psychology of Optimal Experience.* New York: HarperCollins (1990).

Dalio, Ray. *Principles*. New York: Simon and Schuster (2007).

Dane, Erik, and Bradley J. Brummel. "Examining workplace mindfulness and its relations to job performance and turnover intention." *Human Relations* 67, no 1 (2013): 105–128. https://journals.sagepub.com/doi/abs/10.1177/0018726713487753.

Davis, Daphne M., and Jeffrey A. Hayes. "What are the benefits of mindfulness." *American Psychological Association* 43, no. 7 (July/August 2012): 64. https://www.apa.org/monitor/2012/07-08/ce-corner.

Deida, David. *The Way of the Superior Man*. Boulder, CO: Sounds True (2004).

Dube, Rob. "Why More Companies Are Cultivating a Culture of Mindfulness." *Forbes*, March 25, 2019. https://www.forbes.com/sites/robdube/2019/03/25/why-more-companies-are-cultivating-a-culture-of-mindfulness/.

Elrod, Hal. *The Miracle Morning*. Temecula, CA: Hal Elrod International (2014).

Emmons, Robert. *Thanks! How Practicing Gratitude Can Make You Happier*. New York: Houghton Mifflin (2008).

Epstein, Gerald. *Healing Visualizations*. New York: Bantam Books (1989).

Fadiman, James, and Jordan Gruber. *Your Symphony of Selves*. Rochester, VT: Park Street Press (2020).

Feldenkrais, Moshe. *Awareness through Movement.* New York: HarperOne (1977).

Finger, Alan, and Peter Ferko. *The Genius of Yoga*. Boulder, CO: Shambhala (2020).

Foster, Jeff. *The Deepest Acceptance*. Boulder, CO: Sounds True (2012).

Fouts, Melinda. "Being Mindful in Your Relationships." *Forbes*, July 19, 2018. https://www.forbes.com/sites/forbescoachescouncil/2018/07/19/being-mindful-in-your-relationships/?sh=5b9bfe20ceaa.

Frankl, Viktor. *Man's Search for Meaning.* Boston, MA. Beacon Press (2006).

Gallwey, W. Timothy. *The Inner Game of Work.* New York: Random House (2000).

Gelles, David. *Mindful Work: How Meditation Is Changing Business from the Inside Out.* Boston: Houghton Mifflin Harcourt (2015).

Goldfield, Rose Taylor. *Training the Wisdom Body.* Boston, MA. Shambhala (2013).

Goleman, Daniel, and Richard Davidson. *Altered Traits: Science Reveals How Meditation Changes Your Mind, Brain, and Body.* New York: Avery (2017).

Grant, Adam. *Give and Take.* New York: Penguin (2013).

Greenleaf, Robert. *Servant Leadership.* Mahwah, NJ: Paulist Press (1977).

Greiser, Christian. "How Companies Can Instill Mindfulness." *Knowledge at Wharton*, April 19, 2018. http://knowledge.wharton.upenn.edu/article/how-companies-can-instill-mindfulness/.

Haefner, Joe. "Mental Rehearsal and Visualization: The Secret to Improving Your Game Without Touching a Basketball!" *Breakthrough Basketball.* https://www.breakthroughbasketball.com/mental/visualization.html?filterreviews=upvotes.

Hagen, Steve. *Meditation: Now or Never.* New York: HarperCollins (2007).

Hanh, Thich Nhat. *The Miracle of Mindfulness.* Boston, MA: Beacon Press (1999).

Hanh, Thich Nhat. *The Pocket Thich Nhat.* Boulder, CO: Shambhala Publications (2012).

Harding, Douglas E. *Face to No-Face.* Carlsbad, CA: Inner Directions (2000).

Hari, Johann. *Stolen Focus.* New York: Crown Publishing (2022).

Harris, Dan. *10% Happier.* New York: HarperCollins (2014).

Hill, Napoleon. *Think and Grow Rich.* Shippensburg, PA: Sound Wisdom (2017).

Hoffman, Donald D. *The Case Against Reality*. New York: W. W. Norton (2019).

Hoffman, Donald D. *Visual Intelligence*. New York: W. W. Norton (1998).

Holecek, Andrew. *Dream Yoga*. Boulder, CO: Sounds True (2016).

Holecek, Andrew. *Preparing to Die*. Boston, MA: Snow Lion (2013).

Hyde, Bruce, and Drew Kopp. *Speaking Being: Werner Erhard, Martin Heidegger, and a New Possibility of Being Human*. Hoboken, NJ: Wiley (2019).

Jackson, Phil. *Sacred Hoops*. New York: Hyperion (2006).

Jensen, Michael C. "Integrity: Without It Nothing Works." Harvard Business School, Working Knowledge. December 17, 2009. https://hbswk.hbs.edu/item/integrity-without-it-nothing-works.

Kabat-Zinn, Jon. *Mindfulness for Beginners*. Boulder, CO: Sounds True (2012/2016).

Kabat-Zinn, Jon. "Too Early to Tell: The Potential Impact and Challenges—Ethical and Otherwise—Inherent in the Mainstreaming of Dharma in an Increasingly Dystopian World." *Mindfulness* 8, no. 5 (2017): 1125–1135. https://doi.org/10.1007/s12671-017-0758-2.

Kabat-Zinn, Jon. *Wherever You Go, There You Are*. New York: Hachette (1994).

Kaku, Michio. *The God Equation*. New York: Doubleday (2021).

Kastrup, Bernardo. *Why Materialism Is Baloney*. Hampshire, UK: John Hunt (2012/2017).

Katie, Byron, with Stephen Mitchell. *Loving What Is*. New York: Harmony (2002).

Kelly, Edward F., and Paul Marshall, eds. *Consciousness Unbound: Liberating Mind from the Tyranny of Materialism*. Lanham, MD: Rowman and Littlefield (2021).

Kendall, Larry. *Ninja Selling*. Austin, TX: Greenleaf Book Group (2017).

Klemp, Nate. "5 Reasons Your Company Should be Investing in Mindfulness Training." *Inc.* October 17, 2019. https://www.inc.com/nate-klemp/5-reasons-your-company-should-be-investing-in-mindfulness-training.html.

Knight, Chelsea. "5 Benefits of Mindfulness." *The Psych Professionals* (blog). https://psychprofessionals.com.au/5-benefits-of-mindfulness/.

Kornfield, Jack. *The Wise Heart.* New York: Bantam Books (2008).

Krishnamurti, Jiddu. *On Love and Loneliness.* New York: Harper One (1994).

Lakhiani, Vishen. *The Code of the Extraordinary Mind.* Emmaus, PA: Rodale Books (2019).

Lanza, Robert, with Bob Berman. *Biocentrism.* Dallas, TX: BenBella Books (2009).

Lanza, Robert, and Matej Pavsic, with Bob Berman. *The Grand Biocentric Design.* Dallas, TX: BenBella Books (2020).

Lao-tzu. *Tao Te Ching.* Edited and translated by Stephen Mitchell. New York: Harper and Row (1988).

Leonard, George. *Mastery.* New York: Plume (1992).

Levin, Marissa. "The Top 10 Leadership Blind Spots, and 5 Ways to Turn Them into Strengths." *Inc.*, July 13, 2017. https://www.inc.com/marissa-levin/the-top-10-leadership-blind-spots-and-5-ways-to-tu.html.

Lipton, Bruce H. *The Biology of Belief.* Carlsbad, CA: Hay House (2008).

Loy, David R. *Nonduality in Buddhism and Beyond.* Somerville, MA: Wisdom Publications (2019).

Macioti, Maria. *The Buddha Within Ourselves: Blossoms of the Lotus Sutra.* Translated by Richard Maurice Capozzi. Lanham, MD: University Press of America (2002).

Maharshi, Ramana. *Who Am I? The Teachings of Bhagavan Sri Ramana Maharshi.* Tiruvannamalai, India: Sri Ramanasramam (2008).

McDougall, Christine. "Precession and Integral Leadership." *Integral Leadership Review*, August 2011. http://integralleadershipreview.com/3285-precession-and-integral-leadership-2/.

McGown, Michael. "'Remember to Look Up at the Stars': The Best Stephen Hawking Quotes," *Guardian*, March 14, 2018, https://www.theguardian.com/science/2018/mar/14/best-stephen-hawking-quotes-quotations.

McTaggart, Lynne. *The Field*. New York: HarperCollins (2008).

McTaggart, Lynne. The *Intention Experiment*. New York: Free Press (2007).

McTaggart, Lynne. "Living the Field" Course Lesson Plan.

Miller, Barbara Stoler. *Yoga as the Discipline of Freedom*. New York: Bantam (1998).

Mintz, Laurie. "Mindful Sex Is Mind-Blowing Sex." *Psychology Today*, November 12, 2017. https://www.psychologytoday.com/us/blog/stress-and-sex/201711/mindful-sex-is-mind-blowing-sex.

Mitchell, Stephen, trans. *The Bhagavad Gita: A New Translation*. New York: Harmony (2002).

Muktibodhananda, Swami. *Hatha Yoga Pradipika*. Bihar, India: Yoga Publications Trust (2012).

Mumford, George. *The Mindful Athlete*. Berkeley, CA: Parallax Press (2015).

Murphy, Joseph. *The Power of Your Subconscious Mind*. Radford, VA: Wilder Publications (2007).

Nagoski, Emily. *Come as You Are.* New York: Simon and Schuster (2015).

Nair, Guatam. "Analysis: Most Americans Vastly Underestimate How Rich They Are Compared with the Rest of the World. Does It Matter?" Politics, *Washington Post*, August 23, 2018. https://www.washingtonpost.com/news/monkey-cage/wp/2018/08/23/most-americans-vastly-underestimate-how-rich-they-are-compared-with-the-rest-of-the-world-does-it-matter/.

Olson, Jeff. *The Slight Edge*, Austin, TX: Greenleaf Book Group (2013).

Pachter, David. *Remote Leadership*. Herndon, VA: Amplify (2021).

Parent, Joseph. *Zen Golf: Mastering the Mental Game*. New York: Doubleday (2002).

Paul, Nakai, and Ron Schultz. *The Mindful Corporation*. Los Angeles, CA: Leadership Press (2000).

Pinker, Steven. *Enlightenment Now*. New York: Penguin Random House (2018).

Pollan, Michael. *How to Change Your Mind*. New York: Penguin Books (2018).

Rahman, Khaleda. "MyPillow Products Will No Longer Be Sold by These Companies." *Newsweek*. January 19, 2021. https://www.newsweek.com/mypillow-products-no-longer-stocked-these-companies-1562510.

Rasheta, Noah. "Who Knows What Is Good and What Is Bad?" *Secular Buddhism*. August 2015. https://secularbuddhism.com/who-knows-what-is-good-and-what-is-bad/.

Reps, Paul, and Nyogen Senzaki. *Zen Flesh, Zen Bones*. North Clarendon, VT: Periplus Editions (1957/1985).

Richardson, Alan. "Mental Practice: A Review and Discussion, Part 1." *Research Quarterly* 38 (1967): 95–107. https://doi.org/10.1080/10671188.1967.10614808.

Robinson, Ken, and Lou Aronica. *The Element: How Finding Your Passion Changes Everything*. New York: Penguin (2009).

Rogers, Carl. *On Becoming a Person*. New York: HarperOne (1995).

Ruiz, Don Miguel. *The Four Agreements*. San Rafael, CA: Amber-Allen (1997).

Russell, Peter. *From Science to God*. Novato, CA: New World Library (2002).

Sadhguru. *Karma: A Yogi's Guide to Crafting Your Destiny*. New York: Harmony (2021).

Seppälä, Emma. "20 Reasons to Start Meditating Today." *Psychology Today*. September 11, 2013. https://www.psychologytoday.com/us/blog/feeling-it/201309/20-scientific-reasons-start-meditating-today.

"The Serenity Prayer: Learning to Let Go," Alcoholics Anonymous, North Orange County Intergroup Association blog, May 14, 2020, https://www.aanoc.org/breaking-down-the-serenity-prayer/.

Shafer, Joan, Adam Bryant, and David Reimer. "Revealing Leaders' Blind Spots." *Strategy+Business*, April 29, 2020. https://www.strategy-business.com/article/Revealing-leaders-blind-spots.

Shoemaker, Fred. *Extraordinary Golf.* New York: Tarcher Perigee (1997).

Sinek, Simon. *The Infinite Game.* New York: Penguin Random House (2019).

Singer, Michael A. *The Untethered Soul.* Oakland, CA: New Harbinger (2007).

Spangler, David. *The Laws of Manifestation.* San Francisco, CA: Red Wheel/Weiser (1975/2009).

Spira, Rupert. *You Are the Happiness You Seek: Uncovering the Awareness of Being.* Oxford, England: Sahaja (2022).

Sterner, Thomas. *The Practicing Mind.* Novato, CA: New World Library (2005).

Suzuki, Shunryu. *Zen Mind, Beginner's Mind.* New York: Weatherhill (1970/1997).

Tolle, Eckhart. *A New Earth: Awakening to Your Life's Purpose.* New York: Plume (2006).

Tolle, Eckhart. *The Power of Now.* Novato, CA: New World Library (2004).

Tolle, Eckhart. *Stillness Speaks.* Novato, CA: New World Library (2003).

Walter, Barbara F. *How Civil Wars Start.* New York: Crown (2022).

Wattles, Wallace. *The Science of Getting Rich.* Langhorne, PA: Jon Rose (2015).

Wilber, Ken. *No Boundary.* Boulder, CO: Shambhala (1979/2001).

Young, Emma. "Lifting the Lid on the Unconscious." *New Scientist*, July 25, 2018. https://www.newscientist.com/article/mg23931880-400-lifting-the-lid-on-the-unconscious/.

Zaffron, Steve, and Dave Logan. *The Three Laws of Performance*. San Francisco, CA: Jossey-Bass (2009).

Zukav, Gary. *The Dancing Wu Li Masters*. New York: HarperOne (1979).

Zukav, Gary. *Universal Human*. New York: Simon and Schuster (2021).

ABOUT THE AUTHOR

ERIC HOLSAPPLE is a successful developer and entrepreneur with LC Real Estate Group, in Loveland, Colorado, who has used mindfulness to transform his life and business, and helps others to do the same. Eric has a PhD in Economics, has been a real estate CEO and developer for nearly forty years, has lectured in real estate at Colorado State University for twenty years, and has practiced Yoga and meditation for thirty years. Holsapple has a unique perspective on how merging business and mindfulness can be a catalyst in changing lives.

Eric is the founder of Living in the Gap. His popular workshops teach CEOs and professionals a different way to operate mindfully while improving the bottom line. He has won Entrepreneur of the Year Awards from Colorado State University and *BizWest* magazine.

Eric and his wife, Tracy, have three grown children, Ryan, Kaity, and Kohlton, who all have their own businesses. They summer in Maine, where Eric grew up, and enjoy spending time skiing in Steamboat, Colorado, in the winter.